Theatres of Value

Theatres of Value

Buying and Selling Shakespeare
in Nineteenth-Century New York City

DANIELLE ROSVALLY

SUNY PRESS

Cover art: "The Empire City, Birdseye View of New York and Environs."
John Bachmann (artist and publisher) and Adam Weingartner (printer), 1855.
The Metropolitan Museum of Art. The Edward W. C. Arnold Collection of
New York Prints, Maps and Pictures. Bequest of Edward W. C. Arnold, 1954.

Published by State University of New York Press, Albany

© 2024 State University of New York

All rights reserved

Printed in the United States of America

No part of this book may be used or reproduced in any manner whatsoever
without written permission. No part of this book may be stored in a retrieval
system or transmitted in any form or by any means including electronic,
electrostatic, magnetic tape, mechanical, photocopying, recording, or otherwise
without the prior permission in writing of the publisher.

For information, contact State University of New York Press, Albany, NY
www.sunypress.edu

Links to third-party websites are provided as a convenience and for informational
purposes only. They do not constitute an endorsement or an approval of any of
the products, services, or opinions of the organization, companies, or individuals.
SUNY Press bears no responsibility for the accuracy, legality, or content of a URL,
the external website, or for that of subsequent websites.

Library of Congress Cataloging-in-Publication Data

Name: Rosvally, Danielle, author.
Title: Theatres of value : buying and selling Shakespeare in nineteenth-century
  New York City / Danielle Rosvally.
Description: Albany : State University of New York Press, [2024] | Includes
  bibliographical references and index.
Identifiers: ISBN 9781438498348 (hardcover : alk. paper) | ISBN 9781438498355
  (ebook) | ISBN 9781438498331 (pbk. : alk. paper)
Further information is available at the Library of Congress.

For my Bubby, Shura Saul,
who would have found any spelling or grammatical errors
that I missed and enthusiastically devoured the text nonetheless.

And to my parents, Bill and Jennifer.
Look, Mom, I wrote a book!

Contents

LIST OF ILLUSTRATIONS	ix
ACKNOWLEDGMENTS	xi
INTRODUCTION Deriving a Dramaturgy of Value	1
CHAPTER ONE What William Brown Knew: The African Theatre and the Growing Threat of Legitimacy	29
CHAPTER TWO The Value of a Name: P. T. Barnum's American Dream	59
CHAPTER THREE Taking the Reins: The American Reading Career of Mrs. Fanny Kemble	87
CHAPTER FOUR Both Booth's Brothers: The Bulletproof Brand	115
CHAPTER FIVE Our American Shakespeare: The Central Park Statue and National Identity	139
CHAPTER SIX Erasing the Lines: Editing the Wallack Benefit	161

viii | CONTENTS

CONCLUSION
The Dramaturgy of Value at Large   191

NOTES   197

BIBLIOGRAPHY   237

INDEX   257

Illustrations

E.1	Map of Key Places Mentioned in This Book	x
1.1	1821 Park Row Property Assessment	41
1.2	African Theatre Locations Plotted against Shane White's Map of Free Black Households in New York City	46
2.1	George Catlin's *Five Points*	70
2.2	Top Twenty Most-Performed Shows at Barnum's	78
2.3	Number of Performances per Show at Barnum's	79
2.4	Frequency of Performances at Barnum's	80
2.5	Top Ten Most-Performed Plays at Wallack's	80
2.6	Frequency of Performances at Wallack's	81
2.7	Top Ten Most-Performed Plays at the Park	81
2.8	Frequency of Performances at the Park Pie Chart	82
3.1	Kemble's Appellations in Print over Time	105
4.1	Gramercy Park Booth Statue	121
4.2	Series of Medals Coined in Commemoration of April 23, 1894, *Hamlet*	122
4.3	Teacup and Saucer Set from circa 1895	122
5.1	The Three Theatrical Booth Brothers in *Julius Caesar*	155

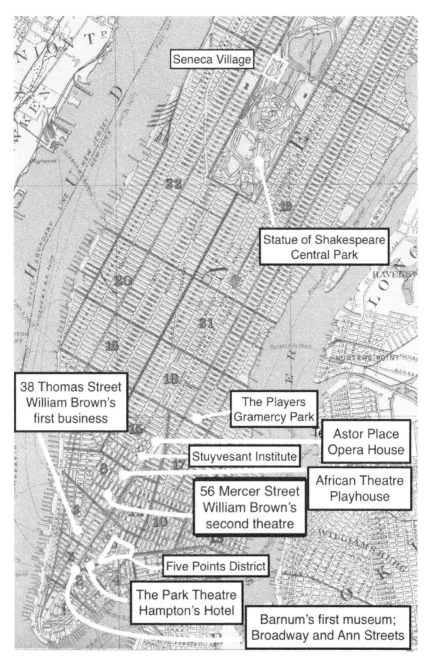

Figure E.1. Overview of Key Places in This Book. *Source*: Created by the author using public domain map.

Acknowledgments

In the more-than-a-decade it took to write this book I've been helped along the way by many, many people.

My thanks go out to Rebecca Colesworthy for believing in this project, her advocacy and allyship, and her unending patience for new-author questions. I also thank the team at State University of New York Press for everything they have done to turn my manuscript into an actual book.

The research this project took would not have been possible without the help of a small army of dedicated archivists and librarians at several institutions: Abbie Weinberg and colleagues at the Folger Shakespeare Library, Micah Hoggatt and colleagues at the Harvard Theatre Collection, Laura Anderson of the National Park Service and her colleagues at Ford's Theatre, Kenneth Cobb at the New York Municipal Archive, Annemarie Van Roessel and colleagues at the New York Public Library Billy Rose Theatre Division, Melissa Houston and colleagues at the Barnum Museum, Elizabeth Van Tuyl and Mary Witkowski at the Bridgeport History Center and Bridgeport Public Library, Morgen Stevens-Garmon and colleagues at the Museum of the City of New York, colleagues at the New-York Historical Society, the New York Public Library's Archives and Manuscripts division, and the American Antiquarian Society.

My research was financially supported by grants from the American Theatre and Drama Society as well as the American Society for Theatre Research. Many thanks to those organizations and the people who gave their time to the various awards committees that recognized my work.

I am extremely lucky to have colleagues who were willing and able to review section drafts of this book (and its proposal), and whose feedback helped shape the project. My eternal gratitude to Trevor Boffone, Meredith Conti, Louise Geddes, Barbara Wallace Grossman, Jennifer Kokai, Jack

Lynch, Lilian Mengesha, and Catherine Young for their time and diligence in caring for my writing. I also thank the two anonymous peer reviewers whose feedback proved valuable in strengthening my arguments. This book would not be the same without all of you.

I wrote this book while working contingently, teaching a 4/4 course load, and being on the job market. My home institution would not lend support for the research or writing process. Still, I had colleagues who supported this work in other ways, ensuring that what I lacked in institutional support could be mitigated as best as possible. My thanks to this community: Meredith Conti, Lindsay Brandon Hunter, Eero Laine, and Ariel Nereson. Thanks also to Ian Downes for their work as my research assistant during sections of my writing process.

This book was the product of a dissertation that was advised by Heather Nathans, and I thank her for years of mentorship and kindness. The world would be a better place if more people were like Heather. My thanks as well to the scholars who sat on that committee and gave their feedback: Barbara Wallace Grossman, Monica White Ndounou, and Virginia Mason Vaughan. My deepest thanks also to Noe Montez for continued mentorship and support over the years.

I thank my family for their patience and never-ending belief in my capabilities as a human: Mom and Dad (Jennifer and Bill), sister Amy, brother Matt, and chosen sister Rachael. Of course, I also thank my four-legged editors: Ares, Artemis, Felix, and Indiana, who provided comfort throughout the writing process.

Last, but certainly not least, I thank my devoted husband Michael, without whose daily support this book would not have been possible.

I can no other answer make but thanks, and thanks, and ever thanks.

—Sebastian, *Twelfth Night*, III.iii

Introduction

Deriving a Dramaturgy of Value

On the night of May 10, 1849, an audience of working-class Americans bombarded the elite Astor Opera House. There, English actor William Charles Macready was giving his Macbeth in direct scheduled opposition to America's Edwin Forrest (performing at the nearby Broadway Theatre). Macready and Forrest had been taking open swipes at each other for some time; Forrest loudly hissed Macready midperformance during an 1846 tour of Britain, while Macready had publicly sneered at Forrest's lack of "taste."[1] Working-class American audiences identified with Forrest, the home-grown star whose muscular physique suggested health and rigor. They took umbrage with the Astor Opera House's audience dress code requiring "freshly shaven faces, evening dress, fresh waistcoats, and kid gloves," thus excluding any who were not of great privilege.[2]

Three days earlier, when Macready opened his performance, the audience hissed him wildly and pelted him with rotten eggs, potatoes, apples, lemons, and copper coins while shouting, "Down with the aristocracy!"[3] Macready left the stage and purposed not to return. In the days that followed, threats were made publicly and privately to Macready, the mayor of New York convened a crisis meeting at City Hall, and the police chief warned that a serious riot would not be quellable, all while Macready's fans implored him to return to the stage.[4] The ensuing riot lasted days, left at least 22 dead and about 240 injured.[5]

The story of the Astor Place Riots is one of theatre history's foundational legends. Here was a moment where the confluence of theatre, society, and economies collided across a veritable tectonic fault line to viscerally demonstrate theatre's power as a site of inscription for values; the force

2 | THEATRES OF VALUE

of Shakespeare in America's imagination and the amount of dissonance this force could sow; the underlying roilings of class division in New York's nineteenth century; and (most pertinently to this work) the value of Shakespeare to his American audience.[6] The central question of this book pertains to "value": What is it? How is it created by theatremakers and audiences? And how can scholars unpack its facets to understand it? Value is sometimes measured in dollars exchanged, but more frequently it is expressed with (and certainly nuanced by) social behaviors. In terms of the Astor Place Riots: it seems odd, nearly unfathomable, that a British playwright would be so strongly accepted into an American repertoire 233 years after the playwright's death and 66 years after a bloody war for independence from England that Americans would be willing to die for him. There are complicated layers to this value expression entwined with audiences, theatre, and a greater cultural zeitgeist. So how do we peel back these layers? How do we begin to understand this behavior as an expression of value?

I propose a methodology that I call the "Dramaturgy of Value." The dramaturgy of value is an envisioning of the social and economic systems that create value within its context. The dramaturgy of value understands value as a thing created and performed, very specifically, by the agents of a free market behaving in accordance with (or as a reaction to) established social codes. These behaviors shape the market on which items are bought and sold, and fluctuations in the market reflect fluctuations in these codes. This method proposes that by understanding one (market or social codes), you can better comprehend the other.

The dramaturgy of value is a form of critical thinking in which one engages with the idea that one's research object (be it a performance, a business enterprise, an object commodity, etc.) is first and foremost an economic exchange. Once this premise is accepted, the dramaturgy of value invites a user to closely consider how value is being created within this exchange. To construct an item's dramaturgy of value, the researcher needs to ask the following questions:

1. What is being sold?

2. What is being bought?

3. How are (1) and (2) different and/or the same?

4. Why is this thing being sold?

5. Why is it being bought?

6. How are (4) and (5) different and/or the same?

7. How is this thing being sold?

8. How is it being bought?

9. How are (7) and (8) different/the same?

These core questions will invariably provoke more situational queries that will require deft and creative methodological shifts to answer. By way of example: each of the following chapters works slightly differently to engage these questions, but the questions remain at each chapter's core.

"Dramaturgy" is a word so vast that when professional dramaturges are asked to define it they will often err toward discussing what dramaturges *do* rather than what dramaturgy *is*.[7] Even the field's foundational text *The Hamburg Dramaturgy* (which introduced the word *dramaturgy* to written language in the late eighteenth century) doesn't define the term so much as demonstrate its methods.[8] One of the better definitions of dramaturgy comes from dramaturge Mark Bly who writes: "When pressed for a definition of what it is that I do as a dramaturg, both in a rehearsal hall and in the theater at large, I generally answer, 'I question.'"[9] Dramaturgy is the art of asking and answering questions that will bolster the process of theatrical creation. Doing dramaturgy involves generating relevant and formative questions in the context of theatrical work, posing these questions to stakeholders in the theatrical process, and researching answers (or facts that can contribute to answers) that help support a theatrical product. Dramaturgy can be a method (the process of doing dramaturgy), a concept (the dramaturgy of *Macbeth*, for instance), or a product ("so-and-so's dramaturgy is clear in their performance of Macbeth"). The term "dramaturgy of value" can be applied in the same three ways: describing the method or process of constructing an item's value by understanding the social and market forces at play in performing that value; describing the concept of these social systems when viewed in conglomerate; or describing the product of this concept. Like its root term "dramaturgy," sometimes the dramaturgy of value is doing the work; sometimes the dramaturgy of value is the work itself.

"Value" is also a word with many shades of situationally created meaning. As such, both "dramaturgy" and "value" are moving targets understood variably in different contexts. The dramaturgy of value must, therefore, be applied individually and situationally depending on the primary object of focus. The methodology is flexible and requires a broad understanding of "market," "commodity," and the social factors engaged with both in order to create a clearer picture of how and why something is valued. Social performances enact value.[10] The dramaturgy of value offers a lens through which to understand how.

This book engages with my method by way of Shakespeare to help answer these questions as they relate to the nineteenth century: Where did Shakespeare's value come from to his nineteenth-century American audience, and how was that value used, accepted, communicated, and invested?

"Masters, here are your parts."

—Peter Quince, *A Midsummer Night's Dream*, I.ii

In the chapters that follow, I will explore six case studies showing how businesspeople in New York City engaged with Shakespeare to claim and use the social and cultural capital he represented. Each of these case studies shows businesspeople with monetary and cultural stakes in the Shakespeare market, and a different end goal that Shakespeare was used to accomplish. The first four case studies share one element: they all represent theatremakers in moments of crisis who looked to Shakespeare to gain something from him—they needed his help to achieve a desired end. The last two case studies mark a shift. In the wake of the Civil War, American invocations of Shakespeare involved a kind of giving back—the perception of giving to Shakespeare and honoring him through noble usage. While Shakespeare was still used as an authority of taste, refinement, and bourgeois values, these invocations become less desperate after Edwin Booth's successful rebranding of himself through and via Hamlet (a phenomenon I explore in chapter 4). Each of the theatremakers I follow constructed Shakespeare's value with and to their audience in different ways. Accordingly, each of the following chapters will take a slightly different approach to drafting Shakespeare's dramaturgy of value within the various contexts they offer and will demonstrate how this process draws different facets of value into critical inquiry.

Chapter 1 examines William Brown's African Theatre as a site of Shakespeare-centric subversive performance and explores the theme of cultural legitimacy. At his theatre for Black audiences William Brown sought to claim a piece of cultural capital in order to prove his endeavor and (by extension) Black theatre in America legitimate. To Brown, Shakespeare's value is crafted via and for the purpose of constructing this legitimacy.

In mounting his productions William Brown faced struggles with the law that led to riots, arrests, and (eventually) the closure of Brown's theatre. In spite of these struggles, Brown continued to find ways to present Shakespeare to his target audience, the newly freed Black residents of New York City. In chapter 1, I explicate the social frameworks that made Shakespeare such a desirable commodity for Brown despite the legal battles he faced.

In chapter 2, I examine how American showman Phineas Taylor Barnum used Shakespeare as a cornerstone to constructing idealized middle-class American life in his American Museum and Lecture Room. Barnum's museum sought to present outward shows of respectability for wide swathes of audiences. Barnum was particularly sensitive to keeping entertainments affordable so as to attract as many costumers as he could. In so pricing his museum, Barnum kicked open his doors to a public close to the class line and otherwise unable to afford the trappings of the middle class. At his museum, Barnum presented an opportunity for audiences to participate in "conspicuous consumption"—outward shows of respectability and self-betterment, performances meant to create a specifically built image of middle-class life.[11]

One of Barnum's major draws was his lecture room (actually a glorified nineteenth-century theatre), a place where Barnum vehemently declared: "No vulgar word or gesture, and not a profane expression was *ever* allowed on my stage! Even in Shakespeare's plays, I unflinchingly and invariably cut out vulgarity and profanity."[12] Chapter 2 examines Barnum's use of Shakespeare in constructing his middle-class American dream, and how and why Shakespeare was valuable to Barnum as part of this dream.

Chapter 3 examines the American reading career of Fanny Kemble and how Kemble was able to use Shakespeare as a vehicle to harness the publicity machine behind her extremely public divorce. In October of 1848, Mrs. Fanny Butler (née Fanny Kemble) returned to the stage as a matter of financial necessity. Mid-divorce from her abusive American husband (Pierce Butler), Kemble cashed in on the cultural capital of her theatrically famous last name. She began a reading series of Shakespeare's works, first in Boston then in New York, which became a sensation. Through these readings, Kemble was able to carefully craft her stage image, select and edit her material, and gain essentially unfettered agency over her performance. With strategic use of the press, Kemble was able to harness the sensational journalism surrounding her divorce and turn a hefty profit from it without sustaining lasting character injury.

To Kemble, Shakespeare had value as a moralizing and empowering force. Reviews and audience diary entries confirm that the readings were viewed by audiences as wholesome entertainment, in keeping with moral and ethical standards of the nineteenth-century bourgeoisie. By creating a domestic setting for these readings, Kemble simultaneously subverted and affirmed traditional nineteenth-century values, particularly those linked to issues of femininity. She purposefully sidestepped conversations surrounding the morality of theatre and engaged with literary tradition as an economic tool to increase both her audience and her prestige. Kemble's American readings show how a nineteenth-century woman was able to use Shakespeare as legitimizing cultural capital to subvert gendered social expectations, even amid a very public exposure of her personal life. In this chapter, I will examine how Kemble was able to do so, how these readings enacted her ideas about the stage and lasting cultural significance, and why this was effective for a nineteenth-century American audience.

One brand that was so economically powerful it could weather the high-profile murder of an American martyr was that of the Booth family. Chapter 4 delves into the careers of the American Booths (Edwin, John Wilkes, and Junius Brutus Jr.), how their brand was built, and the inclusion of Shakespeare as a key feature of the brand. I propose that a purposeful brand elision of Booth and Shakespeare allowed the Booth brand to soak up and retain both Shakespeare's legitimacy as a product and his value as a cultural object.

This is particularly fascinating in light of the brand literally coming under fire when John Wilkes Booth assassinated Abraham Lincoln. Edwin Booth had never agreed with his brother's politics and the two debated so hotly that their mother forbade them from speaking on the topic in her house.[13] John Wilkes Booth was an outspoken proponent of Southern values, including slavery; Edwin was a Lincoln supporter. This divide in the family and the ways it played out publicly means study of the Booth brand must also engage with how the brand constructed whiteness in relation to its reliance on (and support of) the institution of slavery.

The assassination and ensuing fallout kept Edwin from the stage, but after only nine months (at the strong behest of the public), Edwin returned to a packed house, rowdy applause, and ovations that interrupted his performance for five-minute-long intervals of stamping, clapping, and fervent handkerchief-waving.[14] In his return performance, Edwin played Hamlet, which, while unsurprising given his fame in the role, is slightly curious given the play's subject matter in relation to an assassinated ruler. In chapter 4, I will examine the mechanisms that went into bulletproofing the Booth brand, how those mechanisms became synonymous with Shakespeare, and how the Booths' creation of value as associated with white Eurocentrism drafted American Shakespeare that compounded the value of both the Booth brand and Shakespeare's brand to American audiences.

Chapter 5 examines the statue of Shakespeare in New York's Central Park. In 1864, a gathering of actors, businesspeople, and critics came together to erect this statue in honor of the tercentenary of Shakespeare's birth. In so doing, New Yorkers sought to claim Shakespeare as a cornerstone for American national identity as they struggled to create common American myths and historical memories, as well as form a common public culture. Considering the statue as a work of performative memory helps to unravel the ways in which its creators were able to craft a *lieu de mémoire* within Central Park via this Shakespeare.[15] Though a British playwright provided surface inspiration for the piece, everything beneath this mask was thoroughly American: the sculptor, the body model, and the clothing inspiration. Performing Shakespeare as American and Americans as Shakespeareans through this statue allowed Americans to cement Shakespeare within their cultural heritage and link his presence to upper-middle-class sentimental values. While the statue was made for a public park as an outward show of magnanimity, delving into the cultural economics of park usage unveils deeper implications about Shakespeare's place in nineteenth-century class structures and the rhetoric of memorializers' performances.

At face value, the statue might be read as a genuine replica of its English subject placed in a populist locale freely available to audiences of all economic backgrounds. I propose that the work is (rather) an Americanized product of a growing Shakespeare industry, influenced more by native stars such as Steele MacKaye than "genuine" English representations of Shakespeare. The statue's placement is also a statement about its intended audience: the wealthy elite carriage riders of New York's nineteenth century rather than dusty plebeian pedestrians. Additionally,

8 | Theatres of Value

the statue's creation on land seized by law of eminent domain problematizes the place of Shakespeare in Central Park. The law required all land-dwellers (including the residents of nearby Seneca Village, a Black settlement community with decades-old roots) to evacuate by the end of 1857.[16] Chapter 5 examines the erasure of these histories in conjunction with Shakespeare's Americanization and interrogates value building as a violent force of destructive creation.

Chapter 6 examines a moment that represents a pivotal success in American commodification of Shakespeare: the May 21, 1888, benefit performance of *Hamlet* for Lester Wallack. In this performance, an assemblage of commercially thriving late nineteenth-century actors came together to support their well-known theatrical colleague: John Lester Wallack. This benefit was given at the New York Opera house with luminaries including Edwin Booth (Hamlet), Lawrence Barrett (Ghost), and Helena Modjeska (Ophelia) gracing the stage.

Several formal histories of the event were published by the benefit's participants and present simple linear narratives of the evening and the producers' preparations, but these histories are polished-for-publication tellings. In looking closer, I am able to offer a more nuanced version of the story. This study of the Wallack benefit explores the ever-shifting sands of Daly and Palmer's process in the context of its historical moment and uncovers step-by-step how these theatremakers were able to create value and commercial success from what they knew about the workings of nineteenth-century theatre and audiences.

Throughout this book, I understand "Shakespeare" through Robin Bernstein's paradigm of "repertoire." One of the biggest stumbling blocks in discussing "Shakespeare" is ambiguity in the word itself. It might refer to a historical figure—William Shakespeare—the man from Stratford. It might refer to the author of an oeuvre of plays and poetry that is a mainstay in Western literature. It might refer to the texts that comprise this oeuvre. It might refer to the idea of these things, and the cultural capital they represent. Bernstein's work on objects posits that a culturally significant piece of cultural capital might be best understood as a repertoire. To Bernstein, repertoire is (by definition) in constant flux, always being remade. "These re-formations occur deliberately, with the exercise of agency, as well as accidentally, on a small and large scale, through authored and unauthored actions. A repertoire is by definition relational; it exists among people."[17] Bernstein's model makes it possible to encompass all of the aforementioned nuances in the word "Shakespeare."[18] In so understanding "Shakespeare" as a repertoire, one can begin to conceive of these ideas existing harmoniously and often simultaneously in each usage of the term.

I have chosen to focus on New York City as a useful microcosm. Because of its size; diverse racial, ethnic, religious, and cultural population; and, perhaps most importantly, its prosperity as a theatrical community over the course of the nineteenth century, New York offers an excellent sampling of the multitude of issues entwined with nineteenth-century American theatre including Shakespeare's place as a bastion of white Eurocentric authority and the ways buyers and sellers both played into and subverted this supposition.

"Value" and "Worth"

Exploring these case studies will require working definitions of several economic concepts that underlie them. If one is to undertake the labor of composing a dramaturgy of value, first one needs to comprehend the economic foundations of several basic terms. The most deceptively simple of these terms are "value" and "worth." At their core, "value" and "worth" are the medial understandings that allow exchanges to occur on a market. They are the in-between communications that can take a buyer and seller from wanting/having something to a fair exchange of goods/services/capital that satisfies both parties. Generally speaking, "worth" is the countable "value" of something. Value is the thing, positive or negative, that renders worth.[19] In essence: worth can be expressed most easily in a number, value must rather be considered by quality. Worth can be measured in dollars, value is much more difficult to ascertain. Since these are basic economic principles, most of the groundwork done to define them is quite old. For instance: economist L. M. Fraser breaks value down into four aspects or "senses of value" that he calls: "Cost-value" (what a thing costs to make), "Exchange-value" (the amount of stuff, generally money but not necessarily, one can acquire by selling an item and/or the amount of stuff one should be prepared to pay for it), "Use-value" (the thing referenced in speech when one says that something is "valuable" as an equivalent of "useful"), and "Esteem-value" (an item's usefulness in conjunction with the ease with which one might acquire it).[20] In considering Shakespeare's value on an intellectual market, essentially one must make a calculation to convert his use-value as an intellectual commodity into exchange-value by virtue

10 | THEATRES OF VALUE

of audiences paying in time, money, or both to acquire an experience. From there, Shakespeare is converted into esteem-value. The esteem-value of Shakespeare on a nineteenth-century market creates one of the hotly contested historical issues with which this book will wrestle: Who "owns" Shakespeare, how did they acquire that right, and what happens when he is liberated from this ownership? Since esteem-value is market based (valuation in esteem-value relies on a commodity's scarcity within a market), it behooves those who would like to maintain Shakespeare's esteem-value to keep the resource scarce.

Lawrence Levine's work on the transformation of Shakespeare during America's nineteenth century from a "lowbrow" popular culture artifact to a "highbrow" mark of elitism clearly documents the middle- and upper-class desire to preserve Shakespeare's esteem-value by creating market scarcity.[21] In many ways, this drive is also at the heart of the Astor Place Riots. Putting Shakespeare behind cultural barriers increases his esteem-value and cements his place in a bourgeois sphere. Why and how this was done in New York's nineteenth century will be driving forces in chapter 1's discussion of the African Theatre, chapter 2's exploration of P. T. Barnum's use of Shakespeare as legitimizing capital, and chapter 5's account of the Shakespeare statue in New York's Central Park.

Use-value will also be important to this study. While Fraser has provided a preliminary definition, Karl Marx weighs in on an item's "use-value," arguing that "the utility of a thing makes its use-value."[22] Marx's framing of use-value allows the reader to imagine that use-value can directly convert to cost on a market. If utility can be measured in numbers, those numbers provide a direct translation to exchange-value. Envisioning value as a market force also links a commodity into its consumption, which Marx argues plays directly back to its use-value: "Use-values become a reality only by use or consumption."[23] That is: a thing can only have measurable use-value when it is consumed. It is impossible to assign use-value to a thing that has not or cannot be used. The consumptive act is a huge factor in considering value generally and use-value specifically.

Marx gives consumption even greater weight as a market force (especially in thinking about a cultural market) when he argues: "Consumption completes the act of production by giving the finishing touch to the product as such, by dissolving the latter, by breaking up its independent material form; by bringing to a state of readiness, through the necessity of repetition, the disposition to produce developed in the first act of production; that is to say, consumption is not only the concluding act through which the product becomes a product, but also the one through which the producer becomes a producer."[24] Considering a cultural market, the artistic act of production must be consumed both to give the cultural product value and to mark the artist as a "producer." Art for art's sake is not a market force; according to Marx, in order for a thing to have any value on a market, it must be consumed. In terms of the theatre, this resonates even more strongly. Audiences are vital to the very existence of the theatre as a commodity. In conceiving of theatre as a product, Tracy Davis remarks: "In between . . . performances, the show exists only in potential . . . theatre cannot be warehoused for later use, for it is expunged as it is performed: this liveness and inherent temporal fragility are what separates theatre from other arts. . . . It needs to be re-made for each performance, and fully exists only in the presence of consumers in the same space and time as the performers and operatives whose services are being expended."[25] Consumers make theatre as much as theatremakers do and consumption, to Davis as to Marx, is what actually *makes* theatre.

Shakespeare's value on the American market is therefore as much created by the Americans who bought him as it is by the Americans who sold him. In this relationship, value is a function of both producer and audience and creates an important dialogue between the two. This dialogue will be cornerstone to my discussions of brand building in the context of both Fanny Kemble (chapter 3) and Edwin Booth (chapter 4).

Ralph Barton Perry proposes a slightly different theory of "value," engaging with the notion that it can be individual:

> That which is an object of interest is, *eo ipso*, invested with value. Any object, whatever it be acquires value when any interest, whatever it be, is taken in it. . . . The view may otherwise be formulated in the equation x is valuable = interest is taken in x. . . . It follows that any variation of interest or of its object will determine a variety of value; that any derivative of interest or its object will determine value in a derived sense; and that any condition of interest or its object will determine a conditional value.[26]

Perry's theory of value presses further what Fraser established in that value has shades of meaning. Different from Fraser, Perry's shades of meaning derive from interest rather than economic use. Philip Mirowski agrees that value is equal to interest but specifies that this interest must also be large scale (that is: social rather than individual). He proposes a "social theory of value."[27] The sense that value is constructed by consumer forces continues to establish the nuanced space audiences have in creating theatrical value. In these models, consumers create derivative value and new meanings of value itself. As I have already acknowledged, the many permutations of Shakespeare on a market are often conflated. I will demonstrate how this conflation conglomerates value in my discussion of P. T. Barnum's American Museum and Lecture Hall (chapter 2), New York's Shakespeare statue (chapter 5), and the 1888 benefit performance of *Hamlet* to Lester Wallack (chapter 6).

The concept of value stemming from interest is nuanced by other economists, including John Laird who contends that "value in economics is essentially utility."[28] Laird continues to argue that "interest" does imbue items with value, but "interest" should be considered as a function of what humans want and need to survive rather than what their personal preferences are. This sense of value will be deeply important to chapters 4 and 5 as I consider Shakespeare's value to a brand in crisis and his value amid a war-torn America.

Thinking specifically about the value of literary works, Barbara Herrnstein Smith notes that "value" is a moving target: "Evaluation is always compromised because value is always in motion . . . it is constantly variable and eternally indeterminate."[29] Smith reminds us that long-lasting literary works have been valued and revalued by the generations that inherited them: every time they are printed, saved, reprinted, edited, or preserved, they are evaluated. When something is determined "worth keeping," its value is reestablished and affirmed. Literary value, therefore, is the product of a dynamic system and "our experience of the 'value of the work' is equivalent to our experience of the work in relation to the total economy of our existence."[30] With so many variables in the value equation for a piece of literary work, "value is radically contingent, being neither a fixed attribute, an inherent quality, or an objective property of things but, rather, an effect of multiple, continuously changing, and continuously interacting variables or, to put this another way, the product of the dynamics of a system."[31] Smith notes that the supposed "products" of this system are actually symptoms of it: "The value of a literary work is continuously produced and re-produced by the very acts of implicit and explicit evaluation that are frequently invoked as 'reflecting' its value and therefore are being evidence of it. In other words, what are commonly taken to be the signs of literary value are, in effect, its springs."[32]

Value, in Smith's terms, is an intrinsic, created form. It is neither static nor predetermined but a constant negotiation that is highly socially regulated. Looking at why something is valued and how that value is created by both producer and audiences reveals deep things about not just the value of the item but also the society that created this value. In peeling back the layers, one can begin to create the dramaturgy of value, envisioning the social systems that create a thing's value within its context. These systems are constantly changing and shifting, and thus constantly requiring reevaluation. In thinking about value as Smith does, there remains some contingency of social expectations to create this value. Because value is the symptom of a social condition, ever-evolving as it invents and reinvents itself, a thing must be imbued with value by the society surrounding it. Nineteenth-century Americans were simultaneously generating value for Shakespeare as they were generating the market commodity of Shakespeare. In essence, they were marketing a product to each other while also marketing the idea of a market. This dual system is an Ouroboros that feeds even as it expends itself. Because of this paradigm, some of the specific arguments in this book (particularly in chapter 5 concerning Shakespeare's statue in Central Park) may seem circular—but that in itself is telling of a market condition. A self-referential idea of value indicates either an inability or unwillingness to explore where this value originates, or a self-consciousness about this value (and possibly both). These qualities make value difficult to ascertain without an attachment to a historical moment: value is not created in a vacuum and the variation of value trends with the variation of society itself. The dramaturgy of value is a necessary construction for deriving any sense of value at all.

In setting out to define cultural production, Pierre Bourdieu links the creation of value by works of art to their ability to be known and recognized. Art can only hold value if a society recognizes the symbols it represents. As such, valuation of works of art must consider not just material production but also symbolic production.[33] To Bourdieu, the object may hold value only if it is recognizable by an audience and, therefore, evaluation must take into account the systems that make it so. Uncovering and examining these systems is the work of a dramaturgy of value. This does not begin and end with an artwork itself but rather must be constructed from the network to which the piece of art belongs. Key to understanding these systems is the movement of what Bourdieu calls "producers of meaning" (he cites critics, publishers, gallery directors; I add marketers and businesspeople) and how these folks leverage the net-

14 | THEATRES OF VALUE

work's central nodes to create market capital from cultural objects. These actions reveal what marketers believe is "sellable" about a commodity, and this belief unveils the pulse of a social system. I will explore the links between producers of meaning and the social systems they feed in chapters 1 (regarding the African Theatre), 2 (looking at P. T. Barnum), 3 (considering Kemble's readings), and 6 (unraveling Daly and Palmer's benefit to Wallack).

In describing the spheres that interact with and influence value, Bourdieu's concept of "habitus" is useful. "Habitus," according to Bourdieu, is the system of "durable, transposable dispositions, structured structures predisposed to function as structuring structures, that is, as principles which generate and organize practices and representations that can be objectively adapted to their outcomes without presupposing a conscious aiming at ends of an express mastery of the operations necessary in order to attain them."[34] In other words, habitus is the set of guidelines that the individual subconsciously or consciously uses to structure their interactions with the world around them. Habitus formation begins in childhood and continues through a protracted inculcation process over a person's lifetime. It is not a conscious adherence to a set of rules but rather a general feeling about how one should react in specific situations. It is a set of dispositions that influence behavior. Bourdieu claims that habitus is created by "the structures constitutive of a particular type of environment."[35] Bourdieu further claims that the material conditions of a person's environment create their ingrained mental and physical habits and form the way a person interacts with the world. Habitus is the sphere from which people interact with things around them, and to Bourdieu it is heavily mediated by the objects of capital that surround a person, suggesting that social class has a huge impact on habitus.

Because "value" is culturally created, habitus forms the space from which value is judged by an audience. Since habitus is so tightly linked to class, Bourdieu senses a struggle of power relations in literary and artistic fields, represented by a "struggle between the two principles of hierarchization: the heteronomous principle, favorable to those who dominate the field economically and politically (e.g., 'Bourgeois art') and the autonomous principle (e.g., 'Art for art's sake')."[36] In essence, the struggle that Lawrence Levine describes in *Highbrow/Lowbrow* was not just a struggle relevant to Shakespeare in America's nineteenth century but rather a symptom of a greater struggle within literary and artistic fields.[37] Bourdieu points out that bourgeois grip on cultural capital is a power struggle; and so the producing and reproducing of dominant economic capital by those outside of the dominant cultural group is an act of rebellion. I will examine this act of rebellion in chapter 1 as I discuss the African Theatre's productions of Shakespeare and their struggles with legitimacy, and in chapter 3 as I discuss Fanny Kemble's liberation of herself via her Shakespearean readings.

The dramaturgy of value is a method of unpacking and understanding the systems at play that create value. Cultural theorist John Frow describes these systems as "regimes of value": "[A] regime of value, [is] a semiotic institution generating evaluative regularities under certain conditions of use, and in which particular empirical audiences or communities may be more or less fully imbricated."[38] In other words, a regime of value is a sphere from which evaluation can be made and, since value is relative, that value will change as one changes which regime they evaluate from. Frow contends that Bourdieu's theories are not sufficient to explain this phenomenon since (among other complaints) Bourdieu's theories position the relationship of culture and class as too fixed and the positionality of the value analyst / objectified space uncontextualized and unaccounted for.[39] To Frow, Bourdieu does not go far enough toward preventing the observation of a phenomenon to impact the phenomenon. Theorizing regimes of value means that the positionality of the evaluator (a person external to the value equation, that is, neither the buyer nor the seller but rather someone looking to describe the exchange they are making) can also be accounted for in the value equation. By theorizing value as a performance, the dramaturgy of value understands Frow's regimes as fundamental—positionality of commodity, producer, consumer, and evaluator are all critical to value conclusions.

"Commodity," "Brand," and "Market"

With all this talk of "value," my implication is that Shakespeare was a commodity worth buying and selling in the nineteenth century, and that Shakespearean economy was big business monetarily as well as philosophically. Fraser offers a simple-enough definition of four main senses of "commodity": "Either it is anything which has utility: or anything which has exchange value; or any material thing which has utility or exchange value; or any directly consumable thing which has utility or exchange value."[40] Marx defines "commodity" as "an object outside us, a thing that by its properties satisfies human wants of some sort or another."[41] Both

Fraser and Marx lean into the idea that a commodity is a "thing" or an "object," some kind of physically transferable good. In the case of Shakespeare, these items exist in abundance. Take, for instance, the volumes of Shakespearean books and materials that were collected by English people and Americans alike throughout the nineteenth century.[42] Alongside the books were the paraphernalia, the souvenirs and tchotchkes that range from "genuine" items crafted from Shakespeare's mulberry tree in Stratford to the many busts and china sets that featured Shakespearean inscriptions or images.[43] Consider also the value of the intellectual commodity. Shakespeare is more than an object or series of objects, and the buying/selling of Shakespeare-centric objects is driven by his value as an idea. This sense of non-thing commodity, the commodity of ideas, propels all the chapters of this book.

The consideration of Shakespeare's commodity as something that has 1) endured, 2) been valuable to cultural producers and audiences, and 3) been ubiquitous as a means of moneymaking for various businesspeople is not a new phenomenon. Michael Bristol took up these issues up in *Big-Time Shakespeare*, wherein he concluded (among other things) that "the Shakespeare of the culture industry is neither more nor less essential to consumers than Bugs Bunny."[44] Bristol clearly articulated Shakespeare's durability as a commodity and how fame interacted with the Shakespearean product over time, but this conversation leaves more room for engagements with the how and why.

It's worth noting that I've already used the term "brand" to reference the value that Shakespeare imbues on things. Pramod Nayar defines "brand" as "a set of relations between products and services. It is intangible and non-corporeal but it is never immaterial."[45] As I consider the things bought and sold in and around Shakespeare, the term must apply to at least some of these products. Nayar argues that a brand, like value, is coproduced by its users across the many domains that a product is consumed (rather than solely controlled by a corporation), and because of its positionality can function as a quality-testing device for users engaging with the brand.[46] Shakespeare, for instance, might serve as the medium through which Shakespeare-branded products (syllabi, literary theory, pedagogy, etc.) can be gauged qualitatively since, to Nayar, Shakespeare is a fixed standard. Certainly the businesspeople in this book took advantage of this qualitative state associated with Shakespeare and the different ways they engaged with it are explored in the various chapters.

Nayar pushes against the ideas of Kate Rumbold, who argues that to say Shakespeare is a brand is to erase the nuance with which Shakespeare participates in an open market.[47] Rather, Rumbold urges that deeper consideration of Shakespeare's construction on the marketplace is necessary. Since Shakespeare is not a corporation engaging consciously with the usage of itself as a product (like Coca-Cola, for instance, or even Madonna), to Rumbold Shakespeare creates "the impression of a brand" rather than a literal brand.[48] While this nuance is important semiotically, this book will fall more in Nayar's camp. The audiences who used Shakespeare for commerce clearly interacted with his products as branded commodities and it was that brand that helped them to create value. And how do brands create value? Douglas B. Holt theorizes that "cultural brands" (like Nike, Apple, or Budweiser) position themselves as agents of identity upon which consumers can construct their own identities.[49] For many of these brands, consumers value what the commodity *does* rather than what the commodity *is*—what story of themselves can they tell that is engaged with this commodity and that the commodity assists them in telling? This book considers Shakespeare's implementation as a cultural brand across broad spectrums of nineteenth-century American society.

When considering the thing that is bought/sold at the theatre, one considers what Derek Miller calls the "performance-commodity": the thing protected by law that is performed onstage in front of an audience (and, importantly to Miller, does not include the pieces of this thing that are *not* protected by law).[50] While the performance-commodity of Shakespeare is certainly at stake in my examination of the cultural market, Shakespeare's value extends beyond the performance-commodity in all of my case studies.

Commodities are exchanged on a market. In the case of traditional material commodities, this market can be a physical location—a store, a street, a marketplace. In the case of intellectual commodities, the market is more nebulous. Markets for intellectual commodities can come by way of experiences—lectures, classes, readings, theatre performances, and so forth. They can also come by way of demonstrated attachments to the ephemera associated with a cultural object—collections of images, texts, or other items of visual art, for instance. The market as an institution can be helpful in tracing the movement of commodities, as Jean-Christophe Agnew notes in his readings of Marx: "The more frequently commodities are consumed and thereby removed from an expanding circulation, the farther money, as the durable token of equivalence, seems to move away of its own accord from its point of departure in the marketplace. As a result, what begins as a bounded process of the circulation of commodities through the medium of money (C-M-C) ends as the boundless circulation of money via the medium of commodities (M-C-M)."[51] The C-M-C/M-C-M models of circulation are taken directly from Marx and can help unpack the "what" of a Shakespearean marketplace.[52] As Shakespeare-the-commodity is consumed and distributed, he becomes further abstracted from the currency that purchased him. In a way, this book expresses the shift in the Shakespearean market from C-M-C to M-C-M as Shakespeare becomes the vehicle for, and impetus of, the exchange of currency on a sentimental market. Agnew continues on to trace the development of the marketplace and, through this, the development of commodity exchange. He claims: "This historical shift in the market's meaning—from a place to a process to a principle to a power—suggests a gradual displacement of concreteness in the governing concept of commodity exchange."[53] In other words, examining the shifting concept of "market" can help better conceptualize the shift I outlined earlier in what a commodity is and how that commodity is exchanged. Agnew's work tracing "market" from a physical place to a philosophical concept underlies the abstraction of commodities themselves.

The nineteenth century was an important moment in the development of the US marketplace. Ronald Takaki traces America's "market revolution" during this time: the transformation of the American economy from a simple agrarian model into a complex interdependent relational economy with regional specializations.[54] This shift was because of many factors: the increase of urban population (which went from 5% in 1800 to 20% in 1860), the increase in the country's land mass (acquired by imperialistic conquering) and subsequently settled areas of the United States (between 1800 and 1860, the settled area of the United States increased 500%), technological advances in transportation that deisolated farmers from the commercial sector, and all of this resting on the expansion then subsequent abolition of Black slavery as well as the exploitation of Native peoples and their land.[55] These shifts in the very fabric of the United States throughout the nineteenth century had profound impacts on what constituted a market during this time. This book spans almost a century of changes when the United States itself wasn't a settled concept; from chapter 1 to chapter 6, it's important to remember that the market develops along with the nation.

"Capital"

One last key term to understand before undertaking the work of a dramaturgy of value is "capital." Marx equates "capital" with value, and his "general formula for capital" is heavily reliant on money as a symbol of value.[56] Indeed, "capital" and "value" are nearly synonymous. In explicating "capital," Fraser finds that a "sense" of capital is easier to come to than a definition and notes three senses in which it might be used in economic discussion: "It may stand for productive equipment, for the use of purchasing power and the control over resources, and for claims to, or expectation of, that kind of income which goes by the name of 'interest.'"[57] Essentially, "capital" can be used in any moment where the exchange of value is happening. It is the noun that symbolizes value, and amassing capital is equivalent to amassing power (be it spending power or social power, as Bourdieu establishes that the two are very closely linked).

Discussions of capital in this book will oscillate between the acquisition and trade of monetary capital, and the way that interacts with cultural capital. Bourdieu defines cultural capital as a series of social codes, internalized by society, and used to encode works of art with significance and relevance.[58] Possessing knowledge of these codes indicates a person's possession of cultural capital. The ability to decode these social codes is learned throughout life from a person's habitus, institutionalized education, family, and society. Miller hypothesizes the following equation for evaluating cultural capital: "The cultural capital of performance is the surplus value from the production of the performance-commodity."[59] Miller's framing of cultural capital requires an ability to conceive of value simultaneously in multiple forms: money forms, social forms, and intellectual forms; it is therefore key to derive a thing's dramaturgy of value in order to apply Miller's equation to an object of cultural capital.

Returning to Bourdieu, he moves on to argue that there are different forms of capital and that the most unequally distributed form is symbolic capital.[60] He argues, "Symbolic capital . . . is not a particular kind of capital but what every kind of capital becomes when it is misrecognized as capital, that is, a force, a power or capacity for (actual or potential) exploitation, and therefore recognized as legitimate. More precisely, capital exists and acts as symbolic capital . . . in its relationship with a habitus predisposed to . . . know and recognize it on the basis of cognitive structures able and

20 | THEATRES OF VALUE

inclined to grant it recognition because they are attuned to what it is."[61] All capital, according to Bourdieu, is or can be symbolic capital depending on its relation to the predominant habitus in the field where it is being used. Cultural capital's transferal to symbolic capital thus depends upon its usage and the people who shape this usage. By linking the definition of symbolic capital to use, Bourdieu also recognizes that symbolic capital is a product of the market that sells it. In other words: as soon as the piece of cultural capital comes to be recognized as a legitimate market force, it becomes symbolic capital.

As hinted by his emphasis on symbolic capital requiring a certain audience interaction paradigm, Bourdieu explicitly theorizes power in recognition. To Bourdieu, "to be known and recognized also means possessing the power to recognize, to consecrate, to state, with success, what merits being known and recognized, and, more generally to say what is, or rather what is to be thought about what is, through a performative act of speech (or prediction) capable of making what is spoken of conform to what is spoken of it."[62] In Bourdieu's model, the power of recognition not only endows a thing with value but also with the capacity to endow other connected things with value by association. Shakespeare's value to the nineteenth-century businesspeople discussed in this book does not end with the product of Shakespeare but rather extends to the mouthpiece of Shakespeare. It allows them the agency to, using Shakespeare, create the very market upon which they could sell and use the recursive qualities of Shakespeare's value to sell himself and the items he touched.

Building the Nation

These are the terms of buying and selling that will guide this book. There still remains the question of "why." Why would Shakespeare serve as such an important market force, coin-of-the-realm perhaps, for American businesspeople in the nineteenth century? One vital key to answering this question lies with the creation of an American national identity. A great deal of America's attachment to Shakespeare stems from a burning nineteenth-century desire to establish a distinctly American national and cultural identity, and to incorporate Shakespeare into that identity.[63] Theatre has been well expounded as a means for doing so.[64] Earlier American theatres dealt with the fluidity and foreignness of national identity, and the perceived place theatre had in a burgeoning republic.[65] By the mid-nineteenth century, Americans had begun to grapple with understanding their identity, especially during the Civil War when "America" seemed to encompass so many different ideals. Previous scholars explicate efforts that were bound to traditionally theatrical spaces, but what happens when Shakespeare steps off the stage? Removing Shakespeare from the playhouse did not seem to diminish his value as cultural capital and employed other aspects of Shakespeare's legacy to assert cultural dominance in an American canon as well as legitimacy through his literariness. These extra-theatrical performances worked to naturalize Shakespeare-the-man and claim the capital he represented for a bourgeoning American repertoire. Considering these performances, it is helpful to also consider Diana Taylor's argument that "performance makes visible that which is always already there: the ghosts, the tropes, the scenarios that structure our individual and collective life. These specters, made manifest through performance, alter future phantoms, future fantasies."[66] Claiming and naturalizing Shakespeare through any performance (bound to the stage or liberated from it) changes Shakespeare for Americans by rendering visible America's attachment to the idea of Shakespeare and presenting him as a structure of individual and collective American identity.

In discussing how Americans sought to create and structure national identity, two useful ideas about what constitutes a "nation" will prove helpful. Benedict Anderson proposes that a "nation" is "an imagined political community."[67] Anderson claims this community is "imagined" because citizens of a nation will never meet every other member of their nation and, therefore, must imagine them. Anderson further clarifies that a nation is a "community" because of a "deep, horizontal comradeship" that makes the very concept of a nation possible.[68] Anderson's emphasis on the mind creating the space that forms a nation indicates the powerful potential of national consciousness and how Americans' thoughts created the fabric that makes America. Giving Shakespeare space in this imagination also knits him to the essence of the country.

Anderson's conception of "nation" begs questions of boundaries and branding: How is it possible that many people who have never met (and will never meet) might imagine themselves to be contiguous? In order for this group to find cohesion, they need some kind of communally imagined identity. Anthony D. Smith postulates several qualities that he argues create the fundamental features of national identity:

1. An historic territory or homeland

2. Common myths and historical memories

22 | THEATRES OF VALUE

3. A common, mass public culture

4. Common legal rights and duties for all members

5. A common economy with territorial mobility for members

A nation can therefore be defined as a named human population sharing an historic territory, common myths and historical memories, a mass, public culture, a common economy and common legal rights and duties for all members.[69]

In considering these five qualities within the context of this book: Throughout the nineteenth century American territory was still being violently and imperialistically acquired. Americans' common myths were still bourgeoning. Americans struggled to find a common, mass public culture. During and directly after the Civil War, common legal rights and duties for all Americans was a hot-button issue. The country was struggling to establish a stable federal currency.[70] Essentially, all of Smith's required qualities were still in flux. Necessarily, stabilizing these items would indicate a strengthening sense of national identity and that is precisely what Americans did as the century unfolded. As Americans sought to draft their national identity, they incorporated Shakespeare and his cultural capital to help form the fabric that would piece the nation together. The fervor for Shakespeare that I will discuss in the following chapters could be read as an effort to claim a common myth (factor two) as well as mass public culture (factor three) for the American people. Rather than viewing these consumptive moments as Americans memorializing an English playwright, instead they are an attempt to naturalize Shakespeare and claim him as a piece of American cultural heritage and part of America's "imagined nation." By so doing, Americans might use Shakespeare as a touchstone for American mythmaking: he could be a proven piece of legitimate cultural currency upon whose back Americans might build the things they needed to form a national identity.

The tension between the struggle for a distinctly American identity and the fixation upon a decidedly English playwright is both clarified and complicated by an 1864 article published in the *New York Herald*:

Shakespeare is probably nowhere else played or read in the same extent that he is in this country. His works are a household volume. He is the common favorite of all our people, from A.

Lincoln to the urchins that "thunder at a playhouse and fight for bitten apples." He has more phrases that aptly fit our American ideas than any American writer. . . . We are so many separate nations that we have a difficulty about great men. Pennsylvania will believe in no one but the grand noncombatant, William Penn; Massachusetts goes for Franklin, and Vermont will never admire any one but Ethan Allen; Virginia will build monuments to Thomas Jefferson, Tennessee to Andrew Jackson . . . and, though we have bought Washington's homestead, it would be very difficult to get the country to unite in admiration of any other one American . . . ; but we can all unite in our admiration of Shakespeare.[71]

This author's loud and repeated declarations about Shakespeare as a unifying force in a divided America play into Smith's clear directives that national identity must be forged from common materials and may not be created from dissonant parts. The *Herald* article reminds its reader of how divided America is culturally, while simultaneously using Shakespeare as the glue with which the nation may be pieced together. It is, perhaps, because of Shakespeare's Englishness that this is possible: England is the common legacy each of these states enjoyed. In order to create unity, the *Herald* author was forced to trace backward down the branches of America's cultural heritage until the point where they converged, all the way to what Thomas Cartelli calls America's "parent stream" of common language and culture: England.[72] The *Herald* author can't seem to draft Americanness without Englishness precisely because of what Cartelli claims: every river needs a tributary. There can be no garment without raw materials to weave the cloth. Shakespeare is a piece of America's raw materials that Americans cannot do without.

Throughout this piece of writing, the author reiterates how very American Shakespeare is in a plethora of ways: as a widely read literary subject, a totem of household decency, a favored theatrical genre, an apt and fitting writer, and an object of general admiration. The author also explicitly brands Shakespeare as American in this passage's penultimate line ("any other one American").[73] By incorporating Shakespeare as part of an American brand, American nation builders appropriated the cultural capital he entailed to formulate their own imagined identity. In so writing and rewriting Shakespeare as American, the *Herald* author inscribes American values to the English playwright. Predictably enough, the writer continually casts Shakespeare as

24 | THEATRES OF VALUE

"American" and never once mentions England or Englishness. This strategic erasure in conjunction with the inscription of American identity serves as a strong attempt to brand Shakespeare with Americanness.

Of course, both Cartelli's "parent stream" theory and the *Herald* writer's nod toward the assumption that America is drafted in England's image leave wide margins. Those on the outside of this paradigm—the nonwhite, non-European residents and citizens of the United States—still found value in Shakespeare. To them, Shakespeare became a subversive tool, a way to speak the language of the cultural hegemony and introduce their own constructions of "value" and "Americanness" via material already hailed as intrinsically valuable.[74]

Bourdieu calls a sphere of production or circulation a "field." In establishing the ways that a field marks itself as a competitor for cultural legitimacy, Bourdieu remarks that this legitimacy comes from repeated reinscription of the marks of distinction within the field (i.e., producers within the field will orient their product toward the features that most contain value in the field's economy).[75] Repeated assertion of values and valuable capital by producers can, thereby, act as breadcrumbs for the historian—a pattern or flag marking where producers see competition for cultural legitimacy on an open market. Certainly the frequent repetitive use of Shakespeare in the preceding *Herald* quote bears all of these markers, but perhaps there's another element at work here. Bourdieu continues on to argue that spheres on their way to legitimation will confront the question of their own legitimacy far more frequently than accepted legitimate spheres. As such, they will tend to more frequently inscribe legitimacy markers upon themselves in order to meet these inevitable challenges.[76] This redoubled effort to prove, over and over again, why something (specifically Shakespeare-the-idea) is valuable on an American market will be a recurring theme of the following chapters and marks nineteenth-century America's Shakespeare market as a developing sphere on its way to legitimation, but not yet fully legitimate in its own right.

"Put money in thy purse."

—Iago, *Othello*, I.iii

The following six case studies will explore value and worth, buying and selling, markets and consumers, and the socioeconomic systems of power that underlie these concepts in America's nineteenth century. This book is called *Theatres of Value*, which is a bit of a pun. Yes, this book is about theatre (both the art and the place). But also, I invite the reader to consider the idea of a "theatre of value" alongside a "theatre of war." A "theatre of value" is the entire scale and scope of geography where value is crafted—the concept of place (both literal and abstract) that encompasses the exchanges examined by the dramaturgy of value. A theatre of value includes the market, but it also includes the underlying currents of what drives market exchanges. At stake in all of these conversations is the notion of where value comes from. Bourdieu wonders:

> Who is the true producer of the value of the work—the painter or the dealer, the writer or the publisher, the playwright or the theater manager? The ideology of creation, which makes the author the first and last source of the value of his work, cancels the fact that the cultural businessman (art dealer, publisher, etc.) is at one and the same time the person who exploits the labour of the "creator" by trading in the "sacred" and the person who, by putting it on the market, by exhibiting, publishing or staging it, consecrates a product which he has "discovered" and which would otherwise remain a mere natural resource.[77]

If Shakespeare could be considered one of America's natural resources, the American artists and businesspeople who formed and molded him into a product worth buying must also receive due attention from any study of his place in nineteenth-century life. I start this account of Shakespeare in America looking at the claims of legitimacy made on Shakespeare's back, and Bourdieu's acknowledgment of the salesman as a major factor in value creation is a theme that will drive strongly through chapters 1 (Brown and the African Theatre), 2 (Barnum's American Museum and Lecture Room), and 4 (the Booth brand). From there, I will show a change in the way Shakespeare was traded on an American market. While Barnum played a large role in creating the value of his product in an audience's mind, the Booth brand cemented Shakespeare as a thing of value to Americans. After the Booths, Shakespeare retained this value and was able to be used by subsequent businesspeople as an idea inherently valuable. This signals a shift in Shakespeare's place in this economy, a shift (I will argue) pivotally linked to the Booth brand.

In all of these case studies, Shakespeare enters with and as value. He is the control variable (the constant) while the positionality of the

26 | THEATRES OF VALUE

users who extol upon his value changes how they interact with it.[78] The news isn't that these users turned to Shakespeare, but why? What value does he provide to them that can explain this rhetorical strategy? In some ways, the first few chapters seem to represent a false start on the part of American Shakesalesmen. Chapter 1 talks about a theatre company that fell into obscurity for a long time after it closed. Chapter 2 discusses another theatrical enterprise doomed to be literal food for power. Chapter 3 talks about a theatrical event rather than theatre per say. But all of that changes with the Booths—chapter 4. Edwin Booth (arguably America's most beloved theatrical celebrity of his time) was able to successfully marry his brand to Shakespeare, which triggered something in the zeitgeist. Booth's celebrity becoming knit to Shakespeare opened the floodgates for American imagination—suddenly Shakespeare's value was gold-backed. Booth's brand elision created space in the American imagination for a Shakespeare so valuable that he was worth the Central Park statue, that he could power the Wallack benefit, and that he could rehabilitate the Booth brand from the brink of disaster.

When considered in relation to national identity and the argument that Shakespeare's value to nineteenth-century audiences was linked to nation building, this makes sense. Brown's company was creating theatre for a subset of the population marginalized by hegemonic forces and obscured from a cohesive national identity. Try as he might to label his product "American," Barnum's lowbrow popular entertainments were gate-kept from being included as fundamental pieces of national identity due to their nature as artifacts of dubious moral fortitude. Fanny Kemble was British, and though her product was enjoyed by high-status tastemakers, it could hardly be folded into any sense of Americanness. Booth, how-ever, was all-American. His family trauma was deeply connected to the nation's. He stood for everything that white Northern tastemakers desired: intellectual veracity fueled by Eurocentric roots wrapped in a bankably handsome exterior. When Booth called, the Bard answered—and the American public paid attention. As we follow the money, there will be a clear break from the pre-Booth era of American Shakespeare economics and the post-Booth era.

Of course, the theatremakers I'm discussing aren't the only Shake-speare users in this book—I myself am also using him to demonstrate a point. I treat Shakespeare here as a window. Looking through it, one can see these case studies and how they interact with the glass. Sometimes, I will look closely enough that the window will become less visible. Shakespeare is the common variable, but this story is more about his users than Shakespeare himself. This book sees Shakespeare as a device: a tool whose form has great potential to the creative mind. The applications of this metamorphic tool reflect the environments in which it is deployed.

The dramaturgy of value proposes that understanding social phenomena boils down, at its heart, to understanding economics. It offers the theatre historian a way to cross-apply the concepts of dramaturgy, concepts they are already familiar with, to instances of exchange as a means of answering the age-old question of "why." Simplifying a Shakespearean object down to something that has "valuable cultural capital" misses critical opportunities to nuance this understanding. The dramaturgy of value asks and allows scholars to stop taking Shakespeare's value as mere cultural capital for granted without complicating the ways in which this cultural capital intersects with (i.e., shapes and is shaped by) other forms of capital, brand building, and worth.

There is a humanist aversion to this work, and yet it is a necessary foundation to the study of art. When considering a commodity, particularly an intangible commodity, the only way to gauge the magnitude of its impact is to untangle the market forces that led to its creation. The dramaturgy of value provides a vital tool to researchers asking why something matters and how it grew to claim such import; it insists that we dispense with this aversion. "Money talk" needs to be part of the humanist equation; ars gratia artis cannot sustain critical thought.

This book is about process—theatrical and para-theatrical. The Shakespeare users whose work is examined here all come to their own, albeit similar, conclusions about the best use case for Shakespeare's cultural capital in order to achieve their bottom lines. Implementation and its follies are as important to the development of Shakespeare's market space as finished products. In other words: to spot the motivation behind these businesspeople's every movement, one needs to pull back the curtain on their act. This is the dramaturgy of value's primary function: to encourage us to watch the magician's every move in order to spot the trick.

Chapter One

What William Brown Knew

The African Theatre and the Growing Threat of Legitimacy

In September of 1821, the New York State Constitutional Convention sat convened in Albany, New York. On September 12, they were presented with a petition by "the coloured people of the city of New-York," which specifically and emphatically requested legal protections for the rights of the petition-bearers, including suffrage.[1] Prior to this meeting, no distinction had been drawn between voting rights for white and Black citizens in New York State (property and residence requirements were applied equally to all voters).[2] The 1821 convention was a turning point: while some delegates favored abolishing these barriers for all citizens, an outspoken number wished to disenfranchise Black New Yorkers out of fear that a right to vote would mean an influx in Black population as the legalities of slavery shifted.[3] On September 20, 1821, the convention voted to grant full and equal suffrage to Black New Yorkers.[4] This was short-lived; the decision was reconsidered as soon as October of the year.

This decision for suffrage did not come without its detractors. On September 25th, New York sheriff and theatre critic Mordecai Noah wrote in his newspaper, the *National Advocate*, "[Black people] now assemble in groups; and since they have crept in favour with the convention, they are

---

An earlier version of this chapter was published in: Danielle Rosvally, " 'Off with His Head! . . . So Much for Hewlett/Brown': The African Grove Theatre Presents *Richard III*," in *Shaping Shakespeare for Performance: The Bear Stage*, ed. Catherine Loomis and Sid Ray (Madison: Farleigh Dickinson University Press, 2015), 127–40.

determined to have balls and quadrille parties, establish a forum, solicit a seat in the assembly or in the common council, which, if refused, let them look to the elections. They can outvote the whites, as they say. One Black gentleman most respectfully instructed that he thought 'as how he mout [*sic*] be put on the grand jury!' "[5] Noah's recoiling against his perceptions of social change is an indicator flag: change *was* in the air in New York City and it was being felt by many different walks of society. Emancipation was immanent, the free Black population of New York was expanding, and this was going to have profound connotations to the status quo. In this moment, theatre was reacting. A production of *Richard III* was making history in a small residential apartment on the Lower West Side of Manhattan. There, entrepreneur William Brown formed the first theatre of its kind in the United States: a theatre made by Black artists for Black audiences. Predictably, Brown's small theatre met with persecution from its opening days. The way that this persecution interacted with Brown's use of Shakespeare weaves a telling statement about Shakespeare's value to Brown, his actors, and his audiences.

Brown and his company performed Shakespeare from their opening in September of 1821 to a dramatic litigious conclusion in January of 1822. Over the course of this tumultuous five months, Brown turned to Shakespeare as a source of many things. He used Shakespeare as a cultural authority to legitimize his enterprise; he used Shakespeare as a subversive tool to fight oppression; and he used Shakespeare as a viable and marketable commodity. Brown knew Shakespeare was a valuable piece of capital and intentionally used this capital as a foundation upon which to cultivate Black audiences in New York City. He built his business and its claims for legitimacy on the back of Shakespearean performance, and used this legitimacy to assert a place for Black artists and audiences on New York's nascent theatre scene. This chapter will center Brown's experience as it applies the dramaturgy of value. It will unpack the markers of legitimacy that Brown sought in order to establish space (literal and figurative) for Black artists and people in nineteenth-century New York. In so doing, it will use the dramaturgy of value to plumb the depths of Shakespeare's value to the Black audiences Brown served and the white audiences who feared him.

William Brown is the most underrated businessman of the nineteenth-century theatre. Brown was savvy. He saw the places theatre was made in New York, realized the potential of being in those places, observed where his audience demographic lived, and found a way to put his business in spaces that strategically addressed all of these factors in order to turn a profit and allow a burgeoning free Black population to claim places of leisure among the social upheaval prior to the Civil War. Brown was brave. He did not budge when white authorities attempted to overwrite and silence him. Shakespeare, to Brown, was both a moneymaking object and a tool to be leveraged as he fought for a space for Black artists and audiences in New York. This chapter demonstrates the utility of the dramaturgy of value to humanize historical figures by unwrapping their economic choices. William Brown, like Shakespeare himself, has left a very slim archival footprint and most of this footprint is economic data. Absent palpable personal historical evidence, the dramaturgy of value allows a careful historian to hypothesize agency—and that is what I hope to do for Brown in the following pages.

The basic tale of the African Theatre (as it has been told) goes like this: Circa 1818, Brown opened a pleasure garden that catered solely to Black clientele. His pleasure garden was located in the lot behind the residential building in which Brown lived at 38 Thomas Street in New York City. In August of 1821, the garden was closed by New York sheriff Mordecai Noah due to noise complaints. In September of 1821, Brown opened a production of *Richard III* in an upstairs apartment of the Thomas Street building. The cast was all Black and white patrons were not allowed inside the space. Barely a week after opening, Brown moved his company to a slightly larger residential apartment located at 56 Mercer Street. In this location he eventually created a separate seating area to accommodate white patrons. Sometime between September of 1821 and January of 1822, Brown's company began to perform *Richard III* at "Hampton's Hotel" located next to New York's most well-known and legitimate theatrical space of the time, the Park Theatre. In January of 1822, Brown and his actors were arrested midperformance, taken to jail where they were held overnight, then (according to popular anecdote) were released only after they had sworn never again to perform from the works of William Shakespeare. In mid-July of 1822, Brown opened a purpose-built playhouse at the south corner of Mercer and Bleecker Streets. In 1823, Brown retired and the African Company faded into obscurity.[6] As I've hinted in the anecdote with which I began this chapter, the story's setting is key to its profundity. The racial tensions of post-slavery New York City combined with an ever-increasing young, free, Black population created both a roiling pot of social upheaval and a ready market space for Brown. The African Theatre was founded in a city full of young Black men and women, many of them newly freed, hoping to create new lives for themselves.[7] Precisely because

32 | THEATRES OF VALUE

of these dynamics, Brown's business was both timely and fruitful, but this success fueled his detractors and increased the threat Brown presented to a white hegemony struggling to establish their own cultural dominance over the resource that was Shakespeare.

Like any historical object, the African Theatre is a construct of the ways it has been documented and discussed. The printed ephemera left by the African Theatre's footprint in time is a legacy that has long outlasted the theatre itself. Particularly because of this dynamic, it is unfortunate that some of the most complete documentation about the African Theatre is written by one of its most outspoken critics: New York sheriff, theatre critic, editor, and playwright Mordecai Noah. Noah's racism is clear in his newspaper writings about the African Theatre and New York's Black citizens more generally. Of course, Noah's worldview was shaped by his own experience as a marginalized other—a Jewish man and himself the target of racist bias.[8] Still, because of Noah's explicit anti-Black racism, it is impossible to implicitly trust every word of his accounts. However, because these accounts are comprehensive (and more prolific than any other historical source) it is difficult to discard them entirely. This is an important caveat when dealing with Noah and his writings about Brown's Theatre: they must be treated with a healthy amount of skepticism.

"Fine word—'legitimate'!"

—Edmund, *King Lear*, I.ii

While Americans struggled to form their national identity, a crucial component was the art that would accompany this identity. What was "American Theatre"? And, most pertinently to this chapter, what constituted "legitimacy" within the American theatre? In England, the definition had long since been established via the patent theatres and accompanying ordinances surrounding theatrical performance. The United States imported many cultural sensibilities from England—Shakespeare and ideas of "legitimacy" among them. Lawrence Levine argues that in England the term "legitimate" was closely linked to spoken dialogue plays (as opposed to plays with musical accompaniment) and nuances: "In 1832 Douglas Jerrold helped to redefine the term when he told a parliamentary committee investigating the state of the drama that a play was legitimate 'when the interest of the piece is mental rather than physical.' In his testimony, the actor William Macready agreed, defining a legitimate play as one possessing poetic quality or superior literary worth. It was in this sense that the term was imported and used in America."[9] Levine's definition, extrapolated from the words of various nineteenth-century actors and theatremakers, is entirely invested in the content of a performed piece. What does a play provide to an audience, and how does it provide this thing? Levine's terms link a play's legitimacy to its sense of literariness, in itself a hot commodity to nineteenth-century Americans.

An association between literary value and legitimacy is further enforced by Mark Hodin; legitimate theatre "suggested the sort of literariness associated with legitimate drama, a term familiar to British and American playgoers, actors, and critics in the nineteenth century for distinguishing classic plays (Shakespeare, Molière, Sheridan) from the contemporary melodramas they also enjoyed. . . . The particular value of conventionally staged drama was that it provided the best occasion and opportunity available for acquiring cultural prestige, 'literary' value, commercially."[10] Like Levine, Hodin claims that legitimacy (for a nineteenth-century audience at least) is invariably linked to the material that a play presents. To Hodin, certain playwrights (including Shakespeare) carried with them a sense of this value and their works thus brought it to the stage. Hodin holds up Shakespeare as a benchmark for legitimacy, a measuring stick by which other playwrights (and the material they produced) could be evaluated. Since, as Hodin claims, Shakespeare equated to literariness that directly converted to legitimacy, then a piece might be measured to fit this legitimacy by how Shakespearean it is. How many qualities a piece shares with Shakespeare could be used to determine how "legitimate" the piece might be. In Marxist terms, this creates of Shakespeare a "universal equivalent" with which to measure legitimacy in the nineteenth century.[11] Hodin doesn't rely solely on Shakespeare for this model and brings others—Molière, Sheridan—into the literary fold, but neither Molière nor Sheridan enjoyed the robust afterlife in the United States that Shakespeare did. Hodin also introduces the concept of capitalizing upon literary value; that the social value of literariness could translate directly (for theatremakers) to an economic value. By this logic alone, Shakespeare becomes an innately lucrative product: since legitimacy can be measured (at least according to Hodin) by Shakespearean standards, so too might the economic benefits of legitimacy. This exchange shows Shakespeare becoming the money form of the commodity of theatre, the vehicle by which value can be converted to worth.

Both Levine and Hodin argue that in establishing a working definition of "legitimacy," two facets of a performance must be considered: 1) in America, as in England, the venue in which a piece was performed lent credence and merit to the piece's bid for legitimacy, and 2) in America, as in England, the material being performed had to be considered; as Hodin and Levine contend this material must have a certain cultural worth, a certain literariness, and a certain effect upon the audience (namely to generate and provoke thought) in order to be considered "legitimate." Hodin explicitly invokes Shakespeare as a benchmark for facet 2, linking him both to the working definition of "legitimacy" as well as evaluative practices in theatrical economies.

The frame of this conversation about legitimacy highlights its link in nineteenth-century America to a vital economy of value. The fight for and over legitimacy establishes that there is some value (or, as Perry would argue, interest) in the idea of legitimacy and legitimation.[12] Why would a cultural object central to such a feud matter if there were no value in it? And why would it be worth Noah's bother to police (literally and figuratively)? There is no reason to expend the labor cost of anti-action if no benefit can be had from this action. Therefore: Noah's interest in Brown's business endeavors legitimized them as it invested them with Perry's sense of value and indicated that these endeavors were worth the time and action of policing.

Legitimacy is an economic value. Marvin McAllister links Brown's struggle with New York's hegemonic forces to the major/minor struggle in London and the dominance of the patent theatres in English theatrical spaces.[13] This connection underlines how formalizing claims to legitimacy was big business in England and (while the US didn't license theatres officially) was a similarly powerful economic driver for Brown and his detractors. Shakespeare's links to legitimacy (both explicit and implied) made him worth pursuing for all of these parties, and this was as true concretely as it was philosophically: there was money to be had in the Shakespeare trade. Shakespeare's legitimacy (and the legitimacy of the businesses that marketed him) contributed to his ability to be bought and sold.

In addition to being an economic value, legitimacy also had important roots in nation building. The capability to define what could and could not be seen as legitimate was a task still in question in the United States. In London, that authority was issued by the crown and the patent edicts. In America, the question still stood of where this authority might come from. Without a doubt some tensions in the struggle between Brown and New York authorities underlined the American anxiety that Shakespeare was a commodity that belonged to the empowered, a commodity for the white elite. Brown's continued interest in Shakespeare as a cultural object was as much an act of rebellion and defiance as it was an act of asserting presence. By continuing to produce Shakespearean content at the African Theatre, Brown was making and enforcing a model that liberated Shakespeare from the major white theatres and created an American Shakespeare tradition that was directly available to Black communities.

Since there was no American governing body to issue edicts about legitimacy and how performance might be tied to America's cultural identity, these notions underlined Brown's work. As hegemonic cultural institutions struggled to find their own American voice and create a sense of legitimacy for that voice, it follows that they might lash out at minor institutions who "co-opted" this legitimacy. Since the major American theatres' authority over Shakespeare was still in question, their attempts to regulate Shakespeare might be a method of cementing it. Additionally, Brown's pursuit of Shakespeare could be seen as a means of both challenging this authority and claiming space within it for Black people.

As Brown did this, he also seems to have purposefully addressed both the qualities surmised earlier about what can be used to indicate "legitimacy." By choosing to perform Shakespeare, Brown chose capital already valuable on a cultural level. His material had literary value and was already an accepted part of the mainstream theatrical repertoire. As far as the "where" of the performance, it took Brown some time to create a legitimate theatre space, but each step of his process was a clear movement in the direction of legitimation.

"Thou art granted space."

—First Soldier, *All's Well That Ends Well*, IV.i

Brown's first business wasn't the theatre but a pleasure garden referenced variably as a "tea garden" or "ice cream garden." The pleasure garden was a popular nineteenth-century place of leisure, an open-air park where patrons could enjoy walks, scenery, music, or more spectacular entertainments such as balloon ascents and fireworks.[14] When Brown opened his business, there were no other pleasure gardens available to Black patrons in New York City. While accounts differ about its dates of operation, Brown's outdoor space was likely formally opened for business in June of 1821 (though it may have functioned intermittently beginning as early as 1816).[15] One contemporaneous source, "Dr. Smith," describes the business simply as a "tea-garden."[16] Noah's paper describes it with significantly more venom: "We noticed, some time ago, the opening of a tea garden and evening serenades for the amusements of our Black gentry; it appears that some of the neighbors, not relishing the jocund nightly sarabands of those sable fashionables, actually complained to the Police, and the avenues of African Theatre were closed by authority."[17] Amid his jabs and prejudice, Noah indicates that there was much more than tea being served at the African Theatre. He reports music, dancing ("sarabands"), and general joviality resulting in sufficient noise that (presumably white) neighbors took enough notice to report the establishment. Noah's sarcastic jabs also reveal the white onlooker's perspective about Brown's patrons: an underlying class resentment that echoes his previously quoted anxieties surrounding Black civic life.

Brown's garden closed in August of 1821 due to "noise complaints." Despite Noah's railings, there are no complaints in the files of the New York County District Attorney's Office or the New York City Municipal Archive.[18] Several plausible explanations could address this gap, including filing errors, damage to subsets of papers from flood or fire, insufficient documentation practices, or normal loss due to passage of time. It could just as plausibly mean that no complaints were ever filed and the establishment was shut down by Noah in an effort to silence it without due process of the law. Either way, this moment directly shows how this story's paper manifestations have worked to frame narratives. Since the alleged complaint documents are no longer extant, even if they had been filed the only evidence for their verity is Noah's word. Noah's word is flawed when discussing the possibilities of the African Theatre. This white documentation of Black histories as the sole voice of authority asks contemporary audiences to allow the oppressor to frame the history's facts.

Whether or not noise complaints were formally filed, it does seem that Noah's persecution of the tea garden was presented to Brown under the presumed auspices of the law and with accompanying legal theatre.

While Brown's later businesses experienced targeted vandalism, the tea garden didn't seem to be such a target for this type of violence.[19] Noah terrorized Brown through more sinister means: by using his position within the system of oppression to exercise ordered force. Brown's savviness is on full display in the early days of his business, and his ability to beat white detractors at their own game can be traced through the series of events that led to the production of *Richard III*. When noise complaints were made about Brown's tea garden, he moved his enterprise inside. When Noah continued to publish diminutive articles about the content and quality of entertainments at the African Theatre, Brown and his team began to produce Shakespeare.

The African Theatre remained open to Black audiences only until sometime during the autumn of 1821. One of the few surviving playbills for the African Theatre is reprinted in George C. Odell's *Annals of the New York Stage*, and is dated October 1, 1821, a Monday night.[20] The playbill advertises "For the Benefit of Mr. Hewlet" (*sic*) "An Opera" consisting of ten songs sung by Hewlett and others in the company, "After which will be performed, for the last time this season, the Tragedy of Richard the Third," followed by "Pantomime Asama" and a "Ballet." It notes the location of these performances to be "corner of Mercer and Bleecker-st." This is not the Thomas Street apartment, but instead much closer to Brown's eventual purpose-built theatre where he moved his company permanently sometime in the summer of 1822.

This playbill seems nearly identical to one published the week before it and reprinted in the *National Advocate* of September 25, 1821.[21] The 9/25 playbill advertised similar content with a similar cast, but instead of advertising that this would be "the third attempt of this kind in this City, by persons of Colour," it advertised that its performance (on September 24th—also a Monday) would be "the second attempt of this kind in this city by persons of colour." It seems, from these two lines of text on two separate playbills, that Brown's company performed *Richard III* once a week on Monday evenings.[22] Additionally, it is worth noting that the performance on the 24th of September was advertised for admittance at 37½ cents, and October 1st at 50 cents. That is a fairly steep price hike over a single week—a full third higher, and Brown wouldn't have gambled it unless he knew he could fill his audience even at the new price point. This is one indication of Brown's popularity as well as his target clientele: 50 cents (for an unskilled Black laborer at the time) was nearly half a week's salary.[23]

38 | Theatres of Value

Here, Shakespeare's value as a commodity comes into focus. There are several reasons one might justify such a significant upcharge: crowding (a higher price would thin numbers slightly), audience demographic (a higher price would attract clientele who could afford such luxuries—and change the timbre of the audience's energy accordingly), and/or economic necessity (raising ticket cost would mean more profit). Through all of this, Brown's price hike exhibits that Shakespeare's value, to him, was drastically increasing—both in relation to white audiences who were looking at his enterprise from afar and Black audiences who were actually paying his ticket prices. Here is a businessman seeing and recognizing a commodity as holding more value than initially expected and adjusting his business model to suit. Additionally, Brown was able to harness the power of supply and demand to impact his prices. The African Theatre was the only theatre in town that allowed Black patrons anywhere but the galleries. As such, Brown was producing a low-supply commodity under (seemingly) high market demand and was able to adjust his prices in keeping with the market.

Another important change in Brown's business (perhaps linked to this price adjustment) occurred in October of 1821. That is: Brown created a partitioned section for seating white audiences in his theatre. An advert from the *National Advocate* of October 27, 1821, reads: "They have graciously made a partition at the back of their house, for the accommodation of the whites."[24] Allowing white audiences into the African Theatre opened Brown's audience base to a wider demographic (which likely had an impact on ticket sales), but it would be difficult not to imagine that there was an aspect of savviness to this move as well. Enabling white audiences to experience Brown's theatre and Black assembly firsthand might also have been a strategic attempt to circumvent racially loaded concerns about Black congregation that Noah (and, likely, others) dwelt upon in conjunction with the African Theatre.

"Death and danger dogs the heels of worth."

—Steward, *All's Well That Ends Well*, III.iv

Attempts to control Black people and their behavior is a persistent theme in American history, and is particularly complex in the decades leading up to the Civil War. In post-Revolutionary New York, the status of Black residents (slave and free) was an issue rife with anxiety and racial tensions. New York enacted gradual emancipation in 1799, but this act only impacted slaves born after July 4, 1799. All enslaved children born after that date would work in servitude to the slaver who held their mother for a term of twenty-eight years for men and twenty-five years for women. After this time, they would be freed. It was not until eighteen years later (1817) that the legislature agreed to universal freedom for slaves; and this freedom would not be fully enacted until July 4, 1827.[25]

New York's emancipation process created ambiguity for slaves and slave owners. When it became clear that there would be a definite end to slavery in New York, slave owners scrambled to make a final return on what they viewed as investments. Many slaves were able to take advantage of this scramble and negotiated the terms of their freedom so they might be freed sooner. Such negotiations were complicated by a noticeable uptick in cruelty toward slaves as well as an increase in murder attempts (successful and not) on slave owners (both likely the result of an increased pressure on the system of slavery from the imminence of emancipation).[26] Emancipation also created a brewing identity crisis: What would become of newly freed Black citizens? Where would they work? What would they do when they were not working? And how would the state of newly freed Black people impact the lives of white citizens? Such racially rooted fears fostered continued oppression of freed Black people long after the bonds of slavery had been broken.

New York's legislators were prepared for this moment. In 1818, there were several laws that attempted to establish "safe" parameters for Black behavior, including laws that mandated any "negro, mulatto, or Indian slave" to carry a lighted candle in a lantern when traveling the streets after sunset, laws that restricted them from gambling or "gaming with moneys," and laws that gave rewards to white citizens who apprehended Black people breaking the city's law.[27] Many of these laws had been on the books since 1712. When originally passed, the laws were written to apply to "Negro or Indian Slaves." By the mid-eighteenth century, all such laws were reworded to apply to "Negroes *and* Slaves" (emphasis mine) or "any negro, mulatto, or Indian slave." In this way, white lawmakers manipulated the doctrines that governed slave behavior to govern the behavior of freed Black peoples. This codification of white oppression fostered a system of imbalance governing Black behavior before emancipation had been reached. The legal limits of Black freedom were being defined in New York even before Black freedom was a surety.[28]

40 | THEATRES OF VALUE

Considering the legal precedence for white control over Black people in New York, New York slave codes were among the harshest in the Northern states (likely because the enslaved population of New York was greater than any other state in the North).[29] These laws were generally amended to become stricter after major insurrections (after the 1712 uprising, for instance, the laws were tightened to the point that they rivaled slave codes in the Deep South).[30] One of these codes, a 1731 statute, regulated the burial of slaves. This law decreed that it was unlawful for more than twelve slaves to meet together for a funeral because "under pretext whereof they have great Opportunities of Plotting and Confederating together to do Mischief, as well as Neglecting their Masters service."[31] It also allowed the slave owner to select which twelve slaves would be allowed to congregate for the funeral. While this law was never amended to apply to the assembly of free Black people, it was continually reinstated to govern the numbers allowed at slave funerals. This statute specifically states that its purpose is to curtail insurrection and prevent slaves from "plotting," "confederating," "doing mischief," or "neglecting service" to their masters. The first three items mark behaviors that would be infringements upon the law no matter who enacted them; they hint at violence, civil unrest, and general discord. The last item is markedly different. Making it unlawful for Black people to congregate in fear that such gatherings might lead to slaves "neglecting to do service" governs not civil behavior but instead social liberties. The idea that congregation would lead to laziness displays an innate distrust of Black self-governance and exposes the roots of white anxiety over Black free time. This also puts Brown's partition to allow white audience members at the African Theatre into stark relief. Brown was showing white audiences what Black assembly (at least in his establishments) could be—actors performing Shakespeare inside spaces that more resembled receiving rooms than large commercial theatres. Shakespeare, in this case, functions as a buffer for Brown—a way to prove that Black assembly was no threat to white communities. Unfortunately, it seems (from Noah's and others' writings) that this attempt might have backfired and caused white cultural gatekeepers to strengthen their grip on the commodity they viewed as exclusively theirs.

In light of the many racial and economic tensions fomenting in New York City, one can begin to understand how a tea garden might be viewed by the oppressive hegemonic forces of New York's white population as subversive and dangerous. Black congregation incited deep racial anxiety among white New Yorkers and these tensions set the stage for the next chapter of the African Theatre's story. Sometime in the winter of

1821/1822 (likely January of 1822), Brown moved his theatre to a location described in every account of the African Theatre as "Hampton's Hotel."[32] The hotel is generally referenced as being "next door" to the Park Theatre, and some newspaper advertisements even refer to the space as the "Park Theatre Hotel."[33] Considering Brown's work from an advertising standpoint, such a move opens up the possibility that Brown could have advertised or indicated that his performances were happening at the "Park Theatre Hotel" on Theatre Alley right next door to New York's premiere theatre. It doesn't seem like Brown would have to stretch his imagination very far to harness the legitimizing and economic potential of performing at the Park Theatre Hotel.

While there is no listing for a "Hampton's Hotel" in city directories, Longworth's Directory lists a "Porterhouse" belonging to Ephraim Hampton located at 28 Park from 1817 to 1823.[34] In 1823, the listing was adjusted to read "Oysterhouse" and remained that way from 1823 to 1825.[35] After this year, the listing vanishes. The 1821 assessment for Park Row property values suggests the scale and scope of the property. It lists the worth for "E. Hampton," "Hotel" as $12,000 (see fig. 1.1). With the theatre (owned

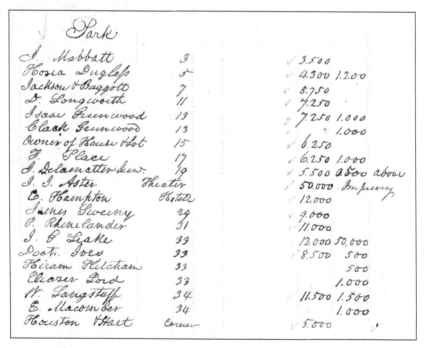

Figure 1.1. 1821 Park Row Property Assessment. *Source*: Public domain.

by J. J. Astor and assessed at $50,000) listed as the most valuable property on the block, Hampton's Hotel is tied for second most valuable (with J. G. Leake at 33 Park).[36]

This evaluation suggests that the property was either: 1) quite large; 2) quite modern with updates to justify its worth; or 3) quite valuable as a commercial location on an otherwise mostly residential street. The buildings of record are listed by ascending lot number and Hampton's is noted just below the Park Theatre, presumably right next door. The Hotel and the Theatre are unique in this list as they are the only properties not denoted by lot number (Ephraim Hampton's property is listed as "Hotel" while the Park is marked "Theatre"). This might indicate that the Park and the Hotel were the only two businesses on the block and perhaps also that their locations were well enough known that even an official record could use the name of the business as a specific reference of place. Additionally, it cements the worth of Hampton's Hotel as a commercially viable space on a block that already was well known for its legitimacy as a theatrical space.

Brown's move and its proximity to traditionally white theatrical spaces was evocative to Noah who, in the *National Advocate* of January 1822, wrote: "It appears that the sable managers, not satisfied with a small share of profit and a great portion of fame, determined to rival the great Park Theatre . . . and accordingly hired the Hotel next door to the Theatre, where they announced their performances."[37] This myth that Brown's move to Hampton's Hotel was an attempt to financially rival the Park is one I will examine in greater depth later, but for the moment it should suffice to say that Brown's contemporaries clearly saw the correlation between the Park Theatre and the Park Theatre Hotel as well as potential motivations for making such a move.

Another noteworthy element of Brown's use of space at Hampton's is the business relationship it required between William Brown and Ephraim Hampton. With all of the previously discussed anxieties in mind, it seems odd, nearly unfathomable, that Ephraim Hampton would go into business with a man who was 1) clearly on the wrong side of the local sheriff who had no qualms about semi-legally shutting down business-related operations and 2) perhaps going to be off-putting to his usual white patrons. Why did Hampton think that encouraging a large Black audience at his establishment on a consistent weekly basis would be a good business move? One plausible explanation incorporates the close proximity of the Park Theatre and the Park Theatre Hotel. Just before Brown moved his company,

Hampton had been forced to close his establishment for repairs. An 1820 fire close the Park Theatre for a time and also caused some damage to Hampton's Theatre Hotel. On January 4, 1821, and January 6, 1821, the *New York Daily Advertiser* ran an advertisement that reads: "E. Hampton respectfully informs his friends and the public, that he has returned to Theatre Hotel, from which he had to retreat rather hastily last spring, in consequence of the last Grand Illumination of the Theatre, which somewhat dazzled his ideas and re-commenced feeding his friends in his usual splendid style."[38] Consider the economic consequences of fire renovations: Hampton would have needed some kind of capital to refurbish his hotel after the fire, and this advertisement makes very clear that he was necessarily looking to reengage his clientele after quite a lengthy pause. The repairs and closure would impact Hampton's business and necessitate a strong base of client support in order to continue operations. Hampton needed Brown's audience. He needed them as patrons in order to keep the lights on. Brown needed the legitimacy Hampton's space offered, and perhaps (also) its protection. Hampton's Hotel had been open on Park Row for some time, according to Longworth's. It was a white-owned business with enough clientele to support its continued operation. It would be much more difficult for Noah to shut this business down in the same way he shuttered Brown's garden.

Returning to the notion that Brown's move to Hampton's Hotel was an effort to directly compete financially with Price at the Park Theatre, it's a myth with deep roots. Noah was among the first to propagate it, then Brown himself took it up. On January 16, 1822, the *Commercial Advertiser* ran a description of the Shakespeare Arrests, which includes an account supposedly quoted from playbills posted throughout the city:

> We published a few days since, a pleasant account from the *Advocate*, of the breaking up of the theatrical establishment of the colored heroes of the sock and buskin, adjoining the New Park theatre. It seems, however, from the following extract from a play bill posted through the city a few days subsequent to the merry farce of *"Turn Out,"* that they are not so easily to be driven from the field in which Shakespeare, Garrick, Cooke, and our right worthy and jolly Sheriff [i.e., Mordecai Noah] have reaped such harvests of glory. The following is the extract: "Mr. Brown, the Manager of the Minor Theatre, respectfully informs the public, that in consequence of the breaking up of

his theatrical establishment, there will be no performance this week. Mr. B. believes it is through the influence of his brother Managers of the Park Theatre, that the police interfered. There is no doubt that in fear of his opposition, they took measures to quell his rivalry. And in consequence of these jealousies, Mr. Brown has been obliged to remove his theatrical corps to the old place, corner of Bleecker and Mercer-streets, where every means will be taken to ensure the public patronage."[39]

If this text is indeed faithfully reprinted from Brown's playbill, it is significant as the only time Brown's voice has been preserved in the telling of his own story. Additionally, it reveals Brown's boldness and savviness: not only did he see to the heart of the matter (that the harassment of his businesses was about more than "noise complaints" or similar smoke-screens), but he was willing to publicly call his oppressors to task. Brown explicitly links the suppression of his theatre to economic fear that his business would create more supply and thus curtail demand on a closely guarded cultural commodity. Brown's understanding perhaps indicates that his minor "fringe theatre" wasn't actually minor. If the undoubtedly major Park Theatre was treating the African Theatre as a threat to be taken seriously, then perhaps it was a threat to be taken seriously. Still, the idea that this threat was purely economic is a bit thin. While Noah and Brown propagate the story of the African Theatre being a financial threat to the Park, contemporary scholars take this cue. McAllister frames this tension as "Manhattan's major-minor struggle" and claims that it began with the fire at the Park (an incident that, to McAllister, caused Price to scramble for business in the same way that I have contended Hampton likely did).[40] Samuel Hay joins this argument with his own, more pointed, take: "Stephen Price's motivation for sabotaging Mr. Brown's productions was economic. From his 'capacious' segregated galleries for African Americans and prostitutes, Price netted approximately nine hundred dollars per week (Price's gallery for African Americans held approximately seven hundred fifty people. If the gallery were only 80 percent filled—a quite conservative estimate—Price, at a ticket cost of twenty-five cents per person, would have made nine hundred dollars for each six-performance week). The galleries met Price's costs."[41] Hay's estimates about Price's galleries represent one telling of the story, but there's more math that needs to be done to reach the conclusion that Price's reasons for sabotaging Brown were purely economic. Running numbers with the realities of Brown's theatre in mind, at least as I have outlined them here, draws a more nuanced conclusion.

At its maximum capacity, George A. Thompson estimates that Brown's theatre could accommodate forty-five to fifty patrons in a given night.[42] As I have discussed, Brown's performances on Thomas and Mercer Streets were both likely held once a week on Monday nights. At Hampton's Hotel, performances were conducted on Monday, Wednesday, and Friday evenings.[43] Price's galleries, according to Hay, had a capacity of 750 patrons. Every six-performance week, he had a potential to sell 4,500 gallery tickets.[44] Assuming that a patron could choose to attend either Brown's performance or Price's performance in a given week (and not both), the Mercer Street space would have only given Brown 50 of these 4,500 potential seats, leaving Price with a large potential audience still available to him. If Price filled his galleries, even with these 50 seats being sold away from him, he might still have netted $1,112.50 per week. If the galleries were 80 percent filled, as Hay presumes, those 50 seats would be subtracted from the 3,600 potential seats per week Price would be selling. According to Hay's model, Price still pocketed a weekly $887.50 even with Brown's involvement. On Mercer Street, Brown would only have been "stealing" $12.50 per week from Price's profits.

The move to Hampton's Hotel and the increased performances there (three rather than one) shifted matters, but not so much as Hay assumes. While I can find no floor plan or interior map of Hampton's Hotel, it's difficult to imagine that Brown would have been able to accommodate more than fifty people in his audience, and the shift to three performances a week might indicate that he could welcome fewer audience members per show (increasing performance numbers in order to keep revenue streams steady). As a conservative estimate, I will maintain Brown's Hampton Hotel audience capacity at approximately fifty people per night. In this model, Brown would only have been capable of pulling 150 audience members a week from Hay's audience estimates.[45] Instead of 4,500 potential seats a week, Price would have been left with 4,350—a potential revenue of $1,087.50 per week. In accordance with Hay's math, Brown (even at his optimal performance conditions) was only threatening $37.50 a week from Price's margins (or approximately 3.4% of Price's potential net revenue). Thus, I find it problematic to claim that Price persuaded Noah to close down Brown's operations due purely to an economic threat. There were clearly other factors unaccounted for by these numbers.

Previously, I have made the argument that Brown was motivated to move to the Park Theatre Hotel by advertising potential and proximity to legitimacy the space held. Additionally, it's worth noting that this move would have put Brown's business closer to its target audience. According to Shane White, "by the early years of the nineteenth century, Theatre Alley was recognized as a Black neighborhood, in 1802, the manager of the theater complained bitterly about the 'noisy mob of Negroes and vulgar boys' who hung around the door begging for checks from patrons, which they then 'promptly sell again at half price, or for what they can get.'"[46] Not only do White's suggestions about the area depict its richness with Brown's target audience (free Black people with hours and money to spare for leisure), but they also include not-so-veiled hints about one of the motivations of Price's behaviors with decidedly racist undertones.

It's possible that these ticket scalpers came to Theatre Alley purely for working purposes or to turn a buck, but again according to White that's clearly not the case. In figure 1.2, I have taken Shane White's map

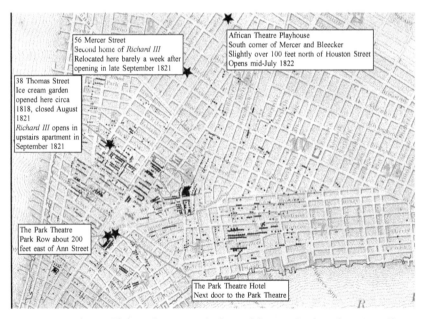

Figure 1.2. African Theatre locations (indicated by stars) plotted against Shane White's map of free Black households (circular dots) in New York City. *Source*: Shane White, "Free Black Households in New York City, 1810," in *Somewhat More Independent: The End of Slavery in New York City, 1770–1810* (Athens: University of Georgia Press, 1991), 176.

of free Black households in New York City and superimposed it upon a detailed street-view map made of the city contemporary to Brown's time.[47] I have then plotted the places on the map where the African Theatre was housed over the course of its life.

As the map suggests, Brown moved his theatre to places where he would find a strong contingent of his target audience (free Black people). His first location, 38 Thomas Street, is in an area densely populated with free Black households. The move up to Mercer was a move away from his primary audience demographic, but consider that this move took place during the time in which Brown first erected his partition and allowed white patrons into the theatre. The partition strategy, one that I have previously suggested was a means to ease white anxieties about Brown's business, might also have been necessary to fill benches and turn a profit. After a time on Mercer Street geographically distant from most of his potential audience (the evidence suggests between one and four months), it stands to reason that Brown might target the Theatre Alley area (with its heavy concentration of Black people and its association with theatregoing) as a key location to generate an increase in business. Moving to Hampton's Hotel and Theatre Alley was not only a move onto a street already associated with theatre and theatregoing, it was also a move closer to where Brown's audience members would have lived.

The timeline of these moves is still hazy, and Michael Warner et al. propose the possibility that Brown and his company performed simultaneously at the theatre uptown and at Hampton's Hotel downtown.[48] The evidence is lukewarm on these things having happened in succession. If they were, as Warner et al. hypothesize, occurring at the same time, that is perhaps further indication that Brown saw the value in the legitimacy lent by the Park Theatre Hotel. Despite already having a performance location for his company, the lure of Theatre Alley was strong enough to chance the economic burden of increasing performance venues as well as the potential social backlash. Consider Brown's presence downtown: despite the fact that Price's theatre was in what had become a Black neighborhood, the comments cited earlier about ticket scalpers suggest that Price's patrons were far from enthusiastic participants in racial integration. The Black residents of Theatre Alley were seemingly viewed as miscreants by white patrons of the area's largest attraction. While Noah's efforts to shut down Brown's enterprise were only nominally linked to economics at the Park, they may have been tied to audience reactions. Extrapolating the potential attitudes of white onlookers to the goings-on at Hampton's Hotel, there is the possibility that white patrons took offense to the thrice-weekly congregation of Black audience members who they saw as an affront to their own theatregoing experience. Such concerns might easily have instigated oppression of these events, and the troubles that led to the forced closure of Brown's enterprise.

There's the equal possibility that these white patrons held a completely opposite point of view. Perhaps being at Hampton's Hotel was a safer place for Brown to run his business because it might have meant a decrease in the congregation of Black citizens on the steps of the Park as they, instead, took in a play by Brown's company. Perhaps moving these people from the streets to a legitimized theatrical space might have been seen as more of a public benefit than public harm. As Hampton looked to reestablish patronage for his freshly rebuilt business, developing goodwill with the community might have been one way to do this. Consequently, positively impacting the Park's loiterers and ticket scalpers and giving them a place to be where they might be closely monitored by white onlookers could have been a prudent business move for Hampton, just as it seemed to be a prudent business move for Brown.

In relocating his theatre to Park Row and the "Theatre Hotel," Brown acquired a venue in what might be considered one of the most legitimate New York theatrical spaces of the time. At Hampton's Hotel, Brown's efforts conformed with the aforementioned expectations of legitimacy. I do not find it incidental that the moment in which this occurred corresponded directly with the alleged Shakespeare arrests; just when Brown had scrambled his way into legitimacy, he began to present a threat too large to be ignored. Perhaps triggered by Brown's ability to fulfill qualifications of legitimacy, Noah made a move that deprived Brown of his legitimate space and his legitimate material, thus hoping to neutralize the threat Brown posed in one fell swoop.

"My language! Heavens!"

—Ferdinand, *The Tempest*, I.ii

The authority that Noah and Price wielded against Brown is one traditionally associated with their status as representatives of a colonizing majority, and Shakespeare has often been viewed as the property of such a force in postcolonial spaces. Thomas Cartelli specifically identifies the United States during the nineteenth century as one such space: "the liminal space between freedom and subjection, independence and dependence."[49] In speaking broadly about Shakespeare's place in postcolonial spaces, Cartelli notes what he calls a "preoccupation of post-colonial cultures with the representational practices of their colonial period" and claims that Shakespeare is America's preoccupation given that it was a British colony.[50] America's postcolonial era can be, effectively, seen in two phases: the split from England, and the nineteenth-century creation of ruler and ruled classes that Cartelli outlines. In this second phase, the preoccupation with Shakespeare by Brown and his contemporaries indicates a preoccupation with the representational practices of the colonizers, that is, white slave owners.

In his manifesto of postcolonial life, Frantz Fanon indicates that language acquisition and use are strong powers of identity for the colonized people: "The more the Black Antillean assimilates the French language, the whiter he gets—i.e., the closer he comes to becoming a true human being. . . . A man who possesses a language possesses as an indirect consequence the world expressed and implied by this language . . . there is an extraordinary power in the possession of a language."[51] Fanon's exploration of language highlights the ways in which it becomes both a tool of oppression and a step toward assimilation. Learning to speak and use the language of the colonizer is one way that the colonized people begin to conform with the culture of the colonizer. Perhaps Shakespeare can be seen, here at least, as one such language of the colonizer. Brown's assimilation into the mainstream theatre was judged by his (and his artists') abilities to—literally—speak the language of their oppressors.

If so, Price and Noah's oppression of Brown and the critiques of the African Theatre must be seen accordingly. There are several reviews of *Richard III* with heavily weighted points of view about the actors' use of language. One was published by Noah on September 21, 1821:

> The courting scene was inimitably fine, particularly when Richard confesses his passion.
>
> > "Ah take de pity in dy eye
> > "And see um here—*kneels*
> > *Ann*—would they were brass candlesticks
> > "to strike de dead."
>
> This, Lady Ann accompanied with a violent action, such as seizing the King by his wool, shaking him furiously, and finally dashing him on the earth. . . . The tent scene was the *chef douvre*: the darkness of the night, the Black face of the

king, the flourish of drums and clarionetts, the start from the dream, the "*Gib me noder horse*," and, finally, the agony of the appalled Richard, the rolling-eye, white gnashing teeth, clenched fists, and phrenzied looks.[52]

The first and most obvious item in this short snippet of text is the pidgin that Noah uses to depict the actors' speech. This version of "literary black-face," Noah writing as Hewlett in Hewlett's voice, harkens to a similar trend observed in Boston broadsides drafted during emancipation that has been termed "Bobalition."[53] In Bobalition broadsides, white writers took on the personas of Black people to satirize Black celebrations of abolition.[54] These broadsides were written using similar pidgin to Noah's telling, and there is every likelihood that Noah had experience with Bobalition writings and emulated the style. Both Noah's work and Bobalition writings preserve a hierarchy of language: Noah's words are written using the standard conventions of English, while the actors he writes about speak (through him) in strange and broken phrases. In recording the event this way, Noah attempted to undermine the actors' use of Shakespearean language and prevent them from advancing into the perceived cultural territory of their oppressor. Here, the power of language that Fanon indicates is revealed by Noah's disallowance of access to that language.

In addition to denoting cultural territory, language also serves as an identifiable class marker. Speaking in a certain way aligns a person with specific values, indicators of status, and positionality with social authority.[55] To Todd Vogel, the use of language by Black citizens in antebellum America was a "cultural code" that indicated relationships between language-users and power.[56] Vogel writes, "If one's manner of speaking illustrated the inner person, then perhaps it could get white society beyond skin color to examine the genuine attributes of blacks. Linguistic capital potentially offered the free black a path to expanded freedoms."[57] Unfortunately for Brown and his actors, Noah's criticisms demonstrate that their bid to use Shakespeare's linguistic capital to illuminate their inner selves and claim expanded freedoms was ultimately unsuccessful.

Another obvious adjustment in this scene is Noah's report of Lady Ann's (played by actress "S. Welsh") use of "brass candlesticks" in place of "basilisks." Assuming that Noah is quoting faithfully from a performance that he saw (not a safe assumption—as I have already discussed), there is the important factor of perception to address here. Was "brass candlesticks" what Welsh *said* or what Noah *heard*? Assuming the former, this might have been a relic of the possibility that Welsh was illiterate and perhaps had her lines read to her so she might memorize them.[58] In this repetition, the word "basilisk" might have transformed to "brass candlesticks."

There's also the possibility that the shift was purposeful—changing the text of a Shakespearean piece was in keeping with the nineteenth-century theatrical tradition of performing Shakespeare. Edwin Booth, for instance, made so many changes to texts in performance that he printed several of his own editions; but even Booth experienced audience pushback. In one instance, Booth was literally shot at midperformance by an audience member disgruntled with his changes to the text of *Othello*.[59] Had Welsh been making a purposeful choice she would have been echoing what the white cultural gatekeepers were doing within their own theatres.

Welsh is not the only actor at the African Theatre who might have made such textual alterations. In the play's opening moments, Noah indicates that Hewlett made shifts of his own:

"Now is de vinter of our dicontent made glorus summer by de son of New-York."

Considerable applause ensued, although it was evident that the actor had not followed strictly the text of the author. Proceeding tranquilly in the soliloquy he made a pause, and continued thus

"*Instead of mounting barbary steeds,*
"*To fright de souls of fearful adversaries,*
"*He caper nimbly in de lady chamber*
"*To de lascivious playings of de flute* . . .[60]

Unlike Noah's account of Welsh's speech, his detailing of Hewlett's "New York" addition is corroborated by other observers. Scottish poet Peter Neilson reminiscences bitingly about an evening at the African Theatre: "One of the theatres is for the Black people of the city; it is really worth one's while to go there for a few nights for the novelty of the thing, and to hear the king's English murdered . . . it is too much for frail flesh and blood to see an absolute negro strut in with much dignity, bellowing forth—'Now is de vinter of our discontent Made glorus summer by de son of New York.' "[61] While these two separate sources seem to corroborate each other, the way they do so begs questions. The mangled English that Noah uses in quoting Hewlett is here repeated, verbatim, by Neilson in a way that makes one wonder if he wrote this himself or simply copied it from Noah's article in the *Advocate*. One way to look at this evidence is as a relic of how influential Noah's writing was to white audiences. While Neilson might have seen a performance at the African Theatre, his use of Noah to quote it directly frames Hewlett in the terms of his oppressor. Rather than allowing Hewlett to speak for himself, Neilson puts Noah's words in Hewlett's mouth—taking the agency of language (and, specifically, of Shakespeare's language) away from him. Still, it remains noteworthy that Neilson quotes the "son of New York" segment rather than any other piece of Hewlett's speech. Was this moment so very striking because of how it was performed at the African Theatre, or was Noah's description what made it stick in Neilson's mind? Did Neilson even see the play, or did he read Noah's account and find that intriguing enough to repeat? Regardless of whether Neilson manufactured this memory, it is significant that he elected this moment specifically to represent the show in its entirety. The moment was salient enough, either in performance or accounts of the performance, to warrant such presence as an avatar of the entire production.

A third corroborating account comes from another white visitor to the African Theatre, "Mrs. Felton," who also noted Hewlett's "New York" addition: "In order to please his audience, wherever the word 'York' appeared, [Hewlett] politely accommodated his language by altering the text to say 'New York.' "[62] According to Felton, this addition was an effort to connect with the audience in a way that made the material directly relevant. Curiously, I've found no accounts of other actors making such accommodations—but it would be strange to think that they did not. It would be odd to hear Richard saying "Duke of New York" while Margaret referred to the "Duke of York." If one can imagine that this was a consistent change, consider what such an alteration might mean to *Richard III*. If Edward is meant to be the "son of New York" that brings about glorious summer and the York house is imagined as a modernized-to-Hewlett New York aristocracy, the African Theatre's *Richard III* actually portrays empowered Black rulers fighting for control of the city and its governance. Even this small element of modernization asks the audience to concede that power of leadership can be endowed to Black statesmen (though *Richard III* is also a parable about the dangers of a maniacal despot). Notably, *Richard III* is a play entirely about nobility. There are very few low-status characters in the show (and those characters were cut from Brown's production).[63] In so fashioning, behaving, and styling themselves, perhaps these actors *were* enacting the thing that Noah feared so deeply.

> "Him I imitate."
>
> —Viola, *Twelfth Night*, III.iv

One very clear pattern that emerges from narratives of the African The-atre is the theme of imitation—that these theatremakers were producing some poor shadow of white performers. Noah writes that "these imitative inmates of the kitchen and pantries, not relishing the strong arm of the law thus rudely exercised, were determined to have some kind of amusement; and after several nightly caucuses, they resolved to get up a play and the upper apartments of the neglected African Theatre were pitched upon for the purpose. *Richard the Third*, after mature deliberation, was agreed upon."[64] Of course, since Brown was producing the first art of its kind in the United States (legitimate theatre made by Black artists for Black audi-ences), there were no Black models for the performers to observe. They necessarily recreated what was generally a white enterprise but with less training, less start-up capital, and fewer financial backers than the major white theatres enjoyed. Shane White indicates that the white audiences might have seen this move as a "bold intrusion onto what had been con-sidered exclusively white cultural terrain."[65] Reviews of the production I have previously cited in this chapter back this claim.

One of the prevailing anxieties surrounding the oppression that Brown and his enterprise met with was the assumption that by "acting white" Black people could and would claim the social and political power of whiteness. This idea that one could be something through performance in the nineteenth century is explored by Naomi Stubbs through her work on the American pleasure garden.[66] The pleasure garden, claims Stubbs, was a seemingly egalitarian place where the restrictions of box, pit, and gallery were lifted, allowing all patrons to spend the evening as "equal." For the price of entry, a pleasure garden allowed guests the opportunity to experience its leisure-time options while engaging with other members of society. Stubbs claims that the nineteenth-century American pleasure garden was deceitful in this social leveling; while on the surface it seemed as though this created utopian social equality, Stubbs argues that equality in the pleasure garden extended only to patrons who behaved as they were expected to within the confines of the garden's rules of propriety. Additionally, as managers saw their patron base shift away from the elite social class they had initially hoped to welcome to a more motley and diverse group, rules of propriety became increasingly strict in order to govern the behavior of the lower classes and ensure that they lived up to the standards of the space. Stubbs argues that this tightening of the rules of engagement encouraged patrons to "perform" class in the pleasure garden setting. Through this performance, pleasure garden guests were able to become what they hoped to be: a bourgeois patron of a culturally enriching leisure activity.[67] Rather than at the theatre where cost of a patron's entry (box, pit, or gallery tickets) designated class, the pleasure garden created a more fluid dynamic of class that might be navigated with the merit of an individual performance rather than the flourish of a purse. Of course, before Brown, Black patrons were barred from pleasure gardens.[68] While Stubbs generally references class ideas connected with white citizens, this mobility via performed behavior was also part of white anxiety surrounding the African Theatre. If Black citizens could advance their status as white citizens had (merely by conforming to the social expectations that white society held of itself), then allowing Black leisure to mirror white leisure would enable this performance.

Imitation was a loaded concept when considered in the light of Black Americans—slaves were considered "imitative" and this, to white onlookers, seemed to prove their simplicity.[69] Imitation was, therefore, a label used as a means of oppression. This is particularly ironic in the context of Shakespeare since Americans were essentially imitating British models with their own appropriations of Shakespeare as theatrical culture. This is almost certainly what Brown's performers were doing—modeling what they saw at large theatres and using it as a basis for their own Shakespearean tradition. Though they started with a template that closely matched what they had seen in spaces like the Park, this template didn't necessarily match the theatre space in which they performed. Consider the show's performance style. Noah's previously cited descriptions depict dramatically exciting action with Lady Anne grabbing Richard by the hair, shaking him, and dashing him to the earth. Another spectator witnessing a production of *Macbeth* in January of 1822 wrote: "When Macbeth came to the last word that we have quoted, he paused, until after he had failed in the fight; and while kicking and writhing upon the floor in the agonies of death, he turned up the white of his eyes, probably thinking of 'The Poet's eye in a fine frenzy rolling,' and cried out 'enough!' This is certainly equal to any improvement in reading made by Kean."[70] These enthusiastic and, perhaps, histrionic descriptions of the shows were clearly attempts by Noah and others to make light of the acting seen at the African Theatre, but perhaps they might be read as depictions of stylized acting performed in a confined space.

In sketching the geometry of Brown's performance space on Thomas Street, it's necessary to take into account room geometry. George A. Thompson estimates the dimensions of Brown's "theatre" on Thomas Street (likely a parlor or drawing room) to be approximately seventeen feet by twenty-five feet, in which, seated upon the same benches that would have furnished the downstairs lot, approximately forty-five to fifty people could be accommodated.[71] Considering Thompson's hypotheses about capacity and seating at the outdoor space, the temporal proximity of Brown's two original business ventures (the pleasure garden and the African Theatre in its first home), and the likelihood that Brown reused seating solutions from one business to the next, I have previously sketched potential layouts for the theatre in the Thomas Street apartment.[72] While these approximations are hypotheses at best, one thing is clear: Brown's actors worked in an incredibly small performance space. African Theatre actors and audience were very close to each other, making the imitation of large-scale theatre such as that performed at the Park infeasible. Being so close to the actors, the audience could clearly see the performers' facial expressions, which meant that standard acting techniques of the time would seem histrionic. The grand gestures and stylistic posturing that were necessary to convey action in giant, dimly lit, nineteenth-century houses would have looked entirely out of place on Brown's tiny stage.

Shane White frames imitation as parody that white people enacted to emulate Black people and performers, but in the case of the African Theatre, Black performers imitated white models.[73] When white performers imitated Black performers (as in minstrel shows), this was parody. When white performers imitated white performers, this was considered legitimate performance. Here, when Black performers are seen as imitating white performers, it constituted trespass.

"Hast thou read truth?"

—Leontes, *The Winter's Tale*, III.ii

I have already posited that the promulgation of Noah's writings about the African Theatre coupled with the dearth of information from Brown is one way that this story has been framed by the very forces that opposed it. Indeed, often the theatre will be referenced as "The African Grove" (the moniker Noah gave it in his writings) rather than "The African Theatre"

56 | Theatres of Value

(the appellation Brown used in marketing materials).[74] This paradigm seems even more sinister to Hay, who argues that Noah's writings about the African Theatre were a contributing factor to the racist stereotyping of Black Americans that emerged as a dominant theatrical trope through minstrelsy.[75] Noah wasn't the only white man to burlesque the theatre's work. Another account of the theatre comes from the minstrel act of Charles Mathews in a bit where Mathews played a minstrel version of Hewlett, interrupted during a *Hamlet* performance by an audience eager to hear a popular minstrel tune.[76] Mathews's ability to have his performance recorded and remembered in more detail than Hewlett's is an act of violence that continues to represent the African Theatre as an artifact of white satire rather than Black art.[77]

In considering *Richard III*'s closure, documentation remains a prevalent theme in the African Theatre's story. The arrests that silenced *Richard III* and led to Brown retreating from Park Row are but a single instance of this. Many accounts of the African Theatre (including Noah's cited earlier) indicate that its closure is closely linked to the Shakespeare arrests. Still, much like the "noise complaints" that closed Brown's tea garden, there remains no evidence that these arrests actually happened. Perhaps the most cited account of the Shakespeare arrests, and certainly the most colorful, once again comes from Noah in the *National Advocate* of January 1822:

> We have heretofore noticed the performances of a Black corps dramatique in this city. . . . The audiences were generally of a riotous character, and amused themselves by throwing crackers on the stage, and cracking their jokes with the actors, until danger from fire and civil discord, rendered it necessary to break up the establishment. The ebony colored wags were notified by the Police, that they must announce their last performance; but they, defying the public authority, went on and acted nightly. . . . On Monday evening a dozen watchmen made part of the audience. The play was Richard. . . . Several immediately ascended the stage and arrested his Majesty. . . . So forthwith Richard, Richmond, Lady Ann, the dead King Henry, Queen Elizabeth, and the two young Princes, were escorted, in their tinseled robes, to the watch-house. . . . Finally they pleaded so hard in blank verse, and promised never to act Shakespeare again, that the Police Magistrates released them at a very late hour.[78]

Despite Noah's account neither myself, Thompson, nor Warner et al. could find record of such arrests occurring.[79] Warner et al. posit that there *were* a series of arrests and police conflicts during Brown's pleasure garden days but make the distinction between the African Theatre uptown on Mercer and Bleecker and the downtown performances at Hampton's Hotel.[80] In this narrative, the arrests at Hampton's likely never happened.

The fact that this story has been told in this way for this long speaks to the lasting power of Noah's words because they were committed to print. The power this advertising wielded was the power to speak, the power to tell the story, and the power to create a preservable artifact. It is almost certain that the African Theatre had other modes of advertising their performances—word of mouth was, for instance, a major one. Shane White notices that most Black communities in early nineteenth-century New York City were probably based out of churches as a pillar of community life. According to census data, a church would be built in an area and then households of free Black families would very closely follow.[81] These patterns clearly indicate that there were centers of community and places where Black congregation would have been a potent tool for oral advertising. Unfortunately, the conversations held behind these walls are not things that history has fully documented—the story that remains is the story of the empowered, the story told by and for the white populace of New York City.

What this telling paradoxically proves is how successful Brown was in employing Shakespeare's worth as a legitimizing force. In creating something that captured and held the attention of the legitimate theatrical power-holders, Brown proved his place among them. His productions of Shakespeare were a threat to the hegemony and, in silencing them, Noah and Price invested them with that value. Brown's theatre was too valuable, and too powerful, to be allowed space in early nineteenth-century New York City.

Chapter Two

The Value of a Name

P. T. Barnum's American Dream

The morning of July 15, 1865, Phineas Taylor Barnum found himself standing among the ashes of what had been, to date, his most successful business. His American Museum and Lecture Room in New York City, a veritable bastion of American popular culture, had burned to the ground in a disastrous fire two days prior.[1] Shortly, his very vocal detractors came out of the woodwork. On July 27, 1865, *The Nation* published a sneering article:

> Barnum's Museum is gone at last. . . . A most dangerous mantrap is removed. . . . It pandered to the most foolish curiosity and to the most morbid appetite for the marvelous. The most gross deceptions were shamelessly resorted to to cause a week's wonder and to swell the week's receipts. The "Lecture Room"— once a sort of "lyceum" hall, latterly a minor theatre in look and character—furnished for the entertainment of its patrons the most vulgar sensation dramas of the day. Its patrons were suitably entertained. It has been many years since a citizen could take his wife or daughter to see a play on that stage.[2]

The Nation author went on for pages of similarly scathing rhetoric—dressing down Barnum's collections to a motley patchwork of random objects and his patrons to sensation-mongers of no taste.

60 | THEATRES OF VALUE

But Barnum knew the age-old axiom that no publicity was bad publicity. He accepted this invitation for public discourse about his business and launched a defense of the museum in the same paper several days later. Among many claims made to protect his integrity and reestablish public goodwill, Barnum specifically addressed the attack on the Lecture Room. He wrote that plays produced on his stage were always of the highest moral fiber and, as an assurance, cited a noteworthy example: "Even in Shakespeare's plays, I unflinchingly and invariably cut out vulgarity and profanity. . . . I was always extremely squeamish in my determination to allow nothing objectionable on my stage."[3] Barnum's use of Shakespeare as the epitome of taste and distinction (though simultaneously not above Barnum's abilities or willingness to sanitize) opens a window to Barnum's construction of value using Shakespeare at his museum. It hints at the magnitude of this value: large enough that Shakespeare's works must be included in Barnum's Lecture Room repertoire despite the admitted need to bowdlerize them; the value was greater than the cost. Barnum's use of Shakespeare as cultural capital in this very public, very vulnerable moment points also to the strategic value Barnum saw in Shakespeare as linked to his enterprise, his audience, and his ability to continue doing business in the wake of this disaster.

Constructing Shakespeare's dramaturgy of value to Barnum reveals, at first glance, quite little. Shakespeare has long been used by businesspeople and cultural gatekeepers as an icon of class and these users had few qualms about redacting Shakespeare for this purpose.[4] The Shakespeare example is also fairly mundane in terms of Barnum's marketing savvy. While infamous for wacky marketing antics, Barnum wasn't necessarily innovating in his use of Shakespeare; in fact he was using Shakespeare almost exactly as we might expect anyone to. But examining this further, the paradigm is telling: the man famous for schemes and creative twists to turn a buck *didn't do that* with Shakespeare's cultural capital. Studying Barnum involves trusting that Barnum knew his business. He was a master at making money when there was money to be had. Believing this also means buying into the notion that the method with which Barnum employed any cultural capital was the method he felt would be most lucrative. As such, it follows that Barnum's straightforward use of Shakespeare as the technique he saw best fit his goal of making money was, perhaps, the best use of Shakespeare to make money. In other words, the dramaturgy of value reveals Barnum's well-studied point of view about the best use for Shakespeare's capital on the market which he served. This reflection also reveals something about said market and its consumers in that they were willing and able to buy Barnum's Shakespearean product. The dramaturgy of value proposes that the market is culture—by using Shakespeare in a straightforward way, Barnum was relying on Shakespeare's universal equivalence to respectability, class, and social status to paint a veneer of these things on his American Museum and his audiences purchased this product to enact their status as cultivated patrons by way of the product.

Bruce McConachie has argued that Barnum's American Museum and Lecture Room was a crucial leisure space for middle-class audiences looking to cement their status through outward shows of gentility.[5] If so, Barnum's inclusion of Shakespeare in this construction demonstrates how valuable Shakespeare was to this performance. Additionally, it shows Barnum co-opting what Kate Rumbold would call the "impression" of a Shakespeare brand and coproducing value from it. Rumbold argues that Shakespeare is not a "brand" because a "brand" is a corporation or individual with control over their own presentation and/or revenue.[6] Rumbold borrows the concept of coproduction from the service industry where it is used to label instances of value creation when one entity entwines its brand with another to generate profit, for instance: a town taking on a certain tourist destination identity (such as Shakespeare's home town of Stratford-upon-Avon branding itself as Shakespeare's birthplace) as a means to generate tourist revenue.[7] As coproducer of value, Barnum uses Shakespeare to brand his museum with the nineteenth-century middle-class values with which Shakespeare was coming to be synonymous.

Barnum's pattern of use for Shakespeare is fairly prominent over the course of the American Museum's life. While Shakespeare featured frequently as a source of worth for Barnum's museum, more often than not the things Barnum was interested in were more spectacle than substance. Take, for instance, the oft-told tale that Barnum tried to purchase the house in which Shakespeare was born and ship it brick by brick to his American Museum.[8] During a European tour in September of 1844, Barnum paid a visit to Stratford-upon-Avon.[9] After this visit, the house was purchased at auction in September 1847 by a "United Committee" of interested persons from Stratford and London. Between the time of Barnum's visit and the purchase, newspapers repeatedly referenced "Yankee Speculators" with interest in the property.[10] This is a compelling story when coupled with an admission from Barnum in his 1872 autobiography that he "obtained verbally through a friend the refusal of the house in which Shakespeare was born, designing to remove it in sections to my museum in New York;

but the project leaked out, British pride was touched, and several English gentlemen interfered and purchased the premises for a Shakespearean Association. Had they slept a few days longer, I should have made a rare speculation, for I was subsequently assured that the British people, rather than suffer that house to be removed to America, would have bought me off with twenty thousand pounds."[11] Barnum's admission of interest in the house focuses less on its cultural value than the value of the investment. While he would not have hesitated to move the building to the United States, the idea that it might make him money without this necessity seemed equally appealing. In this admission, Barnum divulges that to him an item's moneymaking potential is far more important than its value as a cultural product. To Barnum, value is a construction of utility rather than intellectual interest.[12] This pattern will remain apparent in Barnum's construction of value through and of Shakespeare.

Another glimpse at Barnum's use for Shakespeare in his museum can be found in an 1850 pamphlet titled "Barnum's American Museum Illustrated," which details the contents of the museum and notes, in particular: "Shakespeare, the poet of all time, has been duly honored by Mr. Barnum, who in the act has done honor to himself."[13] The author's assertion that such a display not only honored Shakespeare but in turn honored Barnum is a curious one. This honor seems to be something Barnum understood: by the inclusion of Shakespeareana and paying homage to "The Bard," Barnum gained the cultural prestige that Shakespeare carried and reinvested his museum with that worth. The logic of this is quite circular: by including Shakespeare at the American Museum, Barnum elevated the museum to a place worthy of hosting Shakespeare. Simplistic as this thought may be, it's an advertising tactic that works and it association with Shakespeare's brand is a tradition unto itself. Both Pramod Nayar and Douglas Lanier note its efficacy in both elevating the mass cultural product involved (in this case Barnum's museum) and adding celebrity to Shakespeare's brand.[14] Lanier calls this "reciprocal legitimation."[15] Barnum's museum certainly benefited from this exchange and so, it seemed, did his audience. By partaking of Shakespeare (using the same circular advertising logic that fueled his inclusion in the museum/lecture room in the first place) Barnum's audiences fashioned themselves into the kind of people who consumed Shakespeare and this transaction cemented Shakespeare as an object of worth for the type of person to whom Barnum was selling at the American Museum and Lecture Room. Barnum thus effectively fused Shakespeare to the performance of middle-class life via his museum.

> "What is your parentage?"
>
> —Olivia, *Twelfth Night*, I.v

Barnum's track record at generating both value and worth is written all over his career, and the American Museum was one installment of his life where Barnum made bank. In his 1888 autobiography, Barnum referred to the American Museum as "the ladder by which I rose to fortune."[16] Barnum's eventual infamy was fueled by a constant desire for the next great thing—a curiosity and creativity about marketing and a willingness to risk losing money to make money. The American Museum was a crucial rung in the ladder of Barnum's businesses as it was the enterprise that made him enough money to buy the circus—the business that would make Barnum a household name. Barnum opened the first iteration of his museum on January 1, 1842, having purchased the building and base collection from the family of George Scudder, who founded the museum on Broadway and Ann Streets in 1810.[17] The 1865 fire shut down Barnum's first museum, but he rebuilt and Barnum's second American Museum and Lecture Room (larger and more grand than the first) opened on September 5, 1865. On March 3, 1868 it, too, burned to the ground, and this ended Barnum's museum career.[18] As a leisure space, the museum was immensely successful. Barnum biographer A. H. Saxon ran the numbers and determined that it was, relative to the American population, more popular than Disneyland.[19] The museum housed a strange conglomeration of items ranging from live exotic animals in a large menagerie (including sloths, giraffes, beluga whales, and a wide array of birds), to portraits of famous personages, to objects of curiosity and wonder (a scale model of Niagara Falls, for instance, with actual running water).[20]

Because of its affordable price of entry (twenty-five cents for adults at the first museum, thirty cents at the second; half price for children under twelve), Barnum's American Museum was a key leisure space for New Yorkers who craved the trappings of middle-class life but lacked the resources to secure them.[21] McConachie notes that Barnum's museum was one way families on the class margin (artisans, shopkeepers, clerks, etc.) could acquire the appearance of middle-class sensibilities when they were unable to afford other outward shows. While most forms of popular entertainment fell distinctly down the class line (opera, for instance, being fare for the upper class while more rough-and-tumble audiences might view a race between fire companies), Barnum's museum occupied at least the appearance of class equity.[22] Barnum's cost of entry meant that most could afford an afternoon at the museum, and the popularity of the space shows that many partook of its wonders. The most major and permanent exhibit at Barnum's American Museum was its Moral Lecture Room, a three-thousand-seat theatre outfitted with the latest scenic technology, spectacular costumes, and a permanent acting company. Much like the ubiquitous movie theatres one finds attached to contemporary museums of natural history, the Lecture Room was an extension of the museum; entry was gained from the museum's lower saloon without a separate entry fee. Lecture Room guests were treated to shows at least twice a day (once in the evening and once in the afternoon, though as frequently as once per hour on holidays).[23]

Barnum's museum was a place where patrons could imagine themselves as part of an economic class they sought to incorporate into, and where those fantasies could become reality as they intermingled with members of their aspirational class. In chapter 1, I discussed Naomi Stubbs's theory of performance as a critical component to the construction of class identity in the nineteenth century, particularly in places of leisure.[24] These performative moments were viably drafted in Barnum's museum—much as they were at the African Theatre, and in Stubbs's pleasure gardens. Barnum's Lecture Room opened the gates of possibility for patrons to unlock areas of the theatre generally heavily restricted by economics. At Barnum's Lecture Room, patrons could seat themselves in any section of a luxurious three-thousand-seat house after gaining access through the museum.[25] Audiences were thus liberated from the nineteenth century's box, pit, and gallery economic sorting mechanism. This allowed Barnum's patrons an ideal setting for their class performance—a setting with all the connotations of exclusivity but unfettered by Barnum. In the museum proper, patrons were similarly presented with domestic luxuries they might not otherwise have been able to afford. They could take in exhibits, including a lady on the fourth floor who "sewed perpetually at one of the latest made machines."[26] They enjoyed novelties like ice water—available for free.[27] Barnum provided entertainments designed, packaged, and marketed as healthful and sensible and sold them at an accessible price. The museum thrived on this presentation—while Barnum was selling sensation, he was also selling the opportunity for class performance that might, as Stubbs argues, translate directly to social climbing.

The connection between enacting class and Shakespeare's voice in this act is made explicit in one of Barnum's many autobiographies. In 1854, early during his American Museum's peak popularity, Barnum published the first edition of *The Life of P. T. Barnum*.[28] This volume chronicles Barnum's ascent from a simple rural stock boy in the family store to an international celebrity fraternizing with monarchs and swimming in cash. Barnum revised *Life* in 1888 and, in this version, included the following epigraph at the very start of the text:

> "——a map of busy life.
> Its fluctuations and its vast concerns."
> "And see what I can show in this
> *****
> Strange eventful history."
> —SHAKESPEARE.
> The noblest art
> Is that of making others happy.
> —P. T. BARNUM.[29]

Barnum's use of Shakespeare as the opening voice in his autobiography does several tasks. First, it intwines Shakespeare in Barnum's brand not only as a value-add but also as an authoritative and (here) authorial voice. Second, it places Shakespeare's name directly above Barnum's—ceding this voice in the place Barnum was most powerfully vociferous—his own autobiography. Third, it hints at a certain blithe dexterity with Shakespearean text. While this epigraph is only credited to two authors (Barnum and Shakespeare), it's actually a conglomeration from three sources: the first two lines come from William Cowper's 1785 epic poem "The Task" while the third is a line of Barnum's invention.[30] The only line of this text from Shakespeare's pen is the "strange eventful history" borrowed from Jaques's "All the world's a Stage" speech from *As You Like It*.[31] This Shakespearean elision allows Barnum to put words in Shakespeare's mouth, then publicly hold those words up as a source of value. It allows Barnum (not for the first or last time) to implicitly claim the cultural and literary authority that comes with Shakespeare, and to immediately put that capital/authority to use. Because *Life* is so entwined with "the making of the man," this epigraph centers Shakespeare in Barnum's narrative, which essentially captures a fantasy of the American Dream. As Barnum created space for his patrons' performance of status, he modeled via *Life* what benefits this performance might reap—and centered Shakespeare's imagined voice as a key component of this performance.

Performing status at the American Museum also enacted a phenomenon that nineteenth-century economist Thorstein Veblen observed and described as "conspicuous consumption." Veblen's 1899 book *The Theory of the Leisure Class* expands Marx's theory that consumption completes the act of production to describe why and how outward shows of consumption are indicators of status.[32] Veblen contends that when consumption is no longer an act of survival (i.e., when someone consumes more than they need or consumes better goods than they need) this is a demonstration or performance of having risen into a higher class. This consumption done publicly signaled upward social progress. As such, the desire to consume that might initiate a visit to Barnum's is one way Barnum's class-conscious audience was able to show they belonged in a bourgeoisie. Through public consumption of the leisure product Barnum offered, museum visitors could assure themselves and others of their desert of inclusion in the middle-class sphere.

Because this class performance was vital to those living liminally on the class line, access was a key component of this performance's success. In New York City, institutions like the Metropolitan Museum of Art and American Museum of Natural History actively fought against mixed-class patronage by consolidating decision-making power into boards dominated by private elite-class citizens and closed their museums on Sundays citing religious observance (this prevented working-class peoples whose only day off was Sunday from visiting).[33] While the Met and AMNH attempted to claim cultural spaces for upper-class audiences (a story that should sound familiar to readers of chapter 1 of this book), they did not hold an absolute monopoly on the supply side of their resource. Their insistence on creating scarcity in fact bolstered Barnum's success since he had no qualms about turning demand for the museum commodity into profit. But contrary to classic models of supply and demand, Barnum knew his maximal potential would be to sell the high-demand low-supply goods he held at a moderate price. When the fire destroyed his first museum, Barnum knew that market demand would remain high and, without his offerings, supply terminally low. Thus, despite advice from Horace Greeley that he should take the museum's destruction as a sign for a vacation and "go a-fishing," Barnum rebuilt.[34]

Considering access, while Barnum was hard at work selling a middle-class dream, it's imperative to remember the audience Barnum specifically marketed to—and the audience Barnum kept out. Like most other institutions of popular culture at the time, Barnum's museum was segregated.[35] An 1849 advertisement to the museum offers a window into the terms of this segregation: "Notice to persons of color—in order to afford respectable colored persons an opportunity to witness the extraordinary attractions at present exhibited at the museum, the manager has determined to admit this class of people on Thursday morning next, March 1 from 8 a.m. till 1 p.m. Special performances in the Lecture Room at 11 o'clock."[36] James Cook remarks that this one advertisement does not clarify whether Barnum's policy on Black patrons extended to every week, if it showed a broader shift in his management, or if patronage continued to be segregated. He finds evidence of Black patrons during the museum's normal hours by the 1860s. Segregation points toward Barnum's target audience: while he was kicking the doors open for lower classes, he was doing so along strictly racialized lines.

This follows because race was part of what Barnum was selling. White audiences of Barnum's exhibits were constantly presented with the opportunity to assure themselves of superiority on the basis of race—as Linda Frost argues: Barnum's presentations of various "freaks" and racially othered peoples consistently used race as a demarcation of identity and class.[37] Gawking at the "missing link" or Joice Heth the "nursemaid of George Washington" allowed white audiences the space to remind themselves of their superiority and turned that assurance into an economic commodity.[38] Barnum's exploitation of the racial other to do this was a clear indication of his target audience—and connected to Shakespeare's authority grounded in white Eurocentric culture.[39]

> "Apparel vice like virtue's harbinger."
>
> —Luciana, *The Comedy of Errors*, III.ii

In an effort to conform with the values that the nineteenth-century American middle class espoused, Barnum ensured the museum could read as more than just a space of leisure. He packaged and marketed the museum as a bastion of ethical and sentimental health: from the previously cited sewing demonstrations to the branding of the theatre as a "Moral Lecture Room" in order to eschew nineteenth-century taboos about the ill health of theatrical spaces, Barnum crafted the museum as a space where children and unchaperoned ladies could spend their leisure hours.[40] Barnum saw morality as prime capital—and a space that could combine the marketability of ethical health with the leisure options created by theatre leveraged both these paradigms. Barnum's branding of his "Moral Lecture Room" was a veil that afforded respectability to what was otherwise a dubious enterprise in nineteenth-century cities—the theatre. As suggested by the quotation from *The Nation* with which this chapter began, the veil was thin and moderately effective but not without its detractors. An 1854 article in the *United States Magazine of Science, Art, Manufactures, Agriculture, Commerce, and Trade* also remarked upon the performance of morality by Barnum's museum: "Barnum, who has a sharp eye to business . . . produced at his museum, or rather theatre; for such as it is, although he wisely terms it 'a Lecture Room,' because there are certain people who have a pious horror of theatres—never visit them—but yet freely patronize 'the Lecture Room' of Barnum's museum, which is, in every respect, as much a theatre as any other in the Union; this being a distinction without a difference, made for conscience sake."[41] In this regard, the Moral Lecture Room occupied a space very similar to that which Shakespeare did—invariably and opaquely connected to the theatre but capable through the magic of market demand of being sold as a healthful piece of sentimental life.

This branding of the Lecture Room was an ongoing project that Barnum took every opportunity to engage with. Its posthumous connection to Shakespeare, with which I began this chapter, was one such moment. The other end of the Lecture Room's life—its grand reopening in 1850—was another. After a brief lapse in museum ownership from 1855 to 1860 in order to rid himself of choice debts, Barnum reacquired the building and collections. He promptly closed the facility for a week of repairs and renovation, reopening on March 31, 1860, back under his ownership.[42] Upon reopening, the museum and its Lecture Room were packed to the gills. The *New York Tribune* reports that around three thousand spectators crowded the Lecture Room that afternoon, filling the new space to its capacity.[43] On this occasion, Barnum took the opportunity to underscore the Lecture Room's branding. In an address made from the stage, one of the Lecture Room's actresses declared: "Here vice shall be portrayed, with such a mein/ That all shall hate it when it once is seen—/ And virtue, with its rich rewards and fun / Nightly before this altar, you shall see."[44] Barnum knew that rebranding a commodity about which his audience already had deep-seated opinions (i.e., the theatre) would take work. He would need to take advantage of every opportunity to remind his audience what the space was to be called and why.

Barnum himself took to the stage at the reopening to address the crowd, asserting once more: "The dramas introduced in the Lecture Room will never contain a profane expression or a vulgar allusion; in contrary, their tendency will always be to encourage virtue, and frown upon vice."[45] With careful curating, Barnum (it seems) was able to spread the veil of ethical health over the theatre such that, as an 1865 notice in the *New York Times* cites, "We have rarely met a person, moral or immoral, who had never been to Barnum's Lecture-room, and we never met one who objected to going. A large and well-appointed theatre was this place—nothing more and nothing less."[46]

This rhetoric took a strong and strange Shakespearean bent in Barnum's speech at the 1850 grand reopening. In relating his reasons for crafting the museum and Lecture Room the way that he did, Barnum admitted, "I felt that this community needed and demanded at least one more place of public amusement, where we might take our children, and secure much rational enjoyment, as well as valuable instruction, without the risk of imbibing moral poisons in the chalice presented to our lips."[47] In voicing his objective, Barnum borrows words from *Macbeth* to explain through allusion his alignment with the upper-middle-class values he was packaging at the museum. In this speech, Barnum is explicit about his goals to create an environment that would tap into his audiences' desires to present outward shows of sentimental health because of a market demand for this particular genre of leisure. Strangely, Barnum choses *Macbeth* to do this—a show that one might argue eventually tells a moral story but cycles through all manner of vice to get there. As Barnum frames his Moral Lecture Room in the comforts of domesticity—selling it as a family place for women and children—he invokes one of Shakespeare's bloodiest dramas to do it.

Commending poisoned chalices was an experience Barnum had plenty of. Barnum's history of alcoholism made him a staunch devotee to the temperance cause.[48] But in this as well, Barnum tapped into a market demand for specific, targeted acts of charity. Temperance was the single most popular social cause in the 1800s—perhaps not surprisingly, given that by 1830, New York had one bar for every fifteen individuals over the age of fifteen.[49] Tyler Anbinder claims, "In 1851, there were at least 252 saloons and groceries in Five Points' 22 blocks, or about a dozen per block."[50] The regular availability of liquor (particularly in poor districts) catered to a real market need: because the quality of water was so poor and the cost of tea and coffee so high, alcohol was the common man's drink in nineteenth-century New York.[51] Part of the popularity of ethical behavior was to display the difference between oneself and the rampant displays of immorality (such as could be seen in the notorious Five Points district) that showed a stark contrast to the fervently "upright" characters of the middle class. George Catlin's late 1820s painting of Five Points depicts chaos on the streets; prostitution, liquor stores (some labeled as "grocery stores" in the painting), fights, and drunks fill the scene (see fig. 2.1).[52]

This image is not an exaggeration. Anbinder claims that this notorious neighborhood was so infamous that by the 1830s Five Points was an attraction that drew tourists and "out-of-town visitors [who] went there to see its depravities."[53] While some of the wealthy were busy sightseeing

Figure 2.1. George Catlin's *Five Points*. Source: Public domain.

the horrors of Five Points, others were intent upon proving their moral character by supplying aid to the situation.

The Five Points Mission was explicitly tied to morality at Barnum's by a strategic move Barnum enacted to (according to one reporter) ease moral objections from

> the moral ladies of the Five Points Mission . . . but their scruples were overcome by that eminent tactician, Barnum, who, as a salve to their tender consciences, at once introduced a begging box into his establishment, for the benefit of the Mission, which is thus advertised in his bills:—A box for "Contributions to the Ladies' Five Points Mission" and another one for "Contributions to the Five Points House of Industry," have been placed at the inside doors of the museum, for the attention of those who desire to exhibit, in a tangible manner, their interest in the progress of moral improvement at the five points.[54]

Barnum's engagement with this social issue was a multifold way to incorporate the ethical values of charity into the museum's brand. First and foremost, it allowed Barnum to attach a charitable cause to the museum without having to do any real work, and it also allowed Barnum to pass the benefits of this to his audience. By including the boxes in a public place, Barnum opened the doors for shows of charity that his patrons might partake in without themselves needing to do much labor at all. The preceding ad makes this explicit, citing that the boxes benefited those who wished to "exhibit interest" and highlighting the convenience to perform public acts of charity without the burden of time investment or even thought. In other words, the charitable donation boxes proffered another opportunity for Barnum's audience to participate in the type of conspicuous consumption that would cement their place in an ethical sphere appropriate to their aspirational class.

Both in support of temperance and in support of his "moral" mission at the Lecture Room, Barnum frequently produced temperance dramas and the fourth-most-performed piece at his Lecture Room, *The Drunkard*, was a play specifically written to showcase the horrors of drink. Sobriety was a popular cause in New York because of its obvious social need, as well as its connection to self-control (a value lauded by the middle class). Thus: temperance was a way to use values as social climbing devices

72 | THEATRES OF VALUE

and Barnum was an expert at building ladders when folks would pay to publicly scale them.[55]

> "When I was at home I was in a better place."
>
> —Touchstone, *As You Like It*, II.iv

The emphasis on moral and ethical health as a central marketing device tapped into a zeitgeist that considered large cities (including, of course, the rapidly growing New York) as categorically immoral places. Since the area that was to become the United States was still mostly rural, distrust of the city and the evils that it brought were rampant in the popular imagination. In the city, an unsuspecting country boy could be accosted by prostitutes, theatre, vice, and sin (often all at the same time). Cities lacked the ethical health of innate connection to rurality—and, some nineteenth-century people argued, this meant an urban distance from moral structure.[56] Additionally, as markers of gentility faded (speech became popularized, the middle class more accessible), it became more and more difficult to know upon briefly encountering someone where they belonged in a social hierarchy.[57] This led those of the upper classes to place more and more steadfast barriers around cultural property. Cities were problematic because they meant that (increasingly) people were living among strangers. The anonymity that came along with city living meant that performance of self became an even more essential factor of social interaction.[58] With everyday interactions guided by face value rather than deep preexisting relationships, appearances were critical to casual social transactions—and they were all underlined with a deep-seated fear of what might be beneath a social mask. In this way, cities encouraged anxiety about moral health and ethical well-being, and they necessitated caution both in caring for those aspects of self and in finding these aspects of others. Barnum's market was ripe for the picking.

As far as urban environments go, New York was bustling. It was the fastest-growing city in the country. As New York's population expanded, the city struggled to make room for all of its new residents. Because of the population boom, tenement housing and communal living situations became the nineteenth-century New York City norm. As a result, the

Romantic ideal of domesticity providing stability and comfort was completely subverted.[59] As the cost of living rose, so too did the need for women to work, thus further undermining traditional values of domesticity and placing women, the guardians of ethical domestic life, further from their gatekeeping duties. But this led to further complications: with no one to guard the home, who would upkeep it as an oasis of sentimentality and prevent vice and sin from entering? Because domesticity was so important to the preservation of moral and ethical health, women were also the guardians of this morality. As keepers of the domestic sanctuary, they were the protectors against moral evils.[60] Adrift in the "immoral" city, many working-class city-dwellers were also suddenly left without a familiar home situation and the preservation of the healthful self that came with that situation. Additionally, young men who were first emerging from their rural homes into booming industrialized cities suddenly found themselves with no one to be the "mother" and create the domestic moral refuge of ethics. What would become of them?[61]

Barnum understood the market desire this created and used the American Museum to capitalize on the tension between the city's dangers and the presumed morality of domestic spheres. Barnum ensured that his museum looked and felt like a domestic haven. He advertised his exhibits in hyper-domestic ways. For instance: Barnum billed the large menagerie he kept as the "happy family" in reference to the wonder of creatures "each opposed to other in habits and dispositions" displayed all together.[62] One guidebook noted that this display "presents an amusing picture of the harmony which care and kindness may produce in the brute creation," a triumph of the positive influence of domestic life over the very forces of nature.[63] To further reinforce this, Barnum outfitted the museum like an upscale parlor with a rooftop ice cream garden and meticulous "good taste displayed in its arrangements."[64]

While performance of status and the self became enabled by Barnum's drafting of a domestic paradise, a domestic paradise in public was problematic to Barnum's audience for several reasons. The sanctity of the home was fundamental to the shaping and reflection of a person's inner life. Amy Richter emphasizes that to the nineteenth-century American, "Homes and their contents reflected and shaped character."[65] Barnum's incorporation of domestic setting was thus a call to his audiences to enjoy the respectability afforded by that environment and the contents of the museum were an outward reflection of this respectability. This in

74 | Theatres of Value

mind, attacks upon the museum's collections (such as *The Nation's*) were direct attacks on Barnum's audiences as well. In employing Shakespeare to defend these audiences, Barnum was turning Shakespeare into a kind of superhero—someone who would defend his decent, ethical patrons from the harm of *The Nation's* sensation-bashing.

But Barnum's domestic ideal was only a home in illusion. The public nature of his museum added to the ambiguous moral confusion of it. Nineteenth-century domestic spaces became branded with purpose that aligned with public and private spheres (consider the nineteenth-century proliferation of specialized rooms such as the sitting room, entrance room, library, etc.).[66] Barnum's museum was complicated in this paradigm: the public/private nature of domesticity at Barnum's and the gender of this domestic environment's keeper troubled its presentation as a moral bastion. The transition of public/private in domestic life gave rise to the parlor space—a home space that would serve as a buffer between these two zones.[67] In this regard, one could perhaps see the American Museum as New York City's parlor—a domestic haven somewhere between public and private.

This made female patrons doubly important to the success of Barnum's—their presence actively ensured the ethical health of the entire establishment. Knowing this, Barnum worked to provide a space chaste enough for female patrons, going so far as to hire undercover detectives to escort unwanted guests from the premises.[68] Women's presence at the museum assured, by turns, that the museum was a place worthy of their presence. Here, Lanier's principle of reciprocal legitimacy functions as an ethical safeguard. Andrea Stulman Dennett claims: "As customers, women were 'icons of decency,' and as an audience, they guaranteed respectability, 'a mixed audience was by definition a respectable one, a male-only one indecent.' . . . The American Museum was both affordable and fashionable, and women of all classes were attracted to the wholesome atmosphere stressed by the pedagogical rhetoric of Barnum's museum."[69] The museum was as ethically sound as its audience who, in turn, ensured the moral sanctity of this public parlor.

Barnum advertised the museum as "the wonder of America and unquestionably from its position, character and popularity, the most special place of family amusement in the United States," assuring guests from the outset of the place's merit as a family institution.[70] In addition to curating the feel and scope of the museum to enact a domestic paradise, Barnum ensured the Lecture Room also echoed this sentiment by producing shows that highlighted the values of sentimental domesticity.[71] Advertisements and guides to the museum emphasize over and over that the Lecture Room was a place of familial leisure and free of the dangers that a theatre might pose. One guide from 1850 claims:

> The amusements presented in the elegant Lecture Room . . . are of that pure and domestic character which cannot fail to improve the heart, while they enlarge the understanding. The most fastidious may take their families there, without the least apprehension of their being offended by word or deed; in short, so careful is the supervision exercised over the amusements, that hundreds of persons who are preventing visiting theatres on account of the vulgarisms and immorality which are sometimes permitted therein, may visit Mr. Barnum's establishment without fear of offence on that point.[72]

Broadsides, such as one advertising a performance on Friday, August 19, 1853, tend to emphasize this as well:

> The family entertainments which take place every afternoon at 3 o'clock and also every evening at 8 o'clock, are produced in the spacious, cool, comfortable and splendid Lecture Room! . . . and are presented by a dramatic company of surpassing excellence, whose chief aim is to unite modesty with mirth and give everything calculated to gratify the public taste, without ministering to a depraved or morbid appetite by uttering indecent thoughts or sentiments hostile to pure morals and an honest faith in true religion.[73]

The parallel language used in these two pieces of writing shows a continued emphasis on audience comfort, luxury, and the good taste of mirthful entertainments on offer. These two pieces are written three years apart and thus display a brand continuity that Barnum upheld. This in turn suggests that this branding was successful: since the museum itself was clearly a long-term success and since Barnum's branding here hadn't shifted, it's logical to conclude that the branding worked. Barnum was well aware of how to convert audience desires into profit and at the American Museum this process was explicitly linked to the sale of ethical domesticity.

76 | THEATRES OF VALUE

"It hath been a shield twixt me and death."

—Pericles, *Pericles*, II.i

With all of these elements of market, commodity, and exchange in mind, I would like to circle back to Barnum's promise about sanitizing Shakespeare on the Lecture Room stage. Barnum's boast, to me, begs examination—while Barnum was well known to stretch the truth, I have yet to discover an instance where he outright lied to potential customers. So I wondered: How much did the truth bend here? How much Shakespeare was enough Shakespeare to provide the veneer of respectability? And how far would the cultural capital of Shakespeare's name go, even if pulled thin? Through a survey of broadsides, advertising ephemera, and chronicles of the New York stage such as those written by T. Allston Brown and George C. Odell, I documented over 3,500 performances at Barnum's Lecture Room dated between January 27, 1845 (three years into Barnum's first stewardship of the museum), and February 24, 1868 (one week before the fire that leveled the second museum).[74] Of the 3,547 performances I have documented to date, only ten were performances of plays written by William Shakespeare (one performance of *Comedy of Errors*, two of *Romeo and Juliet*, three of *Macbeth*, and four of *Richard III*). An additional eight were what I have categorized as "Shakespeare-inspired pieces" (three performances of *Katherine and Petruchio* and five of a play titled *All That Glitters Is Not Gold*). From a quantitative perspective, 0.28 percent of the performances I have documented at Barnum's were of Shakespeare's plays while 0.51 percent could be said to have Shakespearean content.

This data can be put into better context when compared with similar metrics at two representative legitimate theatres. I mined George C. Odell's *Annals of the New York Stage* to catalogue two seasons at Wallack's Lyceum and the Park Theatre. I chose seasons temporally similar to the seasons at Barnum's in order to represent these theatres' repertoires in relation to each other. The first two seasons of performances at Wallack's Lyceum (September 1852–June 1854) saw 125 catalogued performances of ninety-nine plays. Of these, three plays were Shakespearean pieces (*Much Ado about Nothing*, *The Merchant of Venice*, and *As You Like It*). Performances of Shakespeare at Wallack's constituted seven performances, 5.6 percent of performances during these seasons. The last two seasons of performances at the Park (August 1856–June 1848) consisted of 179 performances of 101 distinct plays. Of these, eleven were Shakespeare (in order of the most frequently performed: *Macbeth, Othello, Hamlet, Richard*

III, King Lear, The Merchant of Venice, Romeo and Juliet, As You Like It, Two Gentlemen of Verona, King John, and *Julius Caesar*). Shakespeare plays were performed thirty-two times over the course of these two seasons; Shakespeare constituted 17.87 percent of the repertory at the Park. Barnum's .28 percent holds no candle to his contemporaries. It becomes clear from these numbers that an audience could not reasonably expect to see Shakespeare upon a casual visit to Barnum's Lecture Room while they could rely on Shakespearean content in traditional theatrical venues.

If Barnum was not producing Shakespeare in the Lecture Room, then what was he producing? My data recognizes 651 separate named pieces that were performed at Barnum's. Figure 2.2 depicts the top twenty most-performed documented shows. *Uncle Tom's Cabin* was by far the most performed show (with 42 documented performances). *Our Irish Cousin* comes next with thirty-six performances. Notably, Shakespeare does not appear anywhere on this top twenty. In fact, Shakespeare's plays do not even break the top one hundred. With four performances, *Richard III* is the most frequently performed Shakespearean piece at Barnum's (ranking 260 on the scale of most-performed pieces overall). Even aggregated to ten total performances of Shakespeare's plays, the oeuvre does not break the top twenty at Barnum's. To put these numbers in perspective, see figures 2.3 and 2.4, two representations of how frequently pieces were performed at Barnum's.

The vast majority of shows at Barnum's American Museum and Lecture Room were one-hit wonders; 150 documented shows were performed a single time before they disappeared. The drop-off into the repertoire is steep; 86.02 percent of shows at Barnum's (560 of 651 unique theatre pieces) were performed less than ten times over the Lecture Room's documented history. Shakespeare's plays at Barnum's all remain in this curve; none of them break it. None of Shakespeare's plays were performed regularly, and (based on a dearth of reviews) the few that were performed do not seem to have drawn particular audience attention.

Again, placing this alongside Wallack's and the Park Theatre, several of Shakespeare's plays break the top ten at both institutions. At Wallack's, *Much Ado about Nothing* is tied with *The Lady of Lyons* and *She Stoops to Conquer* as the third most-performed play, and *The Merchant of Venice* ties several pieces for the sixth most-performed play (see fig. 2.5 for the Wallack's top ten chart and fig. 2.6 for the frequency of performance pie chart).[75]

At the Park, *Macbeth* ties for most-performed with *The Wife's Secret* and *The Lady of Lyons* while *Othello* and *Hamlet* vie among others as the fourth-most performed piece (see fig. 2.7 for the Park top ten chart and fig. 2.8 for the Park's frequency of performance pie chart).

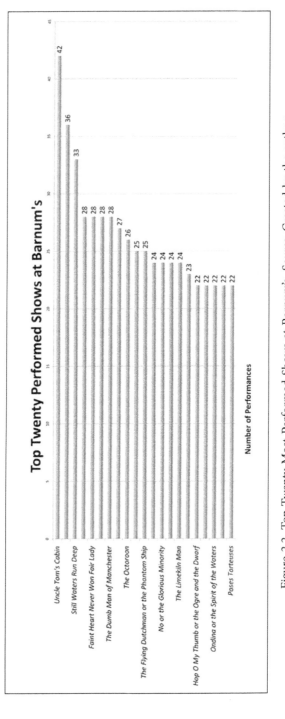

Figure 2.2. Top Twenty Most-Performed Shows at Barnum's. *Source:* Created by the author.

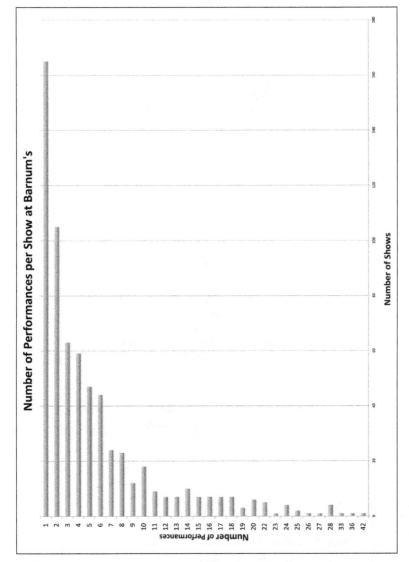

Figure 2.3. Number of Performances per Show at Barnum's. *Source:* Created by the author.

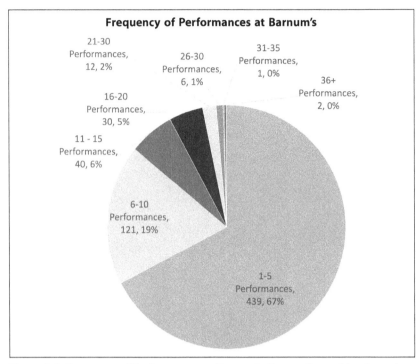

Figure 2.4. Frequency of Performances at Barnum's. *Source*: Created by the author.

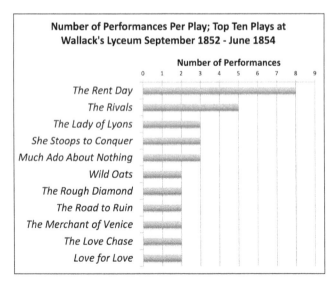

Figure 2.5. Top Ten Most-Performed Plays at Wallack's. *Source*: Created by the author.

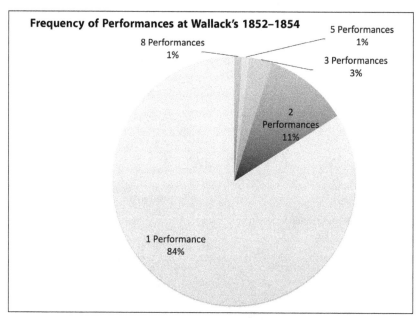

Figure 2.6. Frequency of Performances at Wallack's. *Source*: Created by the author.

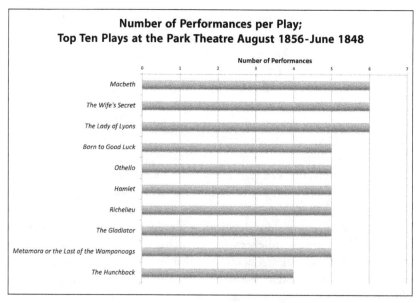

Figure 2.7. Top Ten Most-Performed Plays at the Park. *Source*: Created by the author.

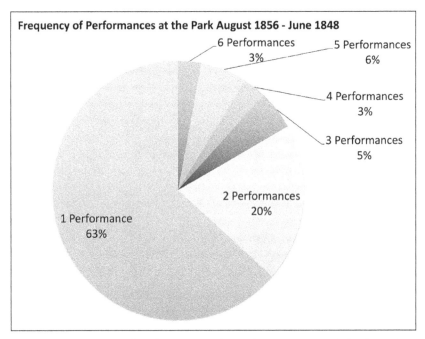

Figure 2.8. Frequency of Performance at the Park. *Source*: Created by the author.

This data may perhaps shed light on Barnum's claim. The established theatres were producing Shakespeare with great frequency. In an effort to seem more like these theatres, Barnum may have attempted to remind the audience of the (albeit small) section of his repertory that most closely matched theirs. By citing Shakespeare as an offering of his Lecture Room, Barnum made a passive comparison between his theatre and other theatrical spaces. In claiming the portion of his repertoire that most closely matched these theatres, Barnum created a link between his theatre and these institutions in the public imagination. This link afforded Barnum the protections of legitimacy but allowed him to continue using the "Lecture Room" moniker to eschew the ethical baggage of calling his space a theatre. In this way, Shakespeare was pulling quintuple duty via Barnum's claim: establishing legitimacy for the theatrical space Barnum maintained; assuring audiences of the status of his establishment and, consequently, theirs for frequenting it; displaying the extent of Barnum's seriousness about maintain these facets; and pulling a veil of Shakespearean legitimacy over Barnum's business like a protective cloak.

The Value of a Name | 83

What is perhaps the most interesting about Barnum's Shakespeare claim is that it is theatrically posthumous. Of the tiny percentage of Barnum's Shakespearean performances, none received top billing (or much fanfare at all). No noteworthy press attention was paid to them during the theatre's lifetime. Barnum, in essence, had little use for Shakespeare as a moneymaking device until a moment of crisis. In hindsight, Barnum was able to spin Shakespeare as a helpful advertising technique even if Shakespearean performances merited small attention prior to this moment. Perhaps even more tellingly, Shakespeare-in-absence seemed more useful to Barnum than any of the active things he *did* do at the Lecture Room. Rather than turn to his proven history of temperance lectures via performances of *The Drunkard* or his support of charitable causes such as the Ladies Five Points Mission, Barnum found Shakespeare the strongest shield—the best evidence to show that the museum was a space of good ethical health.

Perhaps, also, this was a calculated move: Barnum's utterances were about a past that might only be preserved in the memory of those few audiences, those 0.28 percent of audiences, who had been present to see the shows Barnum spoke about. The museum, after all, had burned down. An audience would be hard-pressed to disprove Barnum's words in present action since the Shakespearean object of which he spoke had burned along with it. Barnum's "Shakespeare shield" was, here, only conjurable via memory—a notoriously unreliable device—and Barnum's words—a notoriously semi-reliable device.

Barnum's reliance on Shakespeare's shadowy presence to generate sufficient cultural capital is a pattern that continues with other museum holdings. While Shakespeare's birthplace did not find its way to the American Museum, Barnum did incorporate Shakespearean ephemera into his domestic wonderland, including what seems to be essentially a Shakespeare wing:

> We have many mementos of him: first, his armorial bearings, with the copy of the warrant from the Herald's College, proving his right, by descent, to such honorable distinction. Then we see various models of places connected with his history—among them those of the house in which he was born, in the years 1564, 1767, and 1827, the two latter being "jubilee" years; Daisy Hill Farm House, the lodge of Sir Thomas Lucy's park-keeper, where the poet was confined one night previous to his appearance

before the Knight, for an attempt at deer-stealing on his domain; the Falcon Inn, near the Globe Theatre, Bankside, London; the Jubilee Rotunda; New Place, his residence in Stratford-on-Avon during the latter part of his life; Queen Elizabeth's Nursery, in Golden Lane, London, now a glass warehouse and an "Easy Shaving Shop," but formerly the Fortune Theatre; Charlecote Hall, a choice specimen of Elizabethan architecture, the seat of Sir Thomas Lucy; Stratford-on-Avon Church, in which the poet is buried; the Crown Inn at Oxford, where he used to put upon his occasional journeys to and from Stratford-on-Avon and London; the remains of the Church at Ludington, where he was married to Ann Hathaway; her cottage, &c. Besides these, we have numerous engravings of the interior of Stratford-on-Avon Church, and scenes from the immortal dramatist's plays, not to forget two splendid full-length engravings, respectively of David Garrick and John Phillip Kemble in the character of Richard the Third.[76]

Barnum's collection, essentially, amounted to images and models—place-holders, objects that conjured the feeling of Shakespeare without direct connections to the history. None of these items could be considered historical artifacts but, rather, they entailed some hint of fantasy: some idea that they were connected to a colorful story about Shakespeare. Several of these objects are linked to apocryphal stories of Shakespeare's life: the poaching myth, the crown inn; neither verifiable, but to Barnum both merited collecting. Barnum, here, weaves these anecdotes into his portrayal of Shakespeare perhaps to humanize him and to connect to a pastoral fantasy of the playwright's life that would speak to the urbanite's cravings for such stories as sources of healthful sentiment.

While Barnum was marketing a story about Shakespeare rather than Shakespeare's actuality, he was able to use the verity of present objects to capitalize upon the cultural capital they symbolized. The images of Shakespearean actors in character that Barnum displayed are a special case of this. Barnum used them to conjure the images (literally) of other Shakespearean saviors; by bringing Garrick and Kemble into the museum as ghostly presences, Barnum created a lineage of great Shakespeareans within his museum that pointed directly to himself.

The Shakespeare Barnum weaves from these objects tells of his greatness (the coat of arms, his relationship to Queen Elizabeth) but also reminds the viewer that Shakespeare was human (his marriage venue, the folly of supposed deer theft). In these threads, it is possible to pick apart the value Barnum sees in Shakespeare as an addition to the American Museum. The objects tell a rhetorical story in keeping with the sentimental and domestic factors already discussed: Barnum's Shakespeare reads seamlessly with the glorified story of American bourgeois life painted at the museum. Barnum uses the breadcrumbs he includes of Shakespeare's biography to depict him as a relatable figure of eminence with clear connections to traditional American values: hard work, the rise to renown from humble roots, a man who has not surpassed human concerns like where to stay during a night of travel, but who had found enough infamy to be celebrated by Garrick's jubilee. These aspects of Shakespeare's life that Barnum actively chose to highlight are also the ones he saw as the most worthwhile, the things most apt for selling.

One somewhat curious association packed in Barnum's exhibits is the emphasis on Charlecote and the deer poaching myth. Barnum's faith in this story (or at least his willingness to sell it) as fact is reflected in contemporary writings—an 1863 article published by Nathaniel Hawthorne in the *Atlantic* treats it as gospel.[77] It is a colorful and humanizing anecdote even if historical hindsight has disproven its validity.[78] The nineteenth century's interest in this particular story of Shakespeare's life is, importantly, linked strongly with the cultural interest in the man behind the word and natural genius.[79] It also fits the genre of Barnum's preoccupations: Barnum was notorious for his ability to draft a story (see, for instance, his promotion and display of the so-called "Feejee mermaid": a taxidermic monkey sewn to a fish) and market that story for a profit.[80] In highlighting the poaching story, Barnum takes a kernel of what might be true and immortalizes it as fact. Then, he uses this fact to construct a larger-than-life ideal that audiences consume to excess—not just viewing and appreciating, but sensationalizing. In this method, Shakespeare (or any object of Barnum's interest) becomes a muse for a rhetorical story—the desired end result of which is profit. This link demonstrates Barnum's reliance on the mechanisms of social economies to draft his stories.

The seeming lack of Barnumesque flair in his marketing of Shakespeare is a telling mark straight from Barnum's ledger. Shakespeare's best use, to Barnum, was with the mainstream vogue. Despite the tiny slice of Shakespeare Barnum included in actuality in his packaged-for-consumer middle-class American life, Shakespeare was (continually) included. Shakespeare, to Barnum, was a crucial cog in this machine—unable to be abandoned despite his seemingly small contribution. Put another way: Barnum could not construct the optimized-for-selling version of American middle-class life without at least the veneer of Shakespeare. Still, in this instance, the dramaturgy of value confirms by induction what otherwise might seem anecdotal and demonstrates the marketing power of Barnum's Shakespearean usage for his nineteenth-century class-conscious audience.

Chapter Three

Taking the Reins

The American Reading Career of Mrs. Fanny Kemble

On June 7, 1834, English actress Fanny Kemble married American planta-tion owner Pierce Butler and promised herself it would be the end of her stage career. On April 11, 1834, on the precipice of her nuptials, Kemble admitted: "I did not expect to remain on the stage after the month of May, when my marriage was appointed, and I hoped to be free from a profession which has always been irksome to me."[1] Kemble's hasty retreat from the stage was short-lived; her scintillating public divorce became a tabloid sensation in the late 1840s, leaving Kemble scrambling to make ends meet and the American public at once leery of and fascinated by this vocally liberated woman. Pressed to make a living, Kemble returned to show business in a series of Shakespearean readings. In the United States, Kemble performed first in Boston, then in New York, and finally regionally throughout the Northeast. In New York, Kemble read at the Stuyvesant Institute at 659 Broadway (a few blocks south of Astor Place) and at the Lyceum (in Brooklyn) in March and April of 1849.[2]

In these readings, Kemble secured control of her labor and public image; she selected and cut her texts, had a hand in selecting performance days and venues, costumed herself, and performed each play in solitary reading all the parts herself. By staging these readings, Kemble eschewed the scandal and sensation generally affiliated with theatre and invoked a higher-brow literary engagement with Shakespeare's texts using her English theatrical heritage as capital. Through the readings, Kemble freed herself from traditional theatrical gender roles: she performed every part onstage,

88 | THEATRES OF VALUE

and many offstage as well. This was not the only arena in which Kemble's carefully curated performance harnessed public opinion; Kemble was also doing so in print via newspapers and published diaries. Her performances on all these fronts allowed Kemble to regain control of her public image in order to create a lucrative product while salvaging her reputation. Kemble's use of Shakespeare as a character-saving device employed her status as a woman of English theatrical heritage as she leveraged the cultural capital Shakespeare represented to eschew public scandal, destabilize gendered social expectations, and turn a profit.

To Kemble, Shakespeare functioned in much the same way he did for Brown and Barnum, but unlike these men Kemble was ultimately successful in crafting a lasting set of Shakespearean armor. While Brown's success was ironically proven by the ultimate shuttering of his too-legitimate enterprise and Barnum eventually gave up on rebuilding his seemingly doomed museum, Kemble was able to use Shakespeare to craft a more permanent win. Kemble's Shakespearean usage is, of course, markedly different due to her English theatrical pedigree, but it is significant that Shakespeare's capital created lasting benefit here when invoked by a woman who managed to outmaneuver a patriarchal system when it had seemingly failed others before. The dramaturgy of value allows a closer look into the hows and whys of Kemble's usage and a glimpse at the ways in which Kemble employed Shakespeare as part of her larger performance of self to communicate with her audience and manipulate public opinion.

> "O Jesu, he doth it as like one of these
> harlotry players as ever I see!"

> —Hostess Quickly, *Henry IV, Part 1*, II.iv

Kemble first met Butler during her 1832–1834 American tour: he was an adoring fan who became enamored with her after attending a Philadelphia performance. Butler wooed Kemble for the remainder of the tour and their marriage was quickly appointed. Kemble biographers generally agree that she entered the match as a method of retiring from stage acting.[3] Despite a life of professional stage work courtesy of her theatrically famous family, Kemble was outspoken in her distaste for the vocation.[4] In her widely read journal (originally published 1835), Kemble laments:

How I do loathe the stage! These wretched, tawdry, glittering rags, flung over the breathing forms of ideal loveliness; these miserable, poor, and pitiful substitutes for the glorious with which poetry has invested her magnificent and fair creation. . . . What a mass of wretched mumming mimicry acting is! Pasteboard and paint, for the thick breathing orange groves of the south; green silk and oiled parchment, for the solemn splendor of her noon of night; wooden platforms and canvass curtains, for the solid marble balconies, and rich dark draperies of Juliet's sleeping chamber, that shrine of love and beauty; rouge, for the started life-blood in the cheek of that young passionate woman; an actress, a mimicker, a sham creature, me, in fact, or any other one, for that loveliest and most wonderful conception. . . . To act this! To act Romeo and Juliet! Horror! Horror! How I do loathe my most impotent and unpoetical craft![5]

Kemble's railings against theatre are loud and declarative but there is no small amount of irony in this writing. Despite her vocal revulsion of acting, Kemble's journal can only be viewed as performative. Even if it was originally written for private use, the form of the journal as a published document is an object intended for sale. As such, the journal is a representation of Kemble's public-facing persona as crafted by her own editing hand with a mind toward a wide audience and the hope of its profit-making potential.

By their nature, published journals are deceptive in that they feel personal, intimate, like a close look at the private life and thoughts of their authors, but this is a carefully crafted illusion. Kemble's journals, like any publication, were either written, edited, or some combination thereof with intention for a large reading audience. They should thus be examined with the same critical eye lent to any public performance. Kemble paid careful note to the presentation of her person in her journal and future memoiristic writings (she produced at least six additional memoirs/journals later in her life).[6] The 1835 journal was prepared for publication early in Kemble's marriage to Butler (autumn of 1834 or so). In a public 1850 statement written as supplement to material relevant to the divorce, Butler writes:

During this period, Mrs. Butler was engaged in preparing her "Journal" for the press. I was much averse to the publication of that work: it was the private diary of a young woman, and contained much that was unfit for the public eye; but it was sold to the publishers previous to our marriage, and they would not relinquish their contract. I found it necessary, for her own sake, that many things should be omitted, and accordingly I read the manuscript and proof sheets. Any curtailment greatly irritated her; she opposed the slightest alteration after it was copied for the printer; and as she objected so vehemently to it, I struck out as little as possible, and indeed passed over many parts that I would certainly otherwise have erased. Every sentence, and even word, that I wished to omit or alter, was stately defended, and my suggestions made her very angry. At length she declared she would not submit to further curtailment in her composition, but would leave me. This occurred in November, 1834, less than six months after our marriage.[7]

Butler's insistence upon editing and reediting what Kemble thought best to publish seems to have been the cause of the first fight between them: a fight so bad it ended with Kemble packing her clothes and leaving (though she shortly thereafter returned). The control that Butler wished to exert over Kemble was a theme that would develop into greater trouble later in their marriage. In this instance, it manifested as an effort to control Kemble's public persona via her performance in her edited diaries. This effort to oversee the commodity Kemble was crafting, as well as the persona she was performing, was not something Kemble could abide. The anecdote also elucidates the care that went into the editing of Kemble's public persona—both by Kemble herself, and by Butler on her behalf. Nothing in this journal was accidental, and to Kemble all of it was essential (so much so that Butler's edits were intolerable).

Likely because of Butler's negative reactions to Kemble's writings, this journal would be the last piece Kemble published for a long while. Most of Kemble's memoirs were compiled over a twelve-year period when she was in her mid-sixties and late seventies. This temporal removal of the performer (Kemble) from the means of performance thus drafted a commodity whose success relied upon the credence of the persona Kemble inhabited via her journals. Her performance in this mode is perhaps, then, similar to the Civil War reenactors Rebecca Schneider writes about when she notes that they "fight not only to 'get it right' as it was but to get it right as it will be in the future of the archive to which they see themselves contributing."[8] Kemble's journals self-document a history in hindsight and contribute that history to the archive in hopes of it reading as fact. In publishing her journals, Kemble knew she was writing as her own chief documentarian for a wide public audience, presumably with the end goal of selling the product she drafted for profit. In this act, Kemble edits her memories for their rhetorical significance and fitness for inclusion in her performance. The part she plays via her memoirs is drafted and edited by Kemble's hand (and only Kemble's hand—as her fierce disagreements with Butler elucidate), then told to the audience in her voice and her voice alone—much in the way her readings were.

In terms of the ways in which recorded history reflects the person doing the recording, Ciaran Trace considers how what is recorded (or not) begins to uncover important aspects of the human behind the record that archivists and archive users miss at their own peril.[9] Some critical elements of the way the record is kept (which Trace identifies) include the audience for whom the record is written and the rhetorical desire for outcomes that the recordkeeper has in mind. Diarists such as Kemble use the diary as a rhetorical device and Kemble's diaries, written as both formal archives of her life and profit-generating tools, must be viewed in a similar light to Trace's archives.

The performance Kemble put forth in diaries and public writings (particularly her "Narrative," which I will discuss later) was her way of taking agency in the publicity machine generated in the wake of her sensational public life. Kemble had a massive following because of her career, her divorce, her participation in the dress reform movement, and her significant talents as an equestrian. But newspaper stories *about* Kemble were not sufficient for her—Kemble demanded agency. By speaking directly to her audience about her own story and her own recollections, Kemble created a personal relationship with readers and took the reins of her own archive. The irony of this act—a performance against the theatricality of acting—is underlined by Kemble's heritage. Kemble was born into a family that believed theatre was powerful and that women were crucial components to this power.[10] It's difficult to believe that Kemble *didn't* take this to heart—particularly when performance became such a crucial vehicle for Kemble as a newly single woman. In this light, Kemble's railings against the levels of artifice involved in acting can only be read as performances in and of themselves. Additionally, it is somewhat curious that an actress of some renown would cast aspersions upon her former profession this way.[11] Such public discourse about the distaste of theatrical artifice might make an audience who appreciated Kemble's performances feel foolish. If Kemble vituperated performance as a profession, how does that cast audiences who enjoy the fruits of such labor? To consider that Kemble was business savvy is to consider that this carefully crafted public persona was an illusion built to sell—but how was that interaction taking place in a fruitful way with Kemble's audience and market?

As early as her marriage to Butler, Kemble was looking for ways to retire from the stage to pursue what she viewed as a more prestigious, creative, and lasting profession couched in literature. On December 29, 1832, Kemble wrote to a friend from her American tour: "An actor is at best but a filler up on an outline designed by another—the expounder as it were of things which another has set down, and a fine piece of acting is at best, in my opinion, a fine translation."[12] Here, Kemble's distinction between the value of creation—that is, the object made by a writer—weighed against the value of the actor's craft is clear. What is equally clear is her distaste for the profession of "filling up" the writer's design and romanticization of the source object (the written text). As such, Kemble's memoirs and literary creations take on profounder meaning—Kemble herself understood the value of the written work to be deep, so her self-archiving via published writing bore that authorial weight.

Just as Kemble had a sense for the power of literature in audience's minds, she also knew about the power of marketing and the creation of financial capital from cultural capital. As she wrote in her 1882 autobiography, "The readings were to be my livelihood, and I had to adapt them to the audiences who paid for them:—'For those who live to please, must please to live.'"[13] Kemble was very clear that she understood herself to be a commodity and, in fact, referenced her American tour as a "manufacture of public enthusiasms."[14] The creation of Kemble-centric objects was another aspect of the commodification of the Kemble name. "Kemble" became attached to various material commodities: not just the "Kemble Curls" and "Kemble Caps" that were popular for young ladies but also a proliferation of advertising materials (stores would display Kemble's portrait in a front window as a means to attract customers), equestrians named horses for her, horticulturalists bred a new kind of tulip and christened it with her name.[15] Because of her connection to these products, Kemble was situated within the locus of this market for material commodity long before her divorce and the readings that would reenter her name into the public sphere as a performer. Kemble was a product—and she knew how to sell herself.

> "What great ones do the less will prattle of."

> —Captain, *Twelfth Night*, I.ii

The awareness of herself as commodity and the product she could potentially sell were critical to Kemble's public relations arsenal in the wake of her divorce. As she launched her reading series, Kemble was already making moves to harness public opinion. In 1845, Pierce Butler filed for divorce from Kemble on the basis of abandonment. Kemble had gone to England, purportedly to take care of her aging father, but it became clear that part of Kemble's mission abroad was to escape Butler's abusive and untenable treatment. Most of this would come to light in a series of long narrative statements compiled by Kemble and Butler, and made public over the course of the divorce.[16] Throughout 1845–1848, a series of letters exchanged between Kemble and others were eventually compiled by Kemble into a "Narrative," which she presented to the court of common pleas in Philadelphia.[17] This narrative was written in first person with supplementing documents (letters) meant to stand as proof of its claims. It went into gruesome detail with damning condemnation of Butler and how he had treated Kemble over the course of their marriage. Among the many allegations Kemble leveled at Butler in the narrative were: the withholding of promised allowance money, the prevention of visitation between Kemble and her children, and general harsh and unkind treatment from Butler despite Kemble's many pleas to reconcile. Also in 1848, Kemble formally requested a trial by jury in the divorce case, knowing that it would make all presented documentation (including her narrative) a matter of public record. Accordingly, the narrative was made known to the public early in January of 1849, though the divorce case never came to court. The narrative must then be viewed as a rhetorical document like Kemble's written-for-publication journals—highly performative and meant for a wide reading audience as essentially a plea for favorable public opinion in the matter of her divorce. Kemble's journals taught her how to craft such documents and gave her practice at performing in this mode, so it is no surprise that she would use this familiar means of audience connection as a leverage tool to reclaim the narrative of her ongoing legal saga.

While the narrative quickly became a public document, it wound up having no legal bearings on Kemble's case: the court eventually ruled to

94 | Theatres of Value

strike the narrative from formal records stating it was extraneous and had no evidence to back its sundry claims.[18] But the narrative's purpose wasn't strictly to serve as a legal document; it had perhaps even deeper power as public testimony. Despite being struck from legal record, it was printed in many daily papers and, thus, widely read by a large audience. Predictably, this audience formed their own opinions along gendered lines—women seemed to see the narrative as vindicating and men perhaps less so.[19] J. C. Furnas argues that Kemble was able to directly translate to her success in reaching her audience to success in the readings:

> The Narrative not only secured her useful public sympathy, it was inadvertently good feminist propaganda. It dramatized her poignant case-history as implicitly typifying the married woman's plight as presumed subadult quasi-chattel, her children as inextricably their father's property as if she had been a slave-woman he owned. And her simultaneous career as reader showed that women could stand firmly alone. The audiences to whom she read while Butler Vs. Butler was in the court were mostly people who took for granted the traditional doctrines of husband's hegemony over wife and woman's inferiority to man in all but domestic skills. In that compact, intense, eloquent figure on the platform, however, they were exposed not merely to a woman struggling for freedom. She had the deeper significance of an unmistakable gentlewoman of serene independence supporting herself by giving society a generous money's worth of one of its great cultural by-products.[20]

To Furnas, the narrative was the vehicle through which Kemble was able to solidify herself as righteous and rightful in her domestic claims, and her readings as both political and beneficial to herself and to her audiences. The narrative, according to Furnas, was veritable alchemy—transforming the performative moment of Kemble's divorce and concurrent reading career into a nourishing experience and, consequently, a valuable commodity.

The place Fanny Kemble held in the popular imagination (bolstered by her centrality in a network of already-successful commodities) gave Kemble a firm platform upon which to build the success of her readings. Gail Marshall argues that Kemble's person was itself a spectacle because of her "highly acrimonious and very public divorce hearing" and that many American audiences were drawn to this spectacle.[21] Marshall and others cite an entry from the diary of audience member Philip Hone dated March 13, 1849, as proof of the readings' audience draw: "The fashionable world is agog again upon a new impulse. Mrs. Butler, the veritable Fanny Kemble, has taken the city by storm. She reads Shakespeare's plays three evenings in a week, and at noon on Mondays in the Stuyvesant Institute in Broadway, a room which will hold six or seven hundred persons, and which is filled when she reads by the elite of the world of fashion; delicate women, grave gentlemen, belles, beaus and critics flock to the doors of the entrance, and rush in to such places as they can find, two or three hours before the lady's appearance."[22] Hone's impression of the scale and scope of Kemble's audience clearly articulates the readings' place in polite society, as well as the financial success associated with such a packed house.

This moneymaking accomplishment was born of necessity. Kemble knew she would need to generate income to pay her living expenses, legal fees, and so forth, but she had few ways to protect assets from her husband while they were still married. This was a double bind for Kemble. She did not want to prejudice a jury against herself by invoking the "immorality" of professional stage work but had little recourse to earn money otherwise. This reality, combined with acting's nineteenth-century association with sexuality and the actress's particular linkage to objectification, is another factor that might have made memoir-writing and staged reading appealing vocations for Kemble. Faye Dudden observes:

> To act you must be present in the body, available to be seen. The woman who acts is thus inherently liable, whatever her own intent, to become the object of male sexual fantasy and voyeuristic pleasure. Acting is a particularly acute case of the general phenomenon of woman being reduced to sexual object. . . . The story of the American theatre's two standing offers to women is deeply intertwined with the history of modern women and of public life. Theatre is a quintessentially public activity, and traditionally the public sphere belonged to men.[23]

Kemble clearly had some sense of the precarity of her situation in entering that public sphere not just as an actress but also as a public figure. It would have not been advantageous to Kemble to be seen as an object of sexual fantasy as she petitioned the court for legal freedom from her husband—particularly as she contemplated the fate of her children. Just as the narrative was a calculated move to reclaim agency over the voice

96 | THEATRES OF VALUE

telling her story, the readings were an ideal way for Kemble to harness the potential issues entwined with stage performance and benefit from them—that is, if she could sell them as something other than objectifying.

It wasn't just the presentation of the readings where Kemble took a calculated risk, but also with their success as a commodity. Money, after all, was being made and during the nineteenth century a wife's labor (and its fruits) belonged squarely to her husband.[24] Kemble's divorce had been forthcoming since 1845, but it first came into the public eye sometime in the fall of 1848. The divorce was formally granted September 22, 1849.[25] Despite the ongoing legal battle, profits from the spring 1849 readings were, perhaps miraculously, not a bone of contention in divorce proceedings. Still, either Kemble or her father had some sense that Kemble's earnings would not be safe in her marriage to Butler. While the Butlers had no prenuptial agreement (such an arrangement was rare but extant during the time of their marriage), Kemble's profits from her last English tour were transferred to her father's name and left in London when she came to America to marry Butler in 1834.[26] A warning about the fate of a married woman's money was made explicit in advice given to Kemble by a friend and immortalized in one of Kemble's later-published diaries: "While you remain single and choose to work, your fortune is an independent and ample one. As soon as you marry there's no such thing."[27] Between the advice and the careful protection of Kemble's profits from her premarital tour, Kemble seems to have had an awareness of how her economic independence would suffer with marriage and some understanding that she would need to protect it should she wish to retain options beyond wifehood.

Another moment in which Kemble documents this consciousness can be found in a letter to a friend written in May of 1842 that Kemble published in *Records of a Later Life*. Kemble writes:

> You ask whether it is a blessing or a curse not to provide one's own means of subsistence. I think it is a great blessing to be able and allowed to do so. But I dare say I am not a fair judge of the question, for the feeling of independence and power consequent upon earning large sums of money has very much destroyed my admiration for any other mode of support; and yet certainly my *pecuniary* position now would seem to most people very far preferable to my former one; but having *earned* money, and therefore most legitimately *owned* it, I never

can conceive that I have any right to the money of another person. . . . I cannot help sometimes regretting that I did not reserve out of my former earnings at least such a yearly sum as would have covered my personal expenses; and having these notions, which impair the comfort of *being maintained*, I am sometimes sorry that I no longer possess my former convenient power of coining.[28]

Kemble valued her independence despite the fact that she outspokenly assailed the profession that granted her this independence. She performed this valuation from hindsight in her memoirs, but her hand in the business of her readings continued to display a sense of its valuation.

Kemble employed manager John Mitchell to assist in her American reading tour. Mitchell helped Kemble develop her repertory, engage bookings, and fix prices.[29] Mitchell was not Kemble's first theatrical manager; he took over when Kemble's previous associate Jebediah Barker resigned due to age—but in the interim Kemble did her own management.[30] Even when she worked with a manager, Kemble had an active hand in all aspects of her business. For her reading series, Mitchell tried to insist that Kemble read only the most popular plays as a matter of economics—but Kemble pushed back and expanded her repertoire, claiming man does not live by bread alone:

I was determined, at least, not to limit my repertory to the few most theatrically popular of Shakespeare's dramas, but to include in my course all Shakespeare's plays that it was possible to read with any hope of attracting or interesting an audience. My father had limited his range to a few of the most frequently acted plays. I delivered the following twenty-four: *King Lear, Macbeth, Cymbeline, King John, Richard II., two parts of Henry IV., Henry V., Richard III., Henry VIII., Coriolanus, Julius Caesar, Anthony* [sic] *and Cleopatra, Hamlet, Othello, Romeo and Juliet, The Merchant of Venice, The Winter's Tale, Measure for Measure, Much Ado about Nothing, As You Like It, Midsummer Night's Dream, Merry Wives of Windsor*, and *The Tempest.* These plays I read invariably through once before repeating any of them; partly to make such of them as are seldom or never acted, familiar to the public, by delivering them alternately with those better known; and partly to avoid, what I much

98 | Theatres of Value

> dreaded, becoming mechanical or hackneyed myself in their delivery by perpetual repetition of the same pieces, and so losing any portion of the inspiration of my text by constant iteration of those garbled versions of it, from which so much of its nobler and finer elements are of hard necessity omitted in such a process as my reading of them. I persisted in this system for my own "soul's sake," and not to debase my work more than was inevitable, to the very considerable detriment of my gains.[31]

Kemble's writing indicates a clear sense of the commodity she sold—an invigorating noble reading series of an expansive repertoire of Shakespeare's plays.

This focus on the product she delivered was also a factor in Kemble's insistence on only performing four readings a week—though Mitchell pushed for more since demand was rife. Kemble writes:

> I am afraid my excellent and zealous manager, Mr. Mitchell, was often far from satisfied with the views I took of the duty imposed upon me by reading Shakespeare. My entire unwillingness to exhaust myself and make my work laborious instead of pleasant to me, by reading more than three, or at the utmost four, times a week, when very often we could have commanded very full rooms for the six; my pertinacious determination to read as many of the plays (and I read twenty-five) as could be so given to an audience in regular rotation, so as to avoid becoming hackneyed in my feeling or delivery of them, appeared to him vexatious particularities highly inimical to my own best interests, which he thought would have been better served by reading *Hamlet, Romeo and Juliet,* and the *Merchant of Venice,* three times as often as I did, and *Richard II., Measure for Measure,* and one or two others, three times as seldom, or not at all. But though Mr. Mitchell could calculate the money value of my readings to me, their inestimable value he knew nothing of.[32]

Kemble's sense of value for the commodity she sold is here linked to its quality and esteem value, as well as the sense of joy/purpose Kemble had in the work she performed. The readings were valuable to Kemble both because of something intrinsic to the text (their "inestimable value") and also the impact they had on Kemble and her audience (the way the work was pleasant). The tension between Mitchell and Kemble stemmed from the economic value of Kemble's commodity placed in direct odds with its social value. To Kemble, what she sold was worth more than mere dollar signs. Her noble purpose, or at least the noble purpose performed in these memoirs, was more about the integrity of Shakespeare's work as preserved through her readings. The success of Kemble's product is demonstrable—her audience came and eagerly paid for what she sold. The question at the nexus, then, is what lived between the lines of what Kemble sold and what audiences bought—and how that enabled Kemble to salvage her public image as her divorce raged on.

> "Calpurnia here, my wife, stays me at home."

> —Caesar, *Julius Caesar*, II.ii

Armed with her experience as a public woman onstage and her knowledge of how to work an audience, Kemble was ready to combat allegations of immorality. As Kemble put her readings together, she paid heed to their setting and played upon a sense of domesticity. For the readings, Kemble sat behind a large reading table.[33] At the Stuyvesant Institute, Kemble's table was custom made to her specifications. Generally covered with a cloth that ran to the floor, the table was set with carefully considered domestic trappings—a pile of books, a candelabra, and often a large silver vase with fresh flowers gifted by audience members.[34] A screen was placed behind the table to frame her (it was often red to compliment Kemble's coloring and the elaborate dresses she selected to match the theme of the play she read on a given evening).[35] All of these pieces crafted an air of domestic comfort and made of Kemble's performance space a public parlor from which the fourth wall was conveniently removed. By summoning up that atmosphere, Kemble signaled to her audience that this reading was not, in fact, a stage performance but rather an evening at home—a socially acceptable diversion. In so doing, Kemble situated herself as a standard-bearer of domesticity—a public woman who remained bound to hearth and home.

This was necessary particularly because of how antipathy to performance haunted Kemble's private life. In an 1848 document issued by the

100 | Theatres of Value

court of common pleas of Philadelphia, Kemble noted that performance was something Butler weaponized against her in the disposition of their children:

> At the end of February, 1847, I resumed the exercise of the laborious and distasteful profession of my youth, rendered now doubly laborious and distasteful by the sad circumstances that compelled me to it. . . . My children had till now been permitted to correspond with me; and knowing that they could not fail to hear of my return to a public career, and wishing that my elder child should know the motives which had induced me to such a course, I wrote to tell her that having no secure means of subsistence, and not wishing to deprive my father of any of the comforts of his old age, I had judged it best to work for my own support. This letter the libellant told my child was untrue, and from that moment neither she nor her sister were permitted to write to me again.[36]

Again, Kemble notes her aversion to the profession of the stage—and here she perhaps has cause as Butler used it to keep her from her children. The connection between Kemble's public performances and her correspondence with her children are noteworthy in that they explicitly associate behavior Butler apparently deemed unbecoming with disallowance of engagement with domestic life. Kemble's job as a performer is here the thing that makes her an unfit mother in the eyes of her critic.

Perhaps revealingly considering Kemble's demonstrably savvy use of the press as a public entity, there's a strange disconnect between Kemble's writings about her children and her actions regarding them. Despite writing and publishing about her concern for her kids, Kemble never sought custody. Nan Mullenneaux notes: "Kemble's correspondence does not clearly explain why she never sought custody, except to indicate that she wanted to avoid any kind of public battle. Her letters mask the reasons for her passivity with the rhetoric of a victim."[37] It's difficult to believe Kemble when she "doth protest too much" about her discomfort with a public battle given how she continued to leverage public discourse to her advantage—making her fight in the divorce overt every step of the way. Perhaps, however, Kemble was willing to take up these efforts on her own behalf, but less willing to do so when her children were involved.

Returning to the readings: there are clear stakes for the impressions of this public performance, so it is no strange thing that Kemble developed them into a consistent product that scanned rhetorically to bolster claims of domestic health and intellectual pursuit rather than bodily enactment. Kemble was meticulous in her presentation at the readings, almost ritualized. From her first American reading (Boston at the Masonic Hall on January 26, 1849), she had a specific order of operations to each evening. She would be led to the stage, curtsey to the audience, then sit behind her reading table. She would open her book, say "I have the honor to read . . . ," name the play and read the cast of characters, then begin reading the playtext. She would plan her costume specifically in conjunction with the subject of the play: white satin for *Romeo and Juliet*, deep red for *Hamlet*, and so forth. Her dresses were admired for their fashionable taste.[38] In New York, Kemble read at the Stuyvesant Institute during March and April of 1849 with a few April performances at the Brooklyn Lyceum as her divorce case toiled on (the divorce would finally be settled in September of 1849).

In framing her readings as domestic while simultaneously public-facing, Kemble enacted a dynamic at play for the nineteenth-century woman in which, as Sara M. Evans argues, "the boundaries between work and home remained highly permeable."[39] Evans further argues that between 1820 and 1845 specifically, public space for women was carved between the spheres of home and the public institution of government.[40] These spaces were generally staked in volunteer charity associations that, for Evans, became loaded and liminal for boundary-pressing between the public and private spheres to occur (much like the parlor itself—as I discussed in the previous chapter). Kemble's readings occupied a similar space—sometimes literally since Kemble insisted on offering one reading per run in each city she visited whose funds would be donated to a locally relevant charitable cause.[41] The liminality of Kemble's readings between public and private, domestic and civil, was further enforced by the publication of Kemble's narrative, which opened the door to public views of Kemble as a woman, wife, and mother. In inviting her public audience into her private life both through the narrative and through her readings, Kemble curated a performance of this privacy as these two spheres came crashing together. Through the readings, Kemble harnessed control of this dichotomy; she was no longer simply allowing the public access to her private life but giving them a guided (and carefully curated) tour. She maintained the air of domesticity in public but added a layer of control. The audiences would, through her Shakespeare readings, see her exactly as she wished them to, and that image would be linked to her identity as a literary Englishwoman bringing Shakespeare to the American masses as a wholesome educational experience.[42]

To Nan Mullenneaux, this ability to create a domestic masquerade through public discourse was part of the commodity that nineteenth-century actresses in general sold.[43] Kemble's readings became a cornerstone of her "domestic masquerade" because they produced the illusion of domestic stability at a time when this illusion was fragile and fraught—the public *knew* that, outside of the readings, Kemble's domestic life was anything but stable. Amy Richter argues that women's labor in the nineteenth-century home stood as a bulwark against the immorality of life outside the home.[44] Kemble capitalized on this expectation by invoking domesticity in the setting of her readings—allowing herself to become the guardian of this domestic sphere and, thereby, the moral bulwark even from the public platform of the stage. Additionally, this morality provided a second bulwark against allegations leveled at Kemble personally. The readings were thus cleverly employed as keystone to Kemble's campaign to preserve her public image.

Part of the carefully curated domesticity of this performance was the very book Kemble read from, a performative prop that linked Kemble to both the cultural heritage of her family name and the sense that her readings were wholesome family affairs. Kemble used her father's text for her readings—though whether she read directly out of his book is still a question for debate. In her memoir, Kemble clearly reports that she relied on Charles Kemble's reading texts as the basis for her own: "I gladly availed myself of my father's reading version of the plays, and read those he had delivered, cut and prepared for the purpose according to that."[45] Her reliance on Charles Kemble's texts has been taken at its word by many scholars who argue that Kemble simply took her father's book and read his cuts verbatim.[46] This story seems to have originated with Gerald Kahan's 1983 article, the first and so-far only piece of scholarly writing dedicated solely to Kemble's American reading career.[47] Kahan argues that Kemble read exclusively from a 1744 Hanmer edition held by the Hargrett Library at the University of Georgia. Subsequently, Maria Chappell has made a deep study of this text, and her research clearly shows many instances of Kemble's notes and emendations in this volume (made on several different occasions/passes of the text) but evinces none of Charles Kemble's handwriting.[48] It is likely that rather than literally read from Charles's book, Kemble copied her father's markups into a volume of her own (in point of fact: Kemble herself mentions doing this in her journal).[49] Chappell wonders if the book Kemble copied these annotations into is in fact the Hargrett Hanmer, but she also notes the complexities of the marginalia in this text and calls into question whether this was the volume Kemble used in her readings.[50] Chappell's working theory is that Kemble read from a variety of texts during her readings in England and America, and likely a different text in America than she did in England. While the Hargrett Hanmer may be one of these documents, it is probably not the only one.[51] Still, Kemble's reliance on Charles's notes as a starting point (and her performance via her published diaries about this very fact) allowed her to reap the benefit of Charles's cultural capital: both his name as a brand and her connection to this brand as a dutiful daughter thus perpetuating an idealized domestic myth surrounding her readings.

While she publicized that her father's work was foundational to her reading texts, Kemble also made her own careful study of these texts with a mind toward the product she was drafting. Kemble initially hoped to read the plays in their entirety but realized quickly that this was impractical: "To do so would have required that I should take two, and sometimes three, evenings to the delivery of one play; a circumstance which would have rendered it necessary for the same audience, if they wished to hear it, to attend two and three consecutive readings; and in many other respects I found the plan quite incompatible with the demand of the public, which was for a dramatic entertainment, and not for a course of literary instruction."[52] Charles had settled on a two-hour reading window for the plays and Kemble found herself agreeing to this as well. Of course, she didn't limit herself to her father's repertoire. In exploring pieces beyond her father's canon, Kemble admitted: "When I came to cut and prepare for reading the much greater number which I read, and he did not, I found the task a very difficult one; and was struck with the judgement and taste with which my father performed it. I do not think it possible to have adapted these compositions better or more successful to the purposes for which he required them."[53] While Kemble was effusive in her admiration of her father's editing eye, she was less vociferous about her own contributions to her reading editions. Chapell's findings are fairly clear in that Kemble further adapted the plays that Charles read. Even still, she was careful to be vocal about Charles's work serving as the basis for her success. Kemble ensured that she highlighted Charles's hand in mapping her blueprint

104 | Theatres of Value

despite the fact that she made her own subsequent changes to the documents. In this way, Kemble leveraged her performances via the diaries into her performed domesticity as Shakespearean reader.

Kemble's domestic performance continued beyond the auspices of how she presented her stage work and into the realm of how she presented her own person. After the divorce, Kemble kept her married salutation ("Mrs.") though returned to her family name ("Kemble"). She thus reclaimed the prestige of her theatrically famous last name but released herself from the baggage of being an unmarried women. Furnas argues that this act was to detract from the distraction of having children call an unmarried woman "mother."[54] This is a tough sell to me because (as I've argued) Kemble's relationship with her children remains unclear.[55] In practice, the act of naming seemed much more utilitarian. Mullenneaux argues that actresses who married generally considered marketing when deciding which name to go by professionally (their married name or maiden name) and Kemble's chosen salutation shows her awareness of this power.[56]

Kemble reclaimed her maiden name with explicit instructions to the public regarding how she wished to be referenced. The papers make due note of this request. An October 12, 1849, letter from the editor of the *Wilmington Journal* remarks: "The only attraction of any importance, is Fanny Kemble Butler's Shakespearean readings. Mrs. Kemble, as she now calls herself, is undoubtedly a woman of talent."[57] A similar announcement is made in the *Herald of the Times* of October 11, 1849: "Mrs. Butler has resumed her maiden name; in the announcement of her Shakespearean Readings, she styles herself, Mrs. Frances Ann Kemble."[58] From January 29, 1840, through May 23, 1851, I've tracked forty-eight discreet mentions of Kemble in newspapers from across the United States. Between January and May of 1849, she is referred to using some combination of her chosen appellation and her married name, "Mrs. Fanny Kemble Butler" or "Mrs. Frances Kemble Butler." Twice, she's referenced as "Mrs. Butler"—both times in the *Herald of the Times* (once on June 21, 1849, and once on October 11, 1849).[59] Two articles refer to her as "Mrs. Butler" in the headlines but then use her preferred nomenclature in the article content.[60] Generally, when a paper discusses Kemble's horsemanship, the profit she makes from her readings, or her participation in the dress reform movement, they seem more inclined to call her "Mrs. Butler."[61] The *Daily Union* was sure to specify "Mrs. Fanny Kemble (Formerly Mrs. Butler)" when it published about her readings on November 6, 1849.[62]

Kemble's divorce from Butler was formally granted on September 22, 1849.[63] The first newspaper mentions of "Mrs. Fanny Kemble" or just

"Mrs. Kemble" that I have encountered begin on October 8, 1849 (published in *The Republic* of Washington, DC).[64] After this moment, reports of "Mrs. Fanny Kemble Butler" continue to trickle in. After November 8, 1849, Kemble gradually sheds "Butler" from her public image entirely as papers begin to call her "Mrs. Kemble" or "Mrs. Fanny Kemble." Still, as late as March of 1850 newspapers with a bone to pick (such as one article extremely critical of Kemble's appearance in the *Minnesota Pioneer*) continue to call Kemble "Mrs. Butler" or something such as "Mrs. Kemble (Butler)."[65] For a visualization of this data, see figure 3.1.

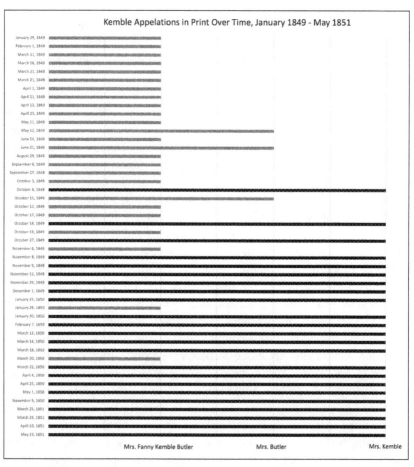

Figure 3.1. Kemble's Appellations in Print over Time. *Source*: Created by the author.

106 | THEATRES OF VALUE

Of course, performing domesticity also allowed Kemble to open her audiences to those who would not deign to set foot in a theatre due to concerns about its moral place in polite society. Furnas notes of Kemble's English readings: "It was an advantage to her and readers after her that many well-to-do families who thought it sinful to enter a theater at all, no matter how innocuous the play or irreproachable the morals of the actors, nevertheless saw no harm in donning their good clothes to patronize a reading of Shakespeare."[66] Furnas's verbiage about Kemble's readings echoes critics' sentiments about P. T. Barnum's Lecture Room. Like Barnum, performing domesticity allowed Kemble to cash in on the benefits of ethical and sentimental health by broadening her audience to reach demographics who otherwise might have turned their noses up at an evening's entertainment on the grounds of moral concerns. In so coding her readings, Kemble expanded her pool of ticket-buyers and, thus, her economic potential. For Kemble, these benefits pulled double duty as they simultaneously created a public image that was beneficial for her personal character.

Also like Barnum, the domestic trappings of Kemble's performance space were not the end of her ethical performance connections. Kemble seems to have cared deeply about the didactic fare on offer via her readings and an audience education about The Bard's work.[67] Kemble admitted: "My first intention in undertaking my readings from Shakespeare was to make, as far as possible, of each play a thorough study in its entireness; such as a stage representation cannot, for obvious reasons, be. The dramatic effect, which of course suffers in the mere delivery from a reading-desk, would, I hoped, be in some measure compensated for by the possibility of retaining the whole beauty of the plays as poetical compositions."[68] Kemble's preliminary thoughts about her readings were commodity-forward—considering deeply the final product on offer and how it filled a market need that stage plays could not. Similarly, Kemble reflected upon the ways a reading might suffer from its form, the loss of dramatic effect that Kemble hoped would be compensated by the poetics of Shakespeare's language. Ultimately, divorcing Shakespeare from bodily enactment and marrying him (through her brand) to the ethical health of domesticity and self-improvement was more important to Kemble's campaign.

As I've previously discussed, Kemble's initial plan with the readings (to read the shows in their entirety) was overrun by practicality. She did eventually forego these notions and cut the shows down to two hours each, but the instinct to read aloud every Shakespearean word as an educational experience tapped into a nineteenth-century market demand for "antiquarian Shakespeare," lavish productions of Shakespeare's work pitched to "learned and respectable audiences" with a mind toward "historical accuracy." In this mode, scenery, costumes, and props were designed with the play's setting as primary focus, and elaborate program notes sought (in the words of David L. Rinear) to make "a trip to this kind of production every bit as learned, self-improving, and respectable as a trip to a museum or the increasingly popular illustrated lectures."[69] Kemble's take on "antiquarian Shakespeare" was more minimalist, but it seemingly played upon similar desires to attract audiences who would seek such self-improving experiences. In this way, Kemble's commodity was as responsive to its market as it was to Kemble's personal tastes and the necessity of her situation.

"Are you a woman?"

—Marina, *Pericles*, IV.ii

While audiences bought Kemble's product and many of them lauded Kemble's efforts, this was not a universal sentiment. In particular (and perhaps predictably) there were fairly extreme reactions to Kemble's ability to so deftly perform male characters. Upon seeing Kemble's readings in London in 1863, fellow actress Ellen Keen née Tree (who had once played Juliet to Kemble's Romeo) wrote (emphasis hers): "It is *monstrous clever*, but *shocking* I think to see a *woman, (a gentlewoman)* so coarsely unsex herself. . . . Her Falstaff I think is good I think [*sic*] for any one (*reading*)—wonderful for a woman—but it made me almost angry that she did it so well. It is *too gross*—it was to me painful—but *very clever* . . . To me her doing Falstaff was as bad as a woman going on for a Clown in a Pantomime—It is such a *coarse unsexing*."[70] According to Tree, Kemble was simply too good at being a man for her performance to sit comfortably with a gender-conscious audience. Tree wasn't the only one to lodge such a complaint. Herman Melville had similar feelings but expressed them much more grossly: "Had she not, on impeccable authority, borne children, I should be curious to learn the result of a surgical examination of her person in private."[71] While Kemble was using domestic discourse to sell her product and maintain her image as a woman in a domestic

108 | THEATRES OF VALUE

sphere, these comments demonstrate how the tension Kemble's readings created between public/private was being read in many different ways. To audiences like Tree and Melville, Kemble's place as a public woman and her performance in traditional male domains opened the door to dangerous transgression in gendered territory. This reaction to Kemble's abilities—that she was *so* good at performing that her performance edged into the uncanny—reflects a discomfort with the public woman manifested in reflection about how behaving in public was, itself, gendered. It is particularly of note that Tree had such a reaction to Kemble's readings— somehow Kemble's performance as Romeo and situated as Tree's romantic lead wasn't enough to evoke the reaction Tree had to Kemble's reading of Falstaff. Something about the situation of reading was, thus, evocative beyond embodiment—too "gross" (as Tree says) for comfort.

These critics' vitriol is perhaps explained by Nancy Isenberg's thoughts on women's roles in public rhetoric of politics during the antebellum period. Isenberg makes specific note that a woman's body in a public space was rhetorically positioned to cause chaos. Her construction of antebellum public life situates women presenting a "special danger" because a woman's physical presence would animalistically create a sexualized desire for onlookers.[72] Kemble's presence in a public sphere, then, created an extremely dangerous space for her audiences who might be lured into viewing her as a sexual object. Additionally, her multigendered presence invoked a fear that Isenberg argues typified nineteenth-century gender relations. This fear (that a woman could somehow pass for a man) is, to Isenberg, linked to a growing nineteenth-century American concern that women might promiscuously and undetectably mix with strangers, not only making men into fools by deceiving them but also gaining access and agency denied to women in their own forms and thus undermining society itself.[73] While Isenberg's example demonstrates the fear taken to a nearly comic extreme, this isn't exactly far from what Kemble effectively did in her performance. By performing as male characters, Kemble generated financial success through her readings. In so doing, Kemble created for herself the ability to buy a house and property in Lenox, Massachusetts (an area she loved and where she eventually found peace). Kemble's performances as men thus gained her access to independently function in traditional male spheres—not just business but also property ownership.

Kemble's domestic performance (which I have already argued was a successful rhetorical device linked to public relations surrounding her divorce) wasn't effective for everyone—especially those already criticizing

Kemble in the vein of gendered trouble. Melville's complaint with its insinuations about genitalia hint toward this imagination. Melville doubled down on his complaint and famously called Kemble "so unfemininely masculine. . . . The Lord help Butler . . . I marvel not he seeks being amputated off from his matrimonial half."[74] Kemble's performance as a man (which Melville found so distasteful) also made Kemble's divorce sensible, and Butler sympathetic. For Melville, Kemble's performance had the opposite of its intended effect because of its intrinsic relationship to and with Kemble's performance of gender.

More locally confined to the stage, Kemble's performance eschewed nineteenth-century performance paradigms and perhaps that led to increased unease from threatened men—she abjured not just traditional lines of business but gender norms in their entirety. Elizabeth Mullenix argues that Kemble's portrayals of both herself and male characters made her own person difficult to read and, therefore, her audience frequently oscillated in reading her as feminine/masculine. This double performance troubled the boundaries of "True Womanhood" since Kemble presented herself as a foil for appropriate female behavior.[75] Kemble's problematization of the dichotomies of man/women, public/private meant that her readings presented a liminal space where all of these spheres meshed and intertwined for better or worse. This liminality (and, of course, the novelty it provided) created value for Kemble's audience within Kemble's product. In other words: this was all part of what Kemble sold.

But as a public woman, Kemble's troubling of the boundaries between men and women did not begin and end on the stage. In her offstage life, Kemble was a noted equestrian and a participant in the dress reform movement. Both these elements of Kemble's public persona gave critics non-gender-normative targets at which to shoot—and shoot they did. The *Staunton Spectator and General Advisor* of Staunton, Virginia, notes on October 17, 1849: "Mrs. Fanny Kemble Butler was at the Fair at Syracuse in full feather, galloping through the throng of horses, carriages, and footmen in the streets, as if it were an everyday pastime. She had the glow of exaltation on her face, which proved that the act of sweeping through the multitude, was rather a pleasant sort of a thing for a bright autumn day.—The following description of this lady is taken from a letter written to the *Cleveland Democrat*, from North Adams, and hits off her ladyship fairly: I was very much disappointed in the person of Mrs. B. She is masculine, very, in mind and body."[76] Kemble's pleasure in the physical exertion of equestrian hobbies gave onlookers the same pause

110 | THEATRES OF VALUE

her readings of Falstaff did. Was it becoming for a woman to so publicly delight in the exertions of her body and the skill she had developed in these exertions? What did that say about Kemble as a woman? To make matters "worse" for Kemble's performed feminine self, newspapers took note of Kemble's "Turkish costume": loose pants and a long tunic/coat rather than the skirts and petticoats expected of women in Kemble's era. Kemble's "Turkish Costume" was called "man's apparel" and her wearing it was deemed eccentric at best, scandalous at worst.[77]

Kemble's appearance was closely knit to the public rhetoric of her greatness—both its detractors and its supporters. For instance, her masculinity was the topic of satirical sneering for the *Minnesota Pioneer* via the *Boston Daily Mail* based on a letter published from March 20, 1850: "Then she was the bright and elegant girl—now she is 'fat, fair and forty,' or thereabouts; she is rather a superior specimen of the stout English woman, at least in her physical proportions; at fisticuffs she would whip Pierce Butler, and give him six for a start."[78] Here, Kemble's appearance stands testament to why her abusive ex-husband would want to be separated from her and also enforces a dialogue that Kemble deserved such treatment because of how she looked. Her martial prowess (linked explicitly to her "unfeminine" appearance) provides further dissolving of the boundaries between public and private, masculine and feminine.

The uproar about Kemble's dress was taken to task by women who admired Kemble. A letter to the *Litchfield Enquirer* of Litchfield, Connecticut, on November 29, 1849, states: "But we cannot still believe that she really dress like a man. If we did, we should think very little of her."[79] Similarly, the women's magazine *The Lily* of December 1, 1849, reports:

> There has been a great cry raised by the gentlemen from all quarters about the male attire which Fanny Kemble is said to have adopted; and their fears seem to be excited, lest the ladies are going to contest their exclusive right to wear pantaloons. We have scarcely taken up a paper these two months but we have seen remarks on the subject, and we really gathered from them (though we never believed it) that several ladies of Lennox with Mrs. Kemble at their head had actually paraded the streets appearing in coats, vests, and pantaloons, and all other paraphernalia of a gentleman's dress. It turns out, however, that the so much talked of, "man's clothes" which Mrs. Kemble has been guilty of putting on is nothing more nor less than a

loose flowing dress falling a little below the knees, and loose pantalets or drawers confined to the ankle by a band or cord. This shows how very sensitive gentlemen are in regard to any infringement on what they are pleased to consider their "rights." They need have no fears however on the subject, for we very much doubt whether even Mrs. Kemble could be willing to don their ugly dress. We wish they could be content with the right of dressing how they please, and not dictate to us what we shall or shall not wear.[80]

The Lily's chiding about how sensitive men can be certainly echoes with Melville's lewd critiques of Kemble's reading skills. These critiques of Kemble—like Butler's attempts at controlling her public image via editing her published journal—demonstrate a discomfort with Kemble's presentation because of its agency, and the perception of that agency's impact on traditional male spheres. But Kemble's dress, like her financial freedom, was an expression of personal liberty that she was not going to allow detractors to steal from her. Kemble did as she pleased and because of her clever application of social capital, she was largely able to use this subversion to increase value to her production—the readings and, arguably, her personal brand.

"She's a most triumphant lady, if report be square to her."

—Mecaenas, *Antony and Cleopatra*, II.ii

One of the continued bones of contention about Kemble's performance as these male characters was her transformative capabilities in the roles she played. Whatever their opinion about the outcome, audiences acknowledged Kemble's reading abilities as so good that she could transform believably into many parts right before their eyes. A review printed in the *Lynchburg Virginian* on April 4, 1850, reports: "It was not Mrs. Kemble on the platform. We were unconscious of her presence from the time she began to read until the performance was closed. It was Shakespeare, Macbeth, Lady Macbeth, the weird sisters, every character, true to nature and in life, that make up the drama. There was nothing left for the listener or the critic to wish for."[81] This disappearance of the woman into the text is corroborated by a report in the *Staunton Spectator and General Advisor* from October 17, 1849, "Her form is not comely—her face anything but beautiful; yet in her reading she would make it radiate with the beauty of life-like expression."[82] When Kemble read, her audiences (even hostile ones) engaged with the performance and allowed it to affect them. Shakespeare worked here as a kind of divine crucible turning the public woman into a conduit for literary genius. Kemble-as-conduit permitted the spectacle of "public woman" to gain the moral and ethical health that enabled Kemble's performances to function rhetorically in the method I have here argued they did. This had a visual element (per the *Staunton Spectator*) as well as a more ephemeral element—the audience could observe great change but some (such as Melville) had trouble describing it. Kemble's transformation was a tangible thing, of which the audience was very aware when it happened. This allowed them to admire her talent since it rendered visible the incredible transformations that a good actor can affect. The readings created the type of contrast that doesn't generally exist in single theatrical roles. In this, Kemble transcended the notion of acting even as she performed—pressing against not just the boundaries of public/private, man/woman but also what constituted performance at all.

Because of this success, it was almost inevitable that the commodity on sale would be brought down to earth: Kemble's fans could hardly contain themselves from guessing at her profits. As audiences flocked to hear Kemble read, newspapers and diarists began to hazard very public estimates about just how much money Kemble might have been making from these readings. On May 12, 1849, the *Columbia Democrat* guessed the sum of $10,000 as potential earnings for her "recent course of Shakespeare readings" (presumably aggregate from her readings so far that year).[83] By way of comparison, in 1831 the earnings of working women almost never exceeded $1.12 a week. By the 1860s, the average salary for thirty thousand female factory workers in New York City was $0.33 a day.[84] Actresses did significantly better, generally by 1850 they could expect $40 to $60 a week with popular actresses commanding between $5,000 and $20,000 a year (a wide range, but highly dependent on popularity and marketability, which were unstable variables at best). Lester Wallack's theatre paid employees (male and female) between $6 and $55 weekly with benefits included in their contracts (a good benefit might net $500 to $1,000 annually).[85]

As time wore on, guesses about Kemble's profits continued to roll in. Philadelphia diarist Sidney George Fisher speculated about Kemble's profits in October of 1849 after having seen her read *As You Like It*: "She makes money rapidly by these exhibitions, having already invested from her profits $20,000. By the terms of her agreement with Butler she is to have $1,500 per annum, so that now she is sure at least of comfort & independence. But she may, if she pleases & probably will, go on making $10 or $20,000 yearly for some time to come, for an exhibition so highly agreeable & intellectual & unique is sure always to please."[86] Fisher's relation of Kemble's profit to the reality of her financial situation brings this glittering dream back to reality—higher purpose aside, the reason why Kemble undertook her readings in the first place was extremely practical.

This is echoed in a "Letter from New York" published in the *Alexandria Gazette* of Alexandria, Virginia, on March 21, 1849, which imagined a projected take for the project:

> Mrs. Frances Kemble Butler's readings from Shakespeare are just now the wonder of the day in New York, in a literary way. She mounts the rostrum thrice a week at the Stuyvesant Institute, where an average of 800 persons go to listen to her, at the moderate charge of $1 each. Her receipts are quite $2,400 per week. This is at the rate of $124,800 per annum—a snug income, indeed, to be derived from reading Shakespeare. Of course, it is not presumable that such enormous receipts from the source can be kept up for any considerable time. But by lecturing or reading thus, here and elsewhere over the country, this talented lady may certainly realize an income which, if prudently husbanded, will soon prove a far more overgrown estate than that concerning which her lord and herself are "at law."[87]

The *Gazette* letter twines Kemble's profit to the sense of her domestic income—though the math and its supposition that Kemble might perform three shows a week to full houses every week of the year (800 x 3 x 52 = 124,800) is, even as the paper concurs, dubious at best. The use of the term "husbanded" to describe prudent money management must be at least a little ironic given Kemble's known situation. The *Gazette* directly links Kemble's profits to her divorce and (rightly) concludes that her income from these readings (and, indeed, perhaps even the fallout from the divorce) might surpass the estate of her ex-husband. In other words—through these readings and because of the divorce, Kemble might come to realize wealth beyond Butler's and an income that surpassed what he had.

114 | THEATRES OF VALUE

If one can quantify joy as an asset to this wealth, that was certainly another contributing factor. Kemble enjoyed her work, and she wrote to her lifelong friend Harriet St. Leger: "The happiness of reading Shakespeare's heavenly imaginations is so far beyond all the excitement of acting them."[88] The readings, to Kemble, were superior to stage productions in many ways—not the least of which was this contentment she drew from the practice. This pleasure seemed to be an appealing feature not just for Kemble but for her audiences as well. Philip Hone guesses in his diary entry of March 13, 1849: "She makes $2,000 or $3000 a week, and never was money so easily earned. There is no expense except the room and the lights, and the performance is 'a labour of love.' Shakespeare was never paid for writing his plays as Mrs. Butler is for reading them."[89] To Hone, not only was Kemble making money on her own terms, but her success was almost legendary—even more, perhaps, than Shakespeare himself.

Kemble's readings were born of necessity—but their power to secure her future even amid public scandal speaks strongly to Shakespeare's value as a cultural commodity to Kemble's audience. In capitalizing on her brand, Kemble played into the brand expectations of her place as a public British woman and was able to use that brand image to challenge her detractors. By divorcing the act of performance from the necessity of embodiment, Kemble was able to activate the liminal space of her reading stage to successfully navigate the aftermath of the Butler divorce. Tracing Shakespeare's dramaturgy of value to Kemble peels back the layers of her strategic maneuverings and, once again, allows a front-row seat to this savvy businessperson's interaction with her market, in turn providing glimpses of how the market reacted to such maneuverings and the nature of the market itself.

Chapter Four

Both Booth's Brothers

The Bulletproof Brand

In late April 1865 in a barn in Charles County, Maryland, John Wilkes Booth was coming to realize that his plan wasn't panning out the way he had hoped. Leg broken from landing poorly on the stage as he fled Ford's Theatre, surrounded by men willing to apprehend him by force or simply kill him, Booth did the last thing he could think to do: he set about justifying his crime in writing. Over the course of several days (likely April 17–22, 1865), Booth wrote two entries in a pocket diary datebook detailing his mental state and thoughts on the country. Booth dated his first entry "the Ides," a clear allusion to the murder of Julius Caesar (a murder he had performed in Shakespeare's play with his brothers five months prior in New York City).[1] In his second entry Booth wrote, "I am here in despair. And why? For doing what Brutus was honored for—what made Tell a hero. And yet I, for striking down a greater tyrant than they ever knew, am looked upon as a common cut-throat."[2] As the country came to terms with the murder of Abraham Lincoln, the parallels between Lincoln and Caesar were iterated and reiterated, and the deed was described continually in Shakespearean phrase. The *Union Vedette* out of Camp Douglas, Utah, published an April 17th editorial on the incident titled "A Deed without a Name" while the *Daily Intelligencer* of Doylestown, Pennsylvania, published one the same day titled "Murder Most Foul."[3] This framing of Lincoln's murder using Shakespeare's language draws a powerful connection between the Booth brand as marked by its most infamous moment and the brand as it was intentionally built.[4]

116 | Theatres of Value

This is a strange dynamic because, by all rights, the high-profile killing of an American hero should be the undoing of a brand, not the cementing of one. Yet publications about Lincoln's murder to this day—from the many volumes about the connection between Lincoln, Booth, and Shakespeare, to the musical *Assassins* by Stephen Sondheim—continually highlight and reinforce this connection.[5] In this chapter, I will use the dramaturgy of value to explore how Shakespeare buttressed the Booth brand before and after the assassination. In particular, Edwin Booth's signature acting style in the role of Hamlet tapped into the nineteenth-century elevation of intellectual labor over bodily labor and the association of this hierarchy with white upper-class sentimental values. This is one iteration of a broader theme: the Booths used Shakespeare to align themselves with the respectability and marketability associated with whiteness and to sell those things to their audiences. To the Booths, Shakespeare was a vehicle to link their brand with desirable cultural values and this provided longevity and fortitude that allowed the brand to persevere through the storm of the assassination.

Again in this chapter we find Shakespeare in the company of theatremakers in crisis. At this point, the reader should sense a pattern emerging: Shakespeare's utility to his nineteenth-century users was like a bung. He appears in these stories as a savior; his use to plug the sinking ship. The Booths' ability to rehabilitate their brand—like Kemble's—relied upon creative application of Shakespearean cultural capital, making the dramaturgy of value critical to explicating why and how.

"Thence comes it that my name receives a brand."

—Sonnet 111

The Booth brand's American presence was hatched from the seed of European theatrics: Booth patriarch Junius Brutus Booth Sr. was particularly well known for his Richard of Gloucester. When Booth emigrated to the United States from London in 1821, he already boasted two things that would help to ensure his legacy in America—a prosperous acting career and a scandalous offstage personality. Booth's emigration was partly the result of a quarrel with Edmund Kean and brought with it enough press to ensure that audiences flocked to his American debut when he played

Richard III at the Park Theatre on October 5, 1821.[6] Booth's move gave America one of its first big-name permanent transplant English actors.[7]

Booth's American career became so successful that upon his death on November 30, 1852, fellow actor Rufus Choate lamented, "Booth dead? Now there are no more actors."[8] In a reminiscence about the aftermath of her father's passing, Asia Booth Clarke remembers, "The walls of the parlors were draped with crepe, pictures and mirrors were covered, and all the ornaments were removed, excepting a marble figure of Shakespeare, which was placed near the coffin, and seemed to gaze down upon the form beneath."[9] Clarke's description of this bereft room decorated only with the trappings of mourning and a bust of Shakespeare personifies Shakespeare as a mourner himself. The bust's presence, strategic display, and inclusion in Clarke's written-for-publication remembrance are all crucial branding artifacts. They incorporate Shakespeare as a friend (or even family member) of the Booths and work to publicly affirm the links established between Booth Sr. as a performer and Shakespeare.

The Booths continued to uphold their father's brand by cementing and marrying the name "Booth" to Shakespearean performance. The most theatrically successful of the Booth children was Edwin, who personally and professionally aligned himself with his most famous role—Hamlet. Booth performed as Hamlet throughout his career.[10] Professionally, Booth became so closely related to the role in the minds of his audience that avid fan Mary Isabella Stone remarked, "Booth's interpretation of the character throughout seems the only possible correct one. He is, indeed, the ideal Hamlet—the noble Prince, and perfect gentleman; he does not act Hamlet, he is Hamlet!"[11] Through his performance, Booth came to embody an avatar: the quintessential American Hamlet.

Perhaps partly because of this professional identification, and partly because of a personal elision with the part of Hamlet, Booth's family reflected on this image as well. His daughter, Edwina Booth Grossman, recalls: "It was long before I could thoroughly disassociate him from the character of Hamlet, it seemed so entirely a part of himself. Indeed, in that impersonation, I think, his confined nature and pent-up sorrows found bent."[12] Grossman notes the particular aptness that Hamlet had for expressing and integrating her father's personal proclivities and history. She was not the only Booth to think so. In one of her memoirs, actress Clara Morris reports to have heard Booth's brother John Wilkes utter in a backstage conversation: "There's but one Hamlet to my mind; that's my brother Edwin. You see, between ourselves, he is Hamlet—melancholy

118 | Theatres of Value

and all."[13] These public reports from family members worked in largely the same way Clarke's tale of Booth Sr.'s funeral did: they cemented Booth branding even as they engaged with the idea that this branding was natural. The connection to Shakespeare was a matter of personality rather than choice—an outcropping of who the Booths were rather than what the Booths did.

The success of this branding (particularly the connection between Edwin and Hamlet) might have been assisted by timing. One of Booth's most triumphant and iconic performances in the role was also his longest run at it. In what came to be known as the One Hundred Nights' *Hamlet*, Booth played Hamlet at New York's Winter Garden Theatre from November 26, 1864, through March 22, 1865. The show closed mere weeks before Booth's brother would assassinate Lincoln. Gary Jay Williams argues that this timing was part of what bolstered Booth's place as Hamlet within the American consciousness: the run began when Northerners craved familiar comfort as the Civil War's darkest hours were recent history. The shock of the assassination meant that Booth's hundred nights' performance became an event of national scale.[14] Between this national attention and Edwin's personal brand having an iconic Hamlet presence, Booth was able to cement himself as a Hamlet equivalent in the American psyche.[15]

Edwin's Hamlet was one aspect of the Shakespeare-Booth elision, but other Booths had similar tightly tied relationships with Shakespeare. John Wilkes Booth worked his entire life to achieve notoriety. From his childhood, likely because of his father's Eurocentric tastes, Booth endeavored to establish mastery over Shakespeare. Clarke recalls: "He could never hope to be as great as father, he never wanted to try to rival Edwin, but he wanted to be loved of the Southern people above all things. He would work to make himself essentially a Southern actor. He applied himself studiously to Shakespeare, and I was made to hear parts over and over again for my slow student. He would not allow a word or syllable to go wrong."[16] Wilkes seemed to be imbued with a sense of how weighty and valuable his last name was. After debuting as Richmond in *Richard III* on August 16, 1855, at the Charles Street Theatre in Baltimore at the age of seventeen, Wilkes realized that he had not yet mastered his craft.[17] Embarrassed by his own performance under the shadow of his father's greatness, Wilkes insisted upon being billed as "J. Wilkes" until he felt comfortable reclaiming the moniker "Booth."[18] In so doing, Wilkes hoped to preserve the brand's value from being marred by his novice performances and also delay the inevitable comparisons to his father and brother.

When these comparisons came, they were often about performance "feel" rather than performance merit. As one source remarks: "Edwin has more poetry, John Wilkes more passion, . . . Edwin has more melody of movement and utterance, John Wilkes more energy and animation; Edwin is more correct, John Wilkes more spontaneous, Edwin is more Shakespearean, John Wilkes, more melodramatic; and in a word, Edwin is a better Hamlet, John Wilkes a better Richard III."[19] These comparisons highlight an important distinction between two iterations of Booth that I will discuss in greater depth later in this chapter: Wilkes's acting was highly physical, Edwin's incredibly intellectual. The nineteenth century saw a similar split between body/mind as workers began to interpolate their relationships to labor and capital, and here that dichotomy plays out in the Booth brothers' theatrical styles.

Wilkes's relationship to his onstage work is complicated by his psychology. He certainly inherited some of his father's "quirks" but it is difficult to determine the precise degree of these delusions from the hindsight of history.[20] John Rhodehamel and Louise Taper suggest that John Wilkes Booth, throughout his life, experienced the line between drama and the real world as "always a little blurred . . . many of the plays he acted were violent, bloody spectacles studded with killings."[21] It is certain that Wilkes's understanding of the world was shaped by the theatrics of his stage career—one very clear example of this can be found in a speech Booth wrote in the last days of December 1860, two months after Lincoln's election and a few days after South Carolina's secession.[22] Booth never delivered this speech, but clearly by the many crossings-out, additions, and added parentheticals it was a document he put great thought into. The manuscript of about five thousand words was preserved by Edwin Booth from his brother's belongings (most of which Edwin burned after Wilkes's death) and is held in the collections of The Players club. In reading the speech, it becomes evident that (subconsciously or otherwise) Booth patterned the speech on Antony's funeral oration from Shakespeare's *Julius Caesar*. Booth began his speech: "Gentlemen Allow me a few words! You ever-where permit freedom of speech. You must not deny me now. My fellow countryman Can I use the liberty of speech among ye. If so hear me. I will not keep you long."[23] In reading this opening, it's difficult not to think of Antony's "Friends, Romans, countrymen, lend me your ears."[24] As Booth continues through an exercise in heavy rhetoric, he includes several other hallmarks that nod back to Antony. Booth wrote call-and-response sections into the speech (harkening to the conversations Antony has with the plebeians in the middle of his oration). He also uses Antony's rhetorical switch—"I come to bury Caesar, not to praise him"—in an appeal at the speech's beginning where Booth promises, "I will not fight for cessation. No I will not fight for disunion. But I will fight with all my heart and soul, even if there's not a man to back me for equal rights and justice to the south."[25] In both instances, these men rely heavily on stating their goals in the negative—saying explicitly that they will not do the very things they intend to do implicitly (a rhetorical move called paraleipsis). This glimpse into Wilkes's mind at the moment of secession shows both Booth's conception of himself as a Shakespearean hero and his machinations for murder entwined in Shakespearean prose. Combined with the way Booth framed his experience in the Charles County barn diary, these moments explicitly show Booth's self-actualization as the Shakespearean hero he imagined himself to be. Crucially, the subject of the murder changes—in the secession speech, Booth as Antony mourns the country in honor of the South. In the diary entries, Booth as Brutus justifies his crime in murdering Lincoln, the tyrant. In both, Booth finds clarity within a Shakespearean role.

Returning to Booth's brother, the personal elision between Edwin Booth and Hamlet is celebrated in many extant pieces of realia and statuary. New York City's Gramercy Park is directly outside of Edwin Booth's The Players, the private club Booth established for actors/socialites in 1888 that remains such to this day. A statue celebrating Booth was erected there in 1916 to celebrate the actor's life. This statue, perhaps the most public and lasting image of Booth, depicts him in the character of Hamlet (fig. 4.1).[26] While this statue was posthumous, a more personal touchstone hints at Booth's meaningful and direct adoption of Shakespeare as an avatar for himself: Booth integrated the bust of Shakespeare as the crest for his personal fob seal.[27]

Other remembrances draft a similar image: a series of medals coined in commemoration of a memorial performance of *Hamlet* on April 23, 1894 (fig. 4.2), bear the image of Booth's bust in the show's title role—a coinage of Booth's coinage.[28]

The production occurred nearly a year after Booth's death on June 7, 1893, and (due to its date and proximity to the day traditionally celebrated as Shakespeare's birthday, April 23) the performance was likely a memorial to Shakespeare rather than Booth, but Booth's figure here serves as an archetypal depiction of this archetypal role. Another item, a teacup and saucer set from circa 1895 (fig. 4.3), shows Booth literally

Figure 4.1. Gramercy Park Booth Statue. *Source*: Photo by the author.

in the shadow of William Shakespeare.[29] Shakespeare's head is depicted just behind Booth's and the two are surrounded by the motto "see the players well bestowed" (an utterance from act 2, scene 2 of *Hamlet*). The set continues to highlight Booth's deep connection to Hamlet while the image contextualizes Booth as a natural progeny of Shakespeare. Considering these items as commodities, the coin and china are both souvenir objects, crafted and sold as keepsakes with little functional purpose. This speaks to their audience (those who would have money to buy items with little function), which in turn speaks to the values of that audience.

Figure 4.2. Series of Medals Coined in Commemoration of April 23, 1894's *Hamlet*, Folger Shakespeare Library Realia collection. *Source*: Photo by the author.

Figure 4.3. Teacup and Saucer Set from circa 1895, Folger Shakespeare Library Realia collection. *Source*: Photo by the author.

Though they could afford any number of leisure objects, they were here given the option of buying Shakespeare. The presence of Shakespeare in the sphere of luxury goods is an indication of his value as an indulgence and the entrenchment of the Booth brand into this mix is similarly telling of the brand's cultural value.

> "Hard-handed men that work in Athens here,/
> Which never labour'd in their minds till now."
>
> —Philostrate, *A Midsummer Night's Dream*, V.i

As I hinted earlier, the mind/body divide that seemed to govern the major differences in Edwin/Wilkes's performance styles was also a major theme of nineteenth-century value construction in regard to labor and the creation of capital. After emancipation, Americans' ideas about labor were politicized in new ways. White wage laborers sought to differentiate themselves from newly freed Black workers, and so class among workers became even further polemicized by the creation of white-only labor unions.[30] As workers sought to align themselves with white values in order to eschew racist stigmas associated with being Black, the value of the labor of the mind became ever-more important.[31] George M. Fredrickson traces the affiliation with intellectualism as a close identification with the culture of an upper class (and cites earlier examples like Jefferson, Hamilton, and the Adamses), but he argues that Andrew Jackson's election in 1828 drove some of this class privilege from the seat of power.[32] As Jacksonian paradigms of physicality decentered intellectualism from power narratives, intellectuals sought to reengage themselves with how to best express sentimental values of self-actualization. In his "American Scholar" address of 1837, Ralph Waldo Emerson proposed: "Private life was a better springboard to self-realization than any public career, because true individuality could be found only by turning away from all forms, traditions, and institutions."[33] Emerson's call for privacy as keystone to the necessities that could unlock self-realization echo strongly in Edwin Booth's life. Booth was an extremely private man—especially in the wake of the assassination—perhaps living (whether purposefully or not) this intellectual ideal. In her memoir, fellow actor Rose Eytinge wrote of Booth, "I have no doubt, that, if I cared to do so, I could string together innumerable anecdotes about Edwin Booth. But he was so sensitive and he so shrank from general public notice, that

124 | Theatres of Value

it seems that to discuss him or his peculiarities would be to take a liberty toward his memory."[34] Here again the parallel between Booth and Hamlet is emphasized through Emerson's musings on the private as a patriotic duty. The heavy solitary philosophical engagements required of Hamlet as Shakespeare's play unfolds might be (and certainly has been) seen as an ideal vehicle for the brooding intellectualism that was quickly becoming popularized as desirable.

Labor division was not the only way the mind/body divide was being explored in the late nineteenth century. In her examination of postbellum portraiture, Sarah Blackwood proposes that the postbellum "problem" of the mind and body can be seen manifesting in portraits—particularly portraits depicting amputees or wounded men from the Civil War.[35] Blackwood contends that the nation's deep anxiety over its bodily scars from the war was part of what led to an increased focus on the psychological world and a decreased focus on the body. This can perhaps help to explain another aspect of the appeal of Booth's deeply intellectual Hamlet—a being that came to life via the mind of Edwin Booth and eschewed the highly physicalized acting style of the Booth family. Considering Edwin Booth's Hamlet in light of the mind/body labor divide, it's difficult not to dwell on the elements of this performance that the audience found captivating. Through Hamlet, Booth was able to capture a white market desire for the marks of intellectualism and harness that in his performance to capitalized upon it.

The highly intellectual nature of Booth's performances not only allowed him to cash in on the mind/body divide and drive for intellectual labor but also unlocked Shakespeare's plays from being purely literary pursuits. One account of the hundred nights' *Hamlet* describes:

> It would, perhaps, not be too much to say that only an actor, and one deep in his business, too, can properly understand the drift and purpose of some scenes in a play like *Hamlet*, and it is certainly true then an actor is a necessary medium between the author and the world. It is for this reason that the performance of Hamlet by Mr. Booth is a continual elucidation of Shakespeare. There are no inconsistencies, no mysteries, no knotty or incomprehensible points in the part of Hamlet as Mr. Booth plays it. We may burn our hundred volumes of commentaries if we will go often enough to the Winter Garden.

All is clear as daylight. The whole history is laid out; we have
every step clearly defined of the intellectual process that the
Prince passes through.[36]

This commentator taps into Booth's audience's craving for literary truth.
His claim that Booth's Hamlet might surpass written analysis identifies
Booth as a medium of communicating Shakespearean essence. In so
doing, Booth was able to deliver a performance with all the marks of
high literary intellectualism—liberating Shakespeare from the page, and
creating some kind of divine understanding about the work at hand via
the conduit of his performance.

The clarity that the previous author identified in Booth's performance
is a frequent comment from audience members. In his biographical writings on Booth, critic and longtime personal friend William Winter also
emphasizes this clarity: "His Hamlet was as near to the truth of Shakespeare
as acting can reach, and it made Hamlet as intelligible as Hamlet can
ever be."[37] To Winter, the clarity Booth brought to the role was enabled
by Booth's intellectual approach spoken through Booth's emotions and
performance of the mind rather than bodily action. Here again, Booth's
success-as-value is enabled by the intellectual labor he undertook—linking the performance closely to white bourgeoise desires and accordingly
drafting this Hamlet's value from such.

"Most radiant Pyramus, most lily-white of hue."

—Flute, *A Midsummer Night's Dream*, III.i

Over the course of the nineteenth century, whiteness was on the rise as
an aesthetic epitome and market demand for it can be spotted in many
spheres. In the theatre, this demand is partly expressed by the popularity
of Booth's Hamlet, which enacted the ideals of whiteness and attached
those ideals to the Booth brand.

The identity politics that accompanied emancipation were complicated. Over the course of America's nineteenth century, the notion of
whiteness was being constructed litigiously as well as ideologically. Socially
and legally, the "one-drop rule" (that a single drop of nonwhite blood

would render a person incapable of claiming white as an identity even if their appearance allowed them to "pass" as white) was emphasized and reemphasized.[38] Legally, this meant whiteness became defined as pristine, "unsullied," and untouched by anything other than whiteness. Rather than a presence of something, whiteness was a lack of something—set to contrast the dark racialized otherness that color (and particularly Blackness) represented.[39] Blackness was also being constructed legally and rhetorically through the courts. In examining just a few of the most prominent Supreme Court cases of the era: The Dred Scott case (1856–1857) ruled that Black people of African descent, whether enslaved or free, were not American citizens. The Civil Rights Cases (1883) held that the Thirteenth and Fourteenth Amendments did not empower Congress to outlaw racial discrimination by private individuals. *Plessy v. Ferguson* (1896) reinforced racial segregation as legitimate. As rhetoric was built by white lawmakers to define "Black" and establish America's treatment of Black peoples, and since whiteness was rendered as an absence of Blackness, the definition of Blackness would define whiteness as well.[40]

Additionally, the institution of slavery was the single most powerful economic force of pre-bellum United States (and, arguably, the single most powerful force of the development of the United States economy). In his opus on reconstruction, W. E. B. Du Bois calls slavery America's "foundation stone."[41] Slavery was also key to the development of white as an identity. I have already briefly touched upon how and why white workers sought to differentiate themselves from Black workers in America's nineteenth century. In investigating the relationship between race and working class in the United States, David Roediger finds that white wage workers (especially those of poorer classes) were particularly eager to distinguish themselves linguistically from enslaved peoples. The identification of freedom became closely linked to the identification of dignity, both crucial components of class formation in the early republic.[42] Because white people could not be enslaved in the United States (again, whiteness being defined by the "one-drop rule"), whiteness became synonymous with the assumption of freedom and Blackness with the assumption of slavery. Cheryl Harris argues that this paradigm means whiteness can be considered a "property."[43] Because of this, the racial line between whiteness and Blackness also became a line of demarcation, a line of protection, and a line of privilege enabling white people to claim the benefits of being white and barring Black people from doing the same.[44]

Whiteness, argues Harris, is thus a crucial property that has been defined and protected by American law: "[Whiteness] can both be experienced and deployed as a resource. Whiteness can move from being a passive characteristic as an aspect of identity to an active entity that—like other types of property—is used to fulfill the will and to exercise power. . . . Thus, a white person 'used and enjoyed' whiteness whenever she took advantage of the privileges accorded white people simply by virtue of their whiteness."[45] Considering whiteness in this fashion, it becomes clearer why white people would look to create as many barriers as possible to the institution of whiteness—to create fences around the properties of whiteness the law was investing it with. If whiteness is a literal property (as Harris claims), then it can be literally stolen and the act of theft not only endows the thief with ill-gotten goods but deprives the original owner of those goods. Nineteenth-century audiences had actual investment in the outcomes of whiteness, its uses, and the populations who were allowed access to those uses. It was a commodity with limits. Assessing this commodity's value and why holders of it treated it so preciously, I turn to the theories of value surveyed in the introduction to this book. Whiteness was invested with esteem-value.[46] Additionally, the idea that whiteness was a property that could be used also invests this commodity with utility—the degree of its usefulness exemplifying the degree of potential value.[47] As whiteness was socially defined, in order to increase its value one would need to increase its utility and decrease the ease with which one might acquire it. Therefore, in order to endow themselves with maximum, white-based property value, the creators of this value needed to keep it both functional and scarce.

Legally and socially these paradigms played out in the courts, but they were also present domestically. While whiteness was being established as a cultural property, beauty standards of the nineteenth century were also starting to prize whiteness as a pinnacle. Nell Irvin Painter examines this phenomenon, especially as a construction of whiteness throughout the nineteenth century.[48] As this was occurring with human skin, it was simultaneously occurring with household objects—James Deetz explicates how whiteness in the material culture of nineteenth-century America was an aesthetic response to the shifts of underlying structures and beliefs that govern the use of objects.[49]

Bridget Heneghan expands Deetz's work to address how this "whitening" of the things of daily life became an expression of socially constructed issues: "White things radiated refinement, order, discipline: but in doing so, they also radiated race. While the proliferation of elite items—porcelain, classical architecture, and imported gravestones—began as an attempt by the upper class to mark its distinction, mass-production made such goods more available to an aspiring middle class."[50] While whiteness in objects once had gatekeepers, those barriers were starting to break down as industrialization made white objects easier to come by. Considering white as an esteem-value commodity, proliferation of whiteness also meant a corresponding crisis in valuation, perhaps leading to an urge to protect whiteness on other fronts.

At home, white reigned supreme. Heneghan highlights that women were the primary consumers of ever-whitening household objects, and thus their primary audience and gatekeepers of the household through them:

> As the main consumers of the family, upper and middle-class white women were responsible for purchasing these white goods. They were responsible for teaching the etiquette that white dishes enforced, and they bore the burden of the ideal purity and spirituality of fiction's white heroines. The white things that flooded households and landscapes in the nineteenth century created an essentially conservative message, telling consumers that the exploitation and miscegenation in slavery were ignorable; that the wage slavery of emerging industrialism was justifiable; that the stricter delineation of gender roles channeled a "greater" power to disfranchised women; and that all of these were mitigated by the sanctified, otherworldly sphere of the home. As the most expensive available, the whitest items—white paint, marble, and porcelain—distinguished the wealthy.[51]

In this way, whiteness was being incorporated into the American household as a bastion of ethics, a source of beauty, a distinguisher of wealth, and a statement of codified bourgeoise values—much as Shakespeare was doing the same.

In the first chapter of this book, I examined why and how Shakespeare was considered white cultural property and how white cultural gatekeepers worked to keep this property from Black theatremakers. The same impulses that led to this protection of white cultural property also led to the evaluation of whiteness as a construction of American Shakespearean value. Through his performances as Hamlet, Edwin Booth tapped into the market value of whiteness to fuel audience demand for the product he was creating. Because his brand was so entwined with America as built by the institution of slavery, the connection to whiteness as a construction of Black exploitation was deeply imbued with the Booth brand as well. Because Edwin the "intellectual" Northern brother remained and Wilkes the "physical" Southern brother perished, the brand was able to claim this family microcosm as an avatar of nineteenth-century America and cash in on the value it brought.

One of the uses of whiteness's value in Booth's Hamlet is connected to the intellectuality I have discussed earlier. Charles Clarke was a clerk who, between January 18 and March 19, 1870, saw Booth perform Hamlet eight times. He painstakingly documented the experience in a line-by-line reconstruction of the show depicting the minutiae of the performance down to enunciation, scansion, stage directions, and so on.[52] Clarke notes that this cerebral quality infused Booth's performance so deeply that it could be seen as a palpable characteristic the moment Booth walked onstage: "The first thing one notices when he appears upon the stage is his intellectuality. This is prominent and it is a living intellectuality. . . . There is a native air of sadness about him. And in Hamlet this finds peculiar aptness and is made distinct."[53] It's odd to think that this impalpable trait—intellectuality—was "the first thing one notices." Clarke depicts Booth turning something invisible about himself (the power of his mind and emotions) into something not just visible but almost overwhelming. The saturation of Hamlet with this "native air of sadness" must be some combination of marketing and presence—how else would one see intellectualism, except if they were primed to do so?

Reviews of Booth's Hamlet tend to highlight his meditative acting style. In a time when declamatory and highly physicalized presentational styles were still in vogue Booth's introspective and intellectual Hamlet was a revelation. Critic Philip Lawrence writes: "In his personification of Hamlet, Edwin Booth possesses every requisite to enable him to portray the intellectual mind, and princely form of the melancholy Dane. His exquisitely modulated voice, his graceful gestures, his natural and elegant manner, delight the ear, gratify the mind, and please the eyes of the appreciative audience."[54] The highlights of Booth's Hamlet—grace, elegance, intellect—are keys to its marketability, especially when considered in light of the marketability of whiteness and the nineteenth-century coding of Blackness.[55]

Considering the rhetorical positioning of Blackness in America's nineteenth century, one first might look to Thomas Jefferson's *Notes on the*

State of Virginia. Jefferson published *Notes* in 1785 and five new editions were published in 1801, indicating the document's popularity in the early nineteenth-century imagination.[56] In *Notes*, Jefferson frames Black people as animalistic and primitive. He alleges that Black skin hides emotion in ways that white skin does not and contends that Black people require less sleep than white people, have simpler minds, and are better disposed to hard labor.[57] This drive to "scientifically" prove that Black people were less than white people continued throughout the century and manifested itself in the popular obsession with phrenology as well as experiments such as Meade Bache's 1895 "Reaction Time with Reference to Race," wherein Bache attempted to "prove" that Black people were more "automatic" of reflex and, therefore, simpler of mind than white people by testing reaction time.[58] Bache's conclusion that "the negro is, in brief, more of an automaton than the white man is" fed into the nineteenth-century rhetoric: "[That] the negro is, in the truest sense, a race inferior to that of the white can be proved by many facts."[59]

On December 3, 1867, Lincoln's successor President Andrew Johnson delivered his third annual message to Congress. In this address, he makes explicit how deeply Jefferson's ideas still permeated American politics: "Negroes have shown less capacity for government than any other race of people. No independent government of any form has ever been successful in their hands. On the contrary, wherever they have been left to their own devices they have shown a constant tendency to relapse into barbarism."[60] The portrayal of Black people as barbarous and simple and the use of this rhetoric from the presidential seat of power stood in stark contrast to the qualities lauded in Booth's Hamlet as exemplary.

This idea that nonwhite peoples were primitive and monstrous was also carried forth in popular entertainments such as minstrelsy and the freak show.[61] In his canonical work on minstrelsy, Eric Lott argues that the appropriation and resulting commodification of Black culture through blackface minstrelsy was "the first appearance in U.S. history of black culture as property."[62] Herein, white performers claimed economic benefit from performed "Blackness" even as they restricted Black citizens from engaging with the property of whiteness. Additionally, Lott argues that white working-class audiences used minstrelsy to configure their relationships to whiteness via their consumption of it. Linda Frost examines the many coded ways that nonwhite representation played out in the popular imagination of the nineteenth century and argues that this had a very definite rhetorical purpose: "Depicting primitives as either inhuman monsters, bestial and cannibalistic, or children, naive and ignorant, conveniently positioned them at the beginning of the story of Western civilization—one that was best exemplified in the form of the United States of America itself. This use of narrative aided in the construction of the nation by creating a hierarchically superior, white, middle-class identity that could claim national membership in a 'natural' or timeless way."[63] Frost's argument that this dichotomy was critical to the formation of nation building also reveals its value as a commodity Americans were hungry for—a paradigm I will examine in more depth in the following chapter. For now, suffice it to say the market value of American brand building was high for Booth's audiences. In previous chapters, I discussed the nineteenth-century middle class's desire to differentiate themselves through outward shows of intellectualism. Here, I propose that the enjoyment of Booth's Hamlet and (consequently) the value of Booth's Hamlet is derived from similar roots to both these sources of value. Booth's Hamlet was coded to align with white cultural values in order to generate a performance that would play to audiences who craved white things. In the same way that audiences participated in acts of conspicuous consumption at Barnum's, or engagement (as Lott argues) with the consumption of minstrelsy, audiences participated in conspicuous consumption of Booth's Hamlet to show outward alignment with whiteness. By consuming this intellectual product, they hoped to enact the white cultural values it was connected to.

> "Good brother, as thou lovest and honourest arms, /
> Let's fight it out and not stand cavilling thus."
>
> —Marquess of Montague, *Henry VI, Part 3*, I.i

In building Shakespeare's dramaturgy of value to the Booth brand, one need recognize the market force of slavery in the nineteenth century and how that force was entwined with the brand. The Booths owned slaves on their Maryland estate. One of Clarke's memories of Wilkes's childhood explicitly draws the connection between the Booths' slaves and Shakespeare as practiced in the Booth household: "*Julius Caesar* . . . was so constantly repeated that even the little darkies . . . were caught repeating after him. 'Hark to that thick-skulled dark! She has sharper wits than I!' Wilkes lamented when vainly trying to give a speech correctly."[64] In constructing his ideal conception of the Shakespearean actor, Wilkes inadvertently also proved the reliance of this construction on the economic forces of slave labor that drove it. Without enslaved people to run their household and work their land, the Booths likely would not have had the necessary leisure time with which to pursue professional theatre.

Additionally, Edwin and John Wilkes's parallel acting careers and the eventual triumph of Edwin's version of the Booth brand onstage is innately tied to the brothers' personal political rivalry, especially because of the circumstances of John Wilkes's demise. Lincoln's assassination should have also been the death knell of the Booth brand and yet, somehow, it seemed to add value to Edwin's Hamlet as performed in the following years.

The brothers had long disagreed about politics. In an 1881 letter to Nahum Capen (a historian who wrote Edwin Booth to inquire about his brother) Booth recalls:

> When I told him that I had voted for Lincoln's reelection he expressed deep regret, and declared his belief that Lincoln would be made king of America; and this, I believe, drove him beyond the limits of reason. I asked him once why he did not join the Confederate army. To which he replied: "I promised mother I would keep out of the quarrel, if possible, and I am very sorry that I said so." Knowing my sentiments, he avoided me, rarely visiting my house, except to see his mother, when political topics were not touched upon, at least in my presence.[65]

The tension within the family, even before Lincoln's murder, was a palpable force.

Clarke reports to have asked Wilkes a similar question, why he never fought for the South. Wilkes's reply is clearly and explicitly tied to the nineteenth-century divide between labor of the mind and body: "I have only an arm to give . . . my brains are worth twenty men, my money worth an hundred."[66] Wilkes's intellectual labor, he argues, is valued more than the bodily labor he might expend as a soldier. His awareness of this coupled with an unwillingness to give the arm (a finite resource) reinforces Booth's conception of upper-class values and of his place within them. Despite being the Southern brother with a heart (so he professed) devoted to the South, Wilkes's ironic unwillingness to give his body displays how deeply he reaped the benefits of aristocracy.

The divide of North/South sentiments played out in the two Booths' stage careers and where they opted to perform: Edwin carved the North and East as his acting territory and left the South to Wilkes. Clarke's recollection of this territorial claiming (reminiscent of *King Lear*) admits no small amount of emotion behind it from both sides:

> Although [Wilkes] by no means ever sought to place himself in opposition to Edwin, he felt it rather premature that Edwin should mark off for himself the North and the East, and leave the South where he no longer cared to go himself, to Wilkes. He felt that he had not had a chance in New York, and his Southern friends were fervid in their desire to make him prove himself in the cities of the North and East. . . . [In the South] even his errors were extolled and his success magnified. The people loved him; he had never known privation or want, was never out of an engagement, while Edwin had the rough schooling of poverty, hardship in far distant cities, struggles in his professional experience, fiercer struggles with himself.[67]

Clarke admits that Wilkes's success in the South was essentially guaranteed and places Edwin on the pedestal of hard work and triumph through intense efforts. The North, while more desirable because of New York and Philadelphia's centralities as theatrical hubs, was also a crueler mistress to would-be theatrical careers. The admission of this tension, that the North was a more difficult market combined with Edwin's unwillingness to go south, idealizes Edwin's career and casts a shadow on Wilkes's success because it was 1) more easily come by, and 2) in a less prestigious market.

The assassination had a profound impact on the Booth brand professionally and the Booths personally. On the morning of April 15, 1865, Edwin Booth was performing at the Boston Theatre when he got the news from manager Henry C. Jarrett that his brother had shot President Abraham Lincoln. In his return letter, Booth acknowledged that Jarrett was closing the Boston Theatre "out of respect to the anguish which will fill the public mind as soon as the appalling fact shall be fully revealed."[68] Booth writes:

> The news of the morning has made me wretched indeed, not only because I have received the unhappy tidings of the suspicions of a brother's crime, but because a good man and a

134 | THEATRES OF VALUE

most justly honored and patriotic ruler has fallen in an hour of national joy by the hand of an assassin. . . . While mourning in common with all other loyal hearts the death of the President, I am oppressed by a private woe not to be expressed in words. But whatever calamity may befall me or mine, my country one and indivisible has my warmest devotion.[69]

The tragedy forced all the remaining Booths from the stage for some time. Junius was arrested, Edwin was also taken into custody, and the Booths' Maryland household was placed under strict surveillance. The Northern Booth survived but—seemingly—the shadow cast by the assassination might forever cloud his legacy.

Though he purposed to retire from show business, Edwin succumbed to what biographer William Winter called "an imperative necessity that Booth should return to the stage."[70] Booth had received a letter signed by "many of the leading citizens of this and other elites" imploring his return, and it seems that he was willing to oblige.[71] But Booth's re-debut wasn't met only by positive response; a series of articles in the *New York Herald* had choice words to say about the announcement of Booth's return:

Is the assassination of Caesar to be performed? The public must be surprised to learn that a Booth is to appear on the New York stage the coming week. We know not which is most worthy of condemnation, the heartless cupidity of the foreign manager, who has no sympathy with this country or the feelings of the American people, in bringing out this actor at the present time, or the shocking bad taste of the actor himself in appearing. Will he appear as the assassin of Caesar? That would be, perhaps, the most suitable character and the most sensational one to answer the manager's purpose. Shame upon such indecent and reckless disregard of propriety and the sentiments of the American people! . . . The blood of our martyred President is not yet dry in the memory of the people, and the very name of the assassin is appalling to the public mind; still a Booth is advertised to appear before a New York audience.[72]

The *Herald* article drew all sorts of responses, most of them emphasizing that this one reporter's opinion was not that of the general public.[73] Still, all of the articles could not ignore the elephant in the room: the Booth brand now had baggage. After a long condemnation of the *Herald* article, even staunch Booth defender Charles Bailey Seymour writing as his byline "Figaro" in the *New York Saturday Press* had to say, "The subject is getting painful: let me change it, therefore, and defer speaking of Booth the actor until he is less prominently before us as Booth the man."[74]

While the *Herald* article was vociferous, it could not drown out the rest of public opinion. Perhaps even more telling of public sentiment about Booth's return was his audience's reaction. During that re-debut performance as Hamlet, upon his first entrance:

> The applause burst spontaneously from every part of the house. The men stamped, clapped their hands, and hurrahed continuously; the ladies rose in their seats and waved a thousand handkerchiefs; and for full five minutes a scene of wild excitement forbade the progress of the play. Mr. Booth was at first overcome by the tremendous ovation. His head dropped low upon his breast, and his frame shook with emotion. The huzzas continuing, and even gathering force and volume as they were prolonged, he arose from his chair and bowed repeatedly. In a moment or two more the agreeable tumult subsided as spontaneously as it had begun, and the play proceeded. At the close of every act the enthusiasm broke forth anew, and Mr. Booth was compelled to cross the stage under a fire of wreaths and bouquets, and saluted by the frantic waving of handkerchiefs and hats and the mighty cheers of the multitude.[75]

The public overwhelmed Edwin Booth with accolades upon his return.

This performance took place at the Winter Garden on January 3, 1866. The previously noted enthusiasm was corroborated by a second reporter: "The house was densely crowded, and he was received with cheers which expressed the sympathy of the public and the general confidence in his patriotism, but, perhaps, indicated quite as clearly the delight of the crowd at the sight of the face of the man who had inevitably become more conspicuous in the common mind since his brother's dastardly crime."[76] In this reporter's opinion, the crime that drove Edwin from the stage eventually did more to preserve the integrity of the Booth brand than deface it. Still, the use of the term "conspicuous" hints at something of infamy rather than fame. While the public rejoiced at the return of

136 | THEATRES OF VALUE

their Booth, they could not help but hold recent history at the back of their minds—accepting, certainly, their Hamlet, but not forgetting the newfound notoriety of the Booth name.

It is no surprise given his close ties to the role that Booth chose Hamlet as his revival piece, though perhaps it should be, given the play's subject matter and the reasons for Booth's absence. Despite political assassination being a key action to the plot of *Hamlet*, the waiting crowds seemed ready and eager to embrace Booth's return. Able to overlook the plotline-driven imperatives of acting Hamlet (that Booth, like his brother, must become a political assassin), the crowd only saw their beloved Edwin Booth once more performing in the role they equally loved:

> It was felt that under the peculiar, unfortunate circumstances of his position, this estimable citizen and honored player deserved an expression of sympathy and a heartfelt greeting from the public that would in some measure encourage him to resume the round of his professional duties. So universal was this sentiment that it needed no concerted action to crowd the theater upon the opening night of the Shakespearean season with an audience that fairly represented the wealth and intelligence of the city, and which eagerly awaited the first opportunity for bestowing upon Booth one of the most remarkably spontaneous ovations ever extended to an actor.[77]

That evening, Shakespeare became a vehicle for mass celebration: America had their Hamlet back.

But the North seemed to be more forgiving of this mark against the brand than the South. In a letter written to William Winter on March 14, 1876, Booth documents his dissatisfaction with playing in the South:

> Except in Phila. I never find in the North or East any reference made to these miserable affairs—wh. shd. in decency & charity have been long ago forgotten. But all through the South— . . . I have been greeted with disgraceful anecdotes about my Father (all in the main false or exaggerated), and the flaunting in my face of buried cerements—raked up by these hyenas. Every little piddling village has stabbed me through & through, wherefore—I know not; it certainly is the most heartless, uncalled for brutality . . . tho' I have read, much to be proud

of & grateful for at the hands of the Southern people this one shameless, devilish act of the press has destroyed all pleasant remembrances I might have borne on this trip through life. I sincerely hope I shall not be invited South again. If ever you have a chance to shame them on this subject I wish you wd.[78]

The South's attachment to Wilkes and the sordid anecdotes of Booth Sr.'s past haunted Edwin, who wished those things forgotten. Try as he might, they were part of the brand he inherited and were tied to the Booth name. In some parts of the United States, this was forgivable and able to be left unspoken as a matter of propriety. In others, it was made explicit.

The survival of Edwin's version of the brand and the demise of Wilkes's contribution to it is another reason, perhaps, why this brand's performance of American Shakespeare was so successful. The clear ties between Edwin and the North and Wilkes and the South allowed a sort of microcosm of the Civil War to play out inside the family on a very public stage. Edwin's Hamlet could be understood as an avatar of the triumphant North emerging from its quarrels with the South. The market value of this, the intellectual Hamlet having overcome the shadow of the Civil War and preserving Northern values as a cultural commodity, spoke strongly to the American zeitgeist—particularly the white Northern audiences who comprised Booth's bread and butter. When audiences saw Edwin Booth as Hamlet in the latter half of his career, they saw a man who had personally triumphed over the hardships of the Civil War—the loss, the blood and violence, even the choice to live a more "enlightened" life, not as a slave owner but as a New York intellectual artist. Perhaps it was because of this that Southern audiences could not leave the shame of Wilkes's deed unspoken—that mark against the family symbolized their failure, and Edwin was an avatar of triumph against them. The same reasons Booth was so successful in the North were why the South would not be silenced in their discussions of the brand's shame. Still, this open conversation (while distasteful to Edwin) does not seem to have been unlucrative. Sympathetic or not, people still had "Booth" on the brain.

The Booth brand's survival in spite of its paradoxical life is deeply engaged with the brand's ties to market-driven forces and audience value declarations. In other words: perhaps Edwin Booth was the Hamlet America needed. Perhaps the value of Booth's Hamlet (and the Booth brand more generally) can be explained by an upper/middle-class white desire to be reminded of what the United States had gained by the North's triumph and the self-assurance of whiteness as a cultural value. Further, in considering *Hamlet* particularly, one cannot escape the grisly, bloody image of the end of act 5—the entire royal court dead on the stage while Horatio works to "draw his breath in pain" to tell the story as a promising new regime takes power in Denmark. Perhaps it was this reminder—that even after a bloody slaughter there can be hope if the story continues to be told—that audiences were so passionate about. The value of Shakespeare to the Booth brand, here, might innately be tied to underlying feelings of sentimental patriotism, and the continued need for a public to deal with the psychological trauma of the postbellum era.

Chapter Five

Our American Shakespeare

The Central Park Statue and National Identity

On May 23, 1872, the crowd had begun to assemble at noon even though formal presentations were not slated to start for several hours. Throngs of onlookers, ticketed and unticketed, arrived in Central Park and stood beneath a tiered pavilion hung with British and American flags. The center of the festivities was the newest addition to Central Park: a bronze statue of Shakespeare by famed American sculptor John Quincy Adams Ward set to be unveiled with great pomp and ceremony that afternoon. The statue had been in the works for some time; an application was first made for it on April 23, 1864, by theatrical impresarios James H. Hackett, William Wheatley, Edwin Booth, and Charles P. Daly in celebration of the tercentenary of Shakespeare's birth. The cornerstone was laid in April of 1864, but completion had met delay amid the Civil War.[1] Despite obstacles, the statue claimed a slice of history in 1872 as the first statue to and of Shakespeare built in the United States, and one of the first in the world.[2]

To this day, the piece stands in Central Park as a public monument to William Shakespeare. This alone is fairly noteworthy when considered in light of Barbara Herrnstein Smith's conception of value as a moving target reevaluated every time something is edited.[3] As the city changed, Shakespeare's continued existence highlights the persistence of this Shakespeare as a mark of endurance. Unlike the other case studies in this book, the Central Park Shakespeare continues to hold space in a prized piece of real estate—just off East Drive at Sixty-Seventh Street nestled closely to the Upper East Side steps away from the modern Fifth-Avenue townhouses that still belong to the generationally affluent.

139

140 | THEATRES OF VALUE

The story of how Shakespeare came to Central Park unravels layers of Shakespeare's value and worth to the nineteenth-century audiences who consumed him, and the artists who marketed him. In drafting this statue's dramaturgy of value, it's necessary to interrogate the various rhetorical intentions and audience interaction paradigms expected and enforced by the people who decided that Central Park needed this Shakespeare. This need was a market desire influenced by the factors that generally impact markets—a sense of lacking that Shakespeare worked to fill, and a perceived social problem that Shakespeare helped to solve. The Central Park Shakespeare was installed as a self-purported public service to educate the lower classes and contribute to a rising sense of national identity at the tail end (and in the wake of) the American Civil War. At its core, this statue is a construct of America's nineteenth-century hunger to create a national identity, incorporate high culture inherited from England into that identity, and simultaneously eschew any associations with Britain while rebranding choice cultural icons as American. Through the Central Park Shakespeare, Americans sought to claim Shakespeare as a vital piece of American cultural heritage by drafting Shakespeare in an American image using an American sculptor, American costumes, and an American body model.

"We'll set thy statue in some holy place
and have thee reverenced like a blessed saint."

—Duke of Alencon, *Henry VI, Part 1*, III.iii

It's not merely a wonder that Shakespeare's statue remains in Central Park but also that it was installed in the first place. Building the park itself was a monumental task. In 1853, the city procured 778 acres of land for the park by law of eminent domain. This was expanded in 1863, an addition that brought the park to its modern 843 acres. Construction began in 1858 with sections of the park opening to the public in the winter of 1859, though the project took an additional fifteen years to complete.[4] Original plans for Central Park included very sparse statuary; an 1873 restriction moved to keep commemorative sculpture to the mall and entrance gate and required "prior review of artistic merit" for a statue's inclusion on park land.[5] This gatekeeping immediately established a narrow corridor both physically and artistically for park aesthetics that would conform with upper-class Eurocentric ideals of taste. Slowly, various groups began to see Central Park as fertile ground upon which to memorialize their cultural heroes and at least the geographic requirement began to fall away. Part of allowing these groups to take over park decoration was economic. While an 1862 plan called for a scant twenty-six statues to adorn the park, this plan was scrapped due to cost overruns.[6] As a result, park commissioners allowed private donors to take on the fiscal burden of statuary and these initiatives were (generally) predictably grouped. Roy Rosenzweig and Elizabeth Blackmar note:

> Organized ethnic groups [sought] concrete public recognition in bronze and stone of great men (and only men) from countries of origin. Indeed, more than half of the fifteen statues of individuals erected in the park in the nineteenth century were financed and promoted by ethnic associations. . . . The choice of the mostly cultural figures is revealing: immigrant New Yorkers were emphasizing their status as "cultivated" people by honoring leading cultural (not political or military) figures in the city's most "cultivated" space. As if to underline the message, the sponsoring associations invariably chose the sculptor from their own ethnic group.[7]

Central Park statuary, in this model, was an established medium to prove cultural status. In a tautology of representation, Shakespeare's presence was required in Central Park because it was a proving ground or hall of noteworthies where inclusion indicated a corresponding degree of social currency for the group whose avatar stood among these collections. At stake in Shakespeare's inclusion was the ability for America to rely on the cultural capital Shakespeare represented as something with proven value. In order for that value to hold merit, Shakespeare *had* to continue showing up in the places that would give him this esteem. In a classic chicken-and-egg scenario, Americans needed to continue putting Shakespeare where cultural prestige lived in order to prove that he merited being there. In prior chapters, I have outlined the variety of modes in which Shakespeare's authority held cultural stakes for Americans—as a legitimizing force, a source of ethical health, and an icon of high culture—and what audiences relied on Shakespeare to do in these models. His presence in Central Park, in many ways, was an effort to gold-back this currency. American

142 | THEATRES OF VALUE

theatre was (at this time) largely derived from English stock.[8] What were American actors but immigrants from England looking to immortalize a cultural hero from their homeland? In this case, the hero held more stakes for a wider public since Americans had already begun to rely on Shakespeare as proven cultural capital. When a group of consumers assumes that a particular object holds certain value by way of its cultural capital and treats it accordingly, this exchange demands other behaviors. The assumption of Shakespeare's value, here, is the driving force behind this circular exchange—consumers needed to back-justify their attachment to Shakespeare's capital.

The Central Park Shakespeare was thus the product of a cultural imperative to ensure that Shakespeare's currency held value. The statue's creation was catalyzed by a moment bardolaters were keen to recognize, the tercentenary of Shakespeare's birth. In deep winter, 1864, it became apparent that an auspicious Shakesdate was upon bard worshipers. Despite the fact that this moment was three hundred years in the making, it seems to have taken the Global Shakespeare community by surprise. In February of 1864, theatre critic William Winter wrote in his Drama column in *The Albion*:

> The twenty-third of April next will be the three hundredth anniversary of the Birthday of Shakespeare. Preparations for its celebration are being made in England, but . . . will the day be celebrated here? Will actors, and men of letters, and artists, of all descriptions unite in honoring the most wonderful Genius ever sent down from heaven? Will there be no assemblage of the arts, to pay homage to their Master? . . . Something surely might be done—here, in the metropolis of the Western World.[9]

Winter goes on to suggest several items that might be suitable to fulfill such honors, including the performance of a banquet of Shakespearean pieces with money earned put toward funding a marble statue of Shakespeare. In this bardolatrous plea to the theatre community, Winter uses England as a rhetorical device to move Americans to action in a self-conscious attempt to stir American pride. If *English* actors and men of letters recognized the bard's birth at such a significant anniversary year, surely this landmark also had a place in America.[10] And, if it didn't, what would that say about American culture? Winter's framing of New York as a natural and necessary locale for American tercentenary celebrations centers the city as a crucial theatrical and cultural hub—the "metropolis of the Western World."

There were good reasons why an American public was distracted enough that this date almost slipped past them. In April of 1864, the Civil War was not yet over. Some of the war's bloodiest encounters (Gettysburg and Chickamauga) had occurred over the summer and early fall of 1863.[11] While Northerners as deeply embedded as New York were, generally, personally safe from the daily implications of life in a war zone, the philosophical and social constructions of a nation at war with itself permeated daily reality. These challenges in mind, the spring of 1864 doesn't seem like a practical time for the creation and installation of large, expensive, public works of art. Indeed, the economic realities of the Central Park statue are overwhelming in scale: the statue cost an approximate $35,000 (equating roughly to $702,507 in 2023 with inflation taken into account).[12] This large number emphasized the value of such an undertaking: the sum of money necessary to make this statue a reality would have been burdensome at any historical moment, but during wartime it seems particularly daunting. Such a high value at such a volatile time indicates a complex dramaturgy of value with critical social functions embedded deeply in the statue's network of worth.

The statue's timing is one key into this network. A statue is the center of a complex web of cultural signifiers wherein its worth is innately tied. As I hinted earlier, the Shakespeare statue held a significant place in a network of American national identity formation. In considering this network, two ideas about "nation" and "national identity" are useful. Benedict Anderson's definition of "nation" as "an imagined political community" with a "deep, horizontal comradeship" emphasizes the mind as a critical component to nation building.[13] Anthony D. Smith's five qualities that form the fundamental features of national identity—1) a historic territory or homeland; 2) common myths and historical memories; 3) a common, mass public culture; 4) common legal rights and duties for all members; and 5) a common economy with territorial mobility for members—expose just how underdeveloped America's sense of national identity was in 1864.[14]

The Shakespeare statue might be a key to building some of these milestones. The creation of the Central Park Shakespeare was a moment in which Americans were able to generate a mass public culture (factor three), and might further be interpreted as a moment where Americans were able to build a common myth (factor two). In this myth, Shakespeare was a critical part of an American canon and the statue canonized him (thus proving by induction his place in American ideals). Returning to Winter's notion that Shakespeare was as valuable to an American audience as he was to an English audience, perhaps the statue might serve as a grand and permanent outward show of cultural liberation. These Americans weren't looking to celebrate England's cultural dominance, but rather Americanize an aspect of this culture. Placing Shakespeare on American soil in grand fashion, they naturalized him—creating literal space for him in the United States and as part of the imaged nation of America. In the act of doing this, they also wrote a version of history where Shakespeare was American—a cultural myth that told how this particular piece of legitimated cultural capital belonged to Americans. These acts of claiming were important foundation stones—pieces of building the American nation that the United States desperately needed at the time the Shakespeare statue was installed. This, perhaps, can help speak to the economic investment audiences were willing to make in order to achieve the statue and their desperation to find some common thread for national consciousness. Investing in the Shakespeare statue wasn't only investing in Shakespeare (though, as I've argued, that had high stakes in its own right) but was also an investment in the American nation itself.

The phenomenon enacted by rewriting Shakespeare into something that would support American identity via the statue creates what Pierre Nora calls a *lieu de mémoire* (site of memory; pl.: *lieux de mémoire*).[15] To Nora, sites of remembering purposefully endowed with material, symbolic, and functional meaning beyond what they naturally encompass become *lieux de mémoire. Lieux de mémoire* are not merely places of memory but places that have been purposefully injected with cultural reminiscence that mark a direct attempt to write history upon the place. Nora makes an important distinction between memory and history—between the way things are remembered, and the way that they happened: "*Lieux de memoire* originate with the sense that there is no spontaneous memory, that we must deliberately create archives, maintain anniversaries, organize celebrations, pronounce eulogies, and notarize bills because such activities no longer occur naturally."[16] Winter's plea for commemoration of Shakespeare's birthday is a clear indication that such spontaneous memory, as Nora notes, was *not* happening organically—and why would it? Why would Americans gather to celebrate the three hundredth birthday of a long-dead English playwright? The artifice of crafting this celebration and the resulting American Shakespeare shows Americans fabricating memory, consciously writing history-as-memory as they navigated the waters of crafting communal myths (that Shakespeare is and was American) and mass common culture (that Americans are people who celebrate such occasions as Shakespeare's three hundredth birthday in monumental ways). This strategic application of memory formation is loud, clear, and declarative. By so writing American history via the Shakespeare statue, Americans were purposefully writing Shakespeare into their history as a crucial player and major national symbol; the fact that this statue endures is a testament to the efficacy of these efforts.

"Come, come, walk in the park."

—Ford, *The Merry Wives of Windsor*, III.iii

Theorizing a tercentenary celebration (as Winter had) was all well and good, but actualizing one was slightly more complicated. In the weeks after William Winter's February article was published, a number of journalists joined his call until New York's own Shakespearean juggernauts James Henry Hackett, William Wheatley, and Edwin Booth took up the mantle.[17] These actors, men who won their bread by embodying English prose in an American mode, had the most to gain from an American claim on Shakespeare. If Shakespeare couldn't be seen as an American entity, then what business did any American have portraying his characters for their countrymen? Suddenly eager to create a lasting physical embodiment of Shakespeare on American soil, the newly assembled "Shakespeare Statue Committee" faced their first major obstacle: Where should such a memorial be placed? In an article describing the statue's eventual unveiling, a *New York Herald* reporter claimed: "A more fitting place . . . could not be selected on the American continent than our own magnificent park."[18] The substance of this claim further unravels the statue's dramaturgy of value as it entwines the piece with nineteenth-century ideals surrounding morality and social economies as exemplified and embodied by a public park.

Central Park was the first park of its kind in the United States—a large green space for urbanites to take a healthful walk while communing with nature and escaping the city smog.[19] Unlike pleasure gardens, Central Park was free to enter and thus economically accessible to most New Yorkers. Public parks, like Barnum's museum, offered a forum where all social classes could walk and mingle—unsorted by the price of entry. Unlike

146 | Theatres of Value

Barnum's museum, public parks were municipal and (in theory at least) thus more freely available to the populace. As a public works project, the magnitude of a large public park suited the magnanimous tastes of wealthy New Yorkers as an appropriate rhetorical statement for the burgeoning republic. Placing Shakespeare in such a significant space sends a clear message about Shakespeare's place in the "democratic experiment" that was the United States at the time—making him a focal and pivotal piece of the people's canon.[20] Considering Benedict Anderson's ideas about a nation being a "community," Shakespeare's placement in the "communal" park further cements his place in the backbone of America.

Central Park's common construction as a communal public space flies contrary to many elements of its history, including its birth. The land that was to become Central Park wasn't exactly an unused, unoccupied waste-land before developers arrived. Roy Rosenzweig and Elizabeth Blackmar tell the in-depth history of Central Park; pertinent to this discussion is the fact that the land wasn't simply free and available for the taking—it had lawful occupants and was being used for their livelihoods before wealthy developers annexed it for their use.[21] The three wards of the city above Fortieth Street (the twelfth, nineteenth, and twenty-second wards) were home to almost sixty thousand occupants in 1855.[22] About two thousand of these residents lived specifically in the area that was to become Central Park.[23] These people, generally, lived in one of a number of large settlement communities spread across the area. Demographically, park dwellers were very similar to occupants of the rest of New York: 53.6 percent of them were immigrants, 1.89 percent of them were Black.[24] Unlike residents of southern New York, 15 percent of uptown occupants lived in one of the area's many orphanages, asylums, hospitals, or old age homes.[25] In order to turn the land these people occupied into Central Park, the city created policy to seize the property through law of eminent domain. Between 1851 when Senator James Beekman introduced an acquisition bill and 1853 when it was finally passed, debates raged hot about the justness or injustice of acquiring the land so.[26] By 1857, the people who made their homes on the area that was to be Central Park were evicted. Landowners were paid for their parcels, but none were allowed to stay.[27]

One of the settlements that was disbanded in this act of imperialism was Seneca Village, which spanned between Seventh and Eighth Avenues, Eighty-Second and Eighty-Eighth Streets. This area is notable for several reasons—how densely it was settled (Seneca Village had at least three times as many residents per block as any other area in the park), the number of residents (it was the largest park settlement and its population comprised more than a sixth of the park dwellers who were removed due to eminent domain), the racial composition of its residents (most of them Black or Irish), and the length the area that had been settled (the settlement was about thirty years old when it was disbanded).[28] Seneca Village was home to Black residents with deep roots—by 1855, Black heads of household in Seneca Village had spent an average of twenty-two years in the area and at least nine families in the settlement could trace ties to the land back over two and a half decades.[29] Black residents owned property here, a marked difference from downtown where they mostly rented.[30]

Seneca Village residents lived largely in single-family homes (an anomaly for workers in New York City at the time and certainly an anomaly for Black workers); sent their children to school at very high rates (about three-quarters of the children in Seneca Village went to school); had three churches, which suggests a bustling community life; and owned enough property that many Seneca Village male heads of household qualified for suffrage.[31] This is to say: Seneca Village was an enclave of Black middle-class peoples and values.

Seneca Village was over a mile away from what was then the city center. By all indications cited earlier, this middle-class community thrived—but that did not stop white policymakers from razing it. One of the arguments used to acquire this land was that it would be put to better use as a public park than a center for "shanties" and the "nuisance industries" that currently occupied the area. It's fairly clear that this argument was a strawman used by white lawmakers to acquire park land in order to make the real estate around it (which, consequently, they owned) accrue even more value.[32] The quality of housing in Seneca Village was drastically better than the tenements of downtown—residents had outdoor space, easy access to fresh air, and much more elbow room than those living in slum housing in the lower wards.[33] In this case, the value of the land was linked strongly to what it could become for wealthy investment stakeholders rather than what it was—a place for families from oppressed demographics to live and work. From the outset, Central Park was clearly established as a playground for the wealthy with no regard for those whose lives they literally paved over.[34] It's difficult to put credence, then, into park developers' purported intentions to create an equalizing space within Central Park.

So, not quite ten years before Shakespeare was placed in Central Park, the land upon which he was placed was seized in an act of racial

148 | THEATRES OF VALUE

violence. The use of this land and the way the park was conceived/constructed continued to weaponize it against the poor even as these efforts were shielded under the vocal pronouncement of supposed ethics and moral health that they were said to embody. A public park was marketed and sold as one potential balm to the perceived sin of city living.[35] It enabled strollers to surround themselves with healthful air, the nobility of nature, and to connect with these important rural luxuries. Thus, the very inception of Central Park was taken up as an ethical imperative. Moreover, it was seen as a valuable opportunity to educate the lower class through use of public spaces. Chief park architect Frederick Law Olmsted famously and notoriously wrote: "A large part of the people of New York are ignorant of a park. . . . They will need to be trained in the proper use of it and be restrained in the abuse of it."[36] Viewing the public park as a means through which to "train" bad habits out of lower-class peoples and, in turn, placing Shakespeare conspicuously within that training ground concretely connects Shakespeare with a white bourgeois attitude about habits and hobbies of people and a pressing interest in how people *should* interact with public land. The point of view that this park would help to raise the standard of behavior for poor audiences displayed a melting-pot-like worldview (with similar problematic destructive tendencies) that centered the park as a means for generating mandated conformity to bourgeoise standards of taste.[37] By placing Shakespeare at the center of this instrument of moral reformation education, nineteenth-century memorializers demonstrated their attachment to and connection with Shakespeare as an important force in this movement and continued to literally center Shakespeare in these dialogues. Like his place at Barnum's, Shakespeare's place in Central Park can be seen as a tacit attempt to include him in a greater body of moral education that was happening via the park—ostensibly for the public good. Because of this land's history, this placement also continues to center Shakespeare in conversations about imperialism—though of course those conversations are largely braced in historical hindsight rather than contemporary intentions.

I've already discussed the ironic place that Shakespeare held in the nineteenth-century imagination when it came to morality. In chapter 2, I discussed this in terms of Barnum's publicity surrounding the American Museum. For Barnum, Shakespeare was a convenient shield that allowed him to operate his theatre under the guise of morality. Consider, in a similar vein, the bowdlerized editions of Shakespeare that were quickly becoming popular in nineteenth-century literary spheres.[38] The nineteenth-century audience's veracity for the high literary concept of Shakespeare and simultaneous distaste for his gross actuality was a fruitful tension for Shakespearean users who effectively inserted premodern fanfiction into this gap between ideal and reality. The Central Park Shakespeare encapsulated these usages—editing Shakespeare to be presented as clean and natural (salubrious genius rather than bawdy upstart) while capitalizing upon the moral currency that Shakespeare stood for. The Central Park Shakespeare perfectly demonstrates nineteenth-century ideals about genius—meant to be seen and contemplated as a wholesome fixture with naughty bits thoroughly redacted. This genius's very presence was a shield similar to Barnum's usage in that it helped work to ensure ethical health and moral reform education by simply existing. Shakespeare's statue was painted by the wealthy elite who installed it as a boon to those who most needed his influence but in actuality created a feedback loop that allowed these influencers to depict Shakespeare in the light of moral reform education without doing the labor of drafting systems to ensure this education. Much like Barnum's alms boxes, Shakespeare was a comforting figurehead for the Americans who installed in him Central Park and a self-assurance of work well done for society's betterment.

> "There has been knights, and lords, and gentlemen,
> with their coaches, I warrant you, coach after coach . . ."
>
> —Hostess Quickly, *The Merry Wives of Windsor*, II.ii

In addition to Shakespeare's presence in Central Park being a rhetorically loaded signifier, where the statue is placed is similarly revealing of its intended audience and, thereby, cultural value construction. Central Park was a high-traffic public space, but the notion of "public" requires further inquiry—especially as it relates to the body of Shakespeare being placed within this park environment.[39] I have framed the park as a mingling-ground for New York's social classes, unmoderated by economic barrier to entry much as Barnum's museum was, but to say that encounters between social classes within public parks were completely unmediated would be misleading. In fact, there was a *huge* distinction made among visitors to Central Park drawn by the methods in which they used the park—specifically, the way they navigated the park.

150 | THEATRES OF VALUE

As New York grew, so did the need for transportation around New York. The owning of a carriage became a popular way to display one's wealth and status. Carriages were prolific among the middle/upper classes and their use as a means to see and be seen in nineteenth-century Central Park is meticulously documented. In his detailed study of carriages in Central Park, Kevin Coffee finds: "Starting from 1862 . . . carriage passengers outnumbered pedestrians, 2.12 million to 2 million; the following year, the ratio increased 2.77 million to 1.47 million. In 1869 . . . carriage users comprised 7.35 million visitors, while pedestrians numbered 3.26 million. Carriage entries to the park rose steadily throughout the 1860s . . . and always outnumbered those arriving on foot and horseback every year from 1862 through 1872."[40] These numbers show a pattern of usage for the park that is immutably linked to economics: the very wealthy consistently comprised a majority of parkgoers, overwhelmingly so in the latter half of the 1860s.

The landscape of New York City was in no small part a factor for this abundance of carriage users (and, consequently, wealthy elite) in Central Park. The time and expense required for a trip to the park could be quite prohibitive to a working family. Though entry into the park was free, travel to the park's gates was not. In 1864, round-trip street railway fare was 12¢ and unskilled laborers made about $1.50 a day.[41] For a family of six, 72¢ could represent roughly half a day's pay. When considered in this light, Shakespeare's majority audience in Central Park becomes clear: Shakespeare was much more readily available to those with the means to get to him. This economic barrier also complicates the performative act of installing a statue for the good of the people. It cannot reasonably be claimed that the Central Park Shakespeare was an equitable moral and ethical behavioral force when the economic divide in park usership and, thereby, audience base existed so clearly. Instead, the act of installation was a show of magnanimity more interested in the trappings of public good than actual endowments of benefit to a wide audience. The wealthy elite imagined themselves proffering moral reform education to the less fortunate but they don't seem to have actually achieved what they set out to do. These "huddled masses" were not present in the spaces they were projected into by wealthy imaginations.

There is, however, something to be said for the power of self-image. Anderson argues that imaginative forces are the backbone of a nation and by imagining something there was power to make it so. By the same logic, the audience drive to install Shakespeare in Central Park as keystone to bettering parkgoers had some power to center Shakespeare in dialogues about how Shakespeare might (and did) fit within these spaces. Much as Americans needed a concrete avatar of Shakespeare to prove his merit in the cultural spaces where merit was proven, they perhaps also needed to continue including him in conversations about ethical health in order to prove his worth as an agent of moral reform. The tautology of representation here continues.

In observing *where* Shakespeare sits in Central park, this divide between intentions toward public good and bourgeois actuality becomes even clearer. Reconsidering Robin Bernstein's notion of a "scriptive thing" is helpful when analyzing Shakespeare's place on the walking mall. The scriptive thing, according to Bernstein, is an object of historical significance whose design gives specific social prompts for audiences to engage with the object using "scripted" behaviors.[42] The Central Park Shakespeare is located at the end of the walking mall, but he is also easily visible from carriage roads. As one travels up Park Drive from the park's south end, Shakespeare appears above the tree line (and when he was installed, there would have been a clear view of Shakespeare from the carriage road as those trees had yet to be planted).[43] Wealthy passengers need not even leave their carriages for the dusty streets to catch a glimpse of Shakespeare but could enjoy his visage from the comfort of their private and showy transport.

Yet, there's an aspect of Shakespeare that carriage riders might miss. As one stands in front of the statue, it's unmistakable that the angle of Shakespeare's gaze is tilted such that he makes eye contact with an observer on foot. Bernstein calls this "enscription": "interpellation through a scriptive thing that combines narrative with materiality to structure behavior."[44] Bernstein further argues that scriptive things beg to be interpolated using a "hail," a mode of engagement suggested by the thing through its design that prompts audience members to embark on the thing's scripted interaction. Shakespeare's "hail" is his gaze combined with his position on the walking mall, but complicated by his proximity to carriage roads. While wealthy carriage riders might see Shakespeare, they must become pedestrians in order to fully experience his offerings. Perhaps passing by in a carriage offers patrons a quick glimpse of Shakespeare, a brief reminder of his presence in the park, but only the foot traveler will enjoy a personal-feeling encounter complete with a soulful gaze into the bard's eyes. Rhetorically, this "hail" seems to reinforce the idea that Shakespeare is an equalizing force in Central Park. Although more available (as I have

152 | THEATRES OF VALUE

argued) to those with the means to get to him, Shakespeare mischievously converts his most meaningfully engaged visitors to groundlings.

> "I'll give thee, ere I leave thee, so much money . . ."
>
> —Antipholus of Ephesus, *The Comedy of Errors*, IV.iv

Returning to Winter's February 1864 article, the piece (published a mere two months before Shakespeare's birthday) catalyzed a historical case of last-minute scrambling. On such short notice, it is no surprise that the entire substantial fund of monies required to complete the statue could not be raised in time for an April celebration. Of course, raising money wasn't the only step in this process: designing, fabricating, casting, and installing the statue would also require time. But these constraints did not deter the community. On the tercentenary, plays were produced across New York City starring the period's most famous leading actors: at Niblo's James Henry Hackett played Falstaff in *Henry IV*, and Edwin Booth played Romeo at the Winter Garden. In the afternoon, Hackett oversaw a ceremony to lay the cornerstone of the statue's pedestal in Central Park.[45]

Cornerstone in place, the next step was to actualize a body to stand atop it. This, of course, required fundraising. One of the most successful fundraising events that contributed to the statue was a production of *Julius Caesar* at New York's Winter Garden Theatre on November 25, 1864. The *Caesar* production's unique value lay in its headliners: it was the first (and, as it turned out, only) time in their careers that all three of the theatrical Booth brothers appeared together onstage.[46] This marketable novelty proved to be advertising gold. That night, the Winter Garden played host to an audience of over two thousand people (the largest Winter Garden audience until that time).[47] The Booths' sister, Asia Booth Clarke, describes the evening:

> The theatre was crowded to suffocation, people standing in every available place. The greatest excitement prevailed, and the aged mother of the Booths sat in a private box to witness this performance. . . . The eldest, powerfully built and handsome as an antique Roman, Edwin, with his magnetic fire and graceful dignity, and John Wilkes in the perfection of youthful

beauty, stood side by side, again and again, before the curtain, to receive the lavish applause of the audience mingled with waving of handkerchiefs and every mark of enthusiasm.[48]

One female admirer was heard by Clarke to sigh, "Our Wilkes is like a young god!"[49] Accounts like these highlight the popularity of the play's leading actors and emphasize how key the Booth brand was to the benefit's success.[50]

Another key can be found in the event's advertising ephemera. One notice claims: "The evening will be made memorable by the appearance in the same piece of the three sons of the great Booth—Junius Brutus, Edwin, and John Wilkes—*Filli patri digno digniores*—Who have come forward with cheerful alacrity to do honor to the immortal bard from whose works the genius of their father caught its inspiration, and of many of whose greatest creations he was the best and noblest illustrator the stage has ever seen."[51] The Booth legacy is portrayed as a key draw to the performance and an inheritance passed down by birthright. In the previous chapter, I argued that the Booth brand was made valuable through its "natural" association with Shakespeare and the ways that association was publicly figured. Here, both those elements come into play to advertise the Booths' benefit. And it worked; the combination of brand, cause, and material was extremely lucrative. Through this benefit performance alone, the Booths raised between $3,500 and $4,000 (approximately 10 percent of the estimated $35,000 it would take to complete the statue).[52]

The timing of this benefit might seem odd—a November performance to support a nebulous future statue commemorating an event that occurred the previous April. The scheduling, apparently, had been messy. Edwin initially conceived of this benefit when he took over management of the Winter Garden in the spring of 1864, but it was not until November that the three brothers could schedule themselves to be in the same place at the same time long enough for the performance to happen.[53]

The cramped rehearsal conditions of this production are brought into sharp focus by Junius Jr.'s records. In his diary, a collection of jottings that he kept in a copy of *Frank Leslie's Lady's Almanac*, 1864, Junius logs: "[November] 23: Left for NY 25: played *Julius Caesar* for the monument fund $3500 in. . . . 26: Ed commences at the W.G. With *Hamlet*. . . . 27: Ed. JW and I stood for characters in JC to be painted. 28: John and I went to Pha."[54] With a day and a half between arrival in New York and curtain up, the brothers didn't have much time at all to convene for rehearsal. Despite the trouble that scheduling proved, the novelty seemed to have added to the benefit's lucrativeness. Ticket prices were high: $1.50 for dress circle and parquette, $1 for family circle, and $5 for orchestra chairs. Compare this to prices listed for an 1862 benefit performance at the Winter Garden for actor-comedian Barney Williams: 50¢ for the dress circle and parquette; 25¢ for the family circle, $1 for orchestra stalls, and $7 for private boxes.[55] Demand seems to have warranted this inflation: despite a 300 percent to 500 percent price increase from other benefits, Edwin reports that tickets sold like "hot cakes."[56]

The irony of the play's subject matter is (of course) a relic of hindsight. That aside, it is not surprising that *Julius Caesar* was chosen for this benefit. As one of the few plays in Shakespeare's canon with three strong male leads, it was a logical option for the three brothers. Edwin had previously played all three roles, though he assigned himself the leading role of Brutus for the occasion. The other brothers' casting is fitting in light of an observation made by John Ripley: "In America Brutus and Cassius were considered the plum parts, while Antony fell to some junior member of the company with athletic good looks and a pleasant voice."[57] Despite the note about Marc Antony being a part for a "junior company member," it's difficult to see Wilkes's casting as a slight since he had made his career on the sorts of athletic performances that were American standard for Marc Antony. Wilkes's athletic desirability in the role, particularly in contrast to his brothers' more stately figures, is highlighted in an image of the trio in character for this production. This portrait is the only surviving image of all three brothers together (fig. 5.1). Wilkes had shaved his trademark moustache for the part. Edwin and Junius are dressed in ankle-length togas with heavily draped fabric. Wilkes is dressed in a knee-length tunic with tights and laced sandals; not only would such costuming display his muscular calves, but it would also allow him greater freedom of movement.

In terms of reception, Clarke's interpretation of audience reaction to the piece is echoed by an external reviewer: "The audience was thus a great success, and the play was a great success also. The audience was fairly carried by storm from the first entrance of the three brothers side by side in their respective parts. Brutus was individualized with great force and distinctness—Cassius was brought out equally well—and if there was less of a real personality given to Marc Antony, the fault was rather in the part than in the actor."[58] This reviewer, positively glowing, places laurels at the Booths' feet and highlights that all three held their own onstage: even Edwin's greatness could not eclipse his brothers.

Figure 5.1. The Three Theatrical Booth Brothers in *Julius Caesar*. *Source*: Public domain.

A reminder, though, of the deep divide playing out onstage was also present the evening of the show. At the time of the *Caesar* performance, the political split in the family was pronounced. An argument in August of 1864 between Edwin and Wilkes had turned heated (Edwin was outspoken that he had only ever cast a single vote in his lifetime—for Lincoln—and Wilkes was outspoken in his belief that Lincoln would become "King of America").[59] The echoes of this conflict were thus plum for ghosting as the brothers enacted Shakespeare's tragedy.[60] A present reminder of the stakes of this argument were made even more pressing when, that night, Confederate sympathizers set fire to several public buildings in New York City including the LaFarge House, which was attached to the Winter Garden.[61] The plot to burn New York to ash wasn't as effective as conspirators had hoped, but the fire did create smoke in the Winter Garden and nearly sent the audience into a panic. Accounts differ about the degree to which audiences experienced by-products of the fire: some say there was merely

156 | THEATRES OF VALUE

the smell of smoke while others claim firemen breached the audience.[62] All accounts agree that the interruption was unsettling, but that Edwin managed to calm the audience through direct address from the stage and convince them to sit and enjoy act 2. The interruption was a prescient harkening of things to come.

The events of November 25, 1864, highlighted the Booth brand's value as linked to Shakespeare and the development of US national identity as a salient piece of successful marketing—the statue, by association with the Booths, could not escape a link with the North's triumph in the Civil War. This association was a powerful driving force of value for the Booths— particularly Edwin. Because of its associations with the Booth brand, the same is true for the statue. As a pillar of national identity, the Shakespeare statue encompassing this triumph and this link, perhaps, can contribute to a deeper understanding of the statue's worth in its historical space.

> "But what need I thus my well-known body
> to anatomize among my household?"
>
> —Rumour, *Henry IV, Part 2*, Prologue

After the Booth benefit, the statue made little progress as the events of the war (including Lincoln's assassination) unfolded. In 1866, almost exactly a year after the war ended, New York City held a public competition to select an American artist to design the monument to Shakespeare. Well-known sculptor John Quincy Adams Ward, a member of the prestigious National Academy of Design and well known for his large-scale statues including the *Indian Hunter* (an earlier addition to Central Park), won based on his sketches for "a standing figure, head bowed in thought and one arm akimbo."[63] The sketch was published in *Harper's Weekly*, and Ward set to work.

Apparently, Ward's job to envision and create America's first whole-body depiction of Shakespeare (one of the first full-body Shakespeare statues in the world) was not easy.[64] There were claims that Ward had trouble visualizing the statue and one can certainly understand why. The intensely public nature of the project as well as its expense to donors, prominent placement, and lauded celebration even before its installation generated an incredible pressure to create something worthy of all this hoopla.

Ward's accounts of his inspirations document a desire for accuracy in the finished production. He writes:

> The Stratford bust I took as the most authoritative of all the representations of Shakespeare. . . . Next to this in authenticity, and evidently founded upon it, I considered the Droeshout etching, prefixed to the first folio. I was in possession, while the studies for the statue were making, of the then recent volume "Life Portraits of Shakespeare" by J. Hair Friswell (London, 1864) and had also woodcuts of the Kesselstadt death-mask. But I attached little importance to any of the speculative material. The Stratford bust and the Droeshout print were the sources upon which I relied.[65]

While Ward was able to rely upon historical sources for Shakespeare's face, Shakespeare's body was left to the sculptor's imagination with no historical sources upon which to rely.[66] Though Ward claims to have "attached little importance" to speculative material, the artist was left with dots to connect and his own speculation to manifest.

A letter from Edwin Booth to Ward reveals several details about an ongoing conversation between the two artists surrounding the body of Shakespeare in the context of Ward's statue. The letter indicates that Ward requested to examine several costumes in Booth's collection as inspiration for Shakespeare's clothing. Booth obliged in the most theatrical way possible:

> It happens, awkwardly enough, that the costumes in question are being used in the play now represented at the Winter Garden. . . . I was perhaps a little officious in calling yr attention to a properly costumed Shakespeare in bronze—the property of Mr. C—, my brother–in–law,—but I thought while it was "seeable" it would be of service. I will obtain you as good seats as I can that you may have a full view of the stage (if you will favor me by accepting them) . . . for I am as anxious that Shakespeare should be properly clothed as Bulwer is in our play of *Richelieu*.[67]

Although I have found no documentation that Ward took Booth up on his offer, there is every reason to believe that he did. The statue certainly shows evidence of Ward's care and attention to the detail of clothing.

158 | THEATRES OF VALUE

Ward's Shakespeare is dressed with immaculate scrutiny including fabric textures—wrinkles in the smooth tights, folds in rich velvet, crinkles in fine lace—that suggest life and movement.

Having dressed Shakespeare in Booth's American wardrobe, Ward seems to have used an equally American source in crafting the figure's body. New York City's *Aldine* of October 1873 describes, "When Mr. J.Q.A. Ward was modeling his now beautiful statue of Shakespeare, he experienced some difficulty in harmonizing the expression of the face with the pose of the figure . . . he called to his aid a friend who had made a study of psychology. The friend at once detected the fault, and stood as a model for the artist."[68] While *The Aldine* gives no further hints at the identity of this "friend," these remarks invite further investigation. Who was this American whose body would be so purposefully, publicly, and expensively memorialized as Shakespeare?

In a volume documenting his father's life in the theatre, Percy MacKaye records an anecdote of American actor Steele MacKaye's life that, though perhaps apocryphal, plausibly explains Ward's inspiration for Shakespeare's body:

> [For] the Shakespeare, on Central Park Mall—young James Steele MacKaye posed on several occasions. . . . The first occasion—as my mother has often recounted to me—occurred in this way. One day, when young MacKaye dropped in to his studio, Ward said:
>
> "Jim, I've been working like the devil on this pose but I can't get what I want. I want the old bard to be thinking—but he ain't! What ails him?"
>
> "That's simple, J.Q." Said Jim, "instead of making him pensive, you've made him sleepy. The difference in pose is slight but radical. It affects the whole body—legs, torso as well as head. The posture of thought should be like this." And Jim illustrated by assuming a posture of absorbed thinking.
>
> "Hold it! Don't move!" cried Ward, and began working furiously at his clay to catch the pose, which MacKaye resumed again on further visits, from which he profited by making clay sketches himself under his friend Ward's supervision.
>
> In Ward's old age, at a dinner of the National Institute of Arts and Letters, the year before he died, wishing to verify the above incident, I said to the venerable sculptor, laughingly,

"Mr. Ward, there's a tradition in my family that the legs of your Shakespeare in Central Park are 'substantially' my father's. Is that so?"

"Yes," he replied with a twinkle, "I guess those are Jim's legs—'substantially,' and so is the pose, too!"[69]

This anecdote might essentially be a published family myth, but when taken in conjunction with *The Aldine*'s assertions, it holds enough credibility to at least be entertained as truth. If MacKaye indeed provided the body model for Ward's statue, this casting represents a purposeful construction of Shakespeare in his American context. Ward relied upon historical sources when possible, purposefully eschewing European speculative models and instead substituting American sources. After all, who was to say that Booth's costuming was more accurate than Friswell's conclusions? Ward's choices in fabricating Shakespeare's person were reliant on the inspiration around him—the American sources that permeated his life. Purposefully or not, Ward chose American models for this Shakespeare over European ones. These choices bring to light how Americanness was woven into the cloth of the statue-as-myth and how the statue's value was fabricated alongside the identity of American. In rendering Shakespeare's bones with American flesh, Ward, Booth, and the many supporters of Shakespeare's statue in Central Park sought to engage with the present moment of crisis for American identity. They were looking to not only reinvigorate Shakespeare as an important cornerstone of American culture but also to inscribe Americanness onto Shakespeare.

As a physical embodiment of memory, Shakespeare's American presence in Central Park also functions as what Joseph Roach would call a "surrogate." This American Shakespeare steps into the role of Shakespeare in Americans' minds—particularly those who pass it and enact its scriptive hail. As Roach declares, "The King is dead, long live the King"; the bard is dead but reborn again American. This surrogation also invokes countermemory, a concept Roach defines as "the disparities between history as it is discursively transmitted and memory as it is publicly enacted by the bodies that bear its consequence."[70] In making an American effigy of Shakespeare, memorializers publicly enact an American history of Shakespeare on American soil with American players, thus creating a *lieu de memoire* within Central Park. As an artifact of the canon, Roach further argues that Shakespeare holds a special place for memorializers: "English classics help control the dead to serve the interests of the living. The

160 | THEATRES OF VALUE

public performance of canonical works ritualizes these devotions under the guise of the aesthetic. . . . In this reinvention of ritual, performers become caretakers of memory through many kinds of public action."[71] The remembrance ritual Winter called for, enacted by Booth, Ward, Hackett, and colleagues, allowed these men to become caretakers of Shakespeare's place within (and, as I have argued, as) America. Since (Anderson claims) the very concept of "nation" is imagined, this strategic caretaking of memory allows memorializers to bond the formation of Shakespeare with the formation of the nation itself.

I have already cited the statue's continued existence as a mark of its success but there were also earlier indications. Upon its unveiling, the statue was heaped with praise. A piece in New York's *Christian Union* of May 29, 1872, lauds the sculpture: "As a likeness, it is at least skillfully compounded of the various most authentic materials which the grudging past has furnished us, while, as an ideal expression of the possible Shakespeare . . . it leaves nothing to be desired."[72] Ward's creation is, here, specifically celebrated for its resourcefulness in the face of adversity. His "ideal expression of the possible Shakespeare" manages to earn marks of both skill and authenticity from this critic. This tension between "authentic" and "possible" seems to be the same tension that birthed the space for an American expression of Shakespeare—had Ward been able to look to an earlier English body model, he would not have needed the help of Booth and MacKaye to fill the void of imagination. The imagined space of Shakespeare's body thus allowed for the possibility to recast Shakespeare and, thereby, claim him for the American nation.

Shakespeare's pivotal place in the economic, ethical, and cultural life of America's nineteenth century is epitomized by the Central Park statue. An outwardly egalitarian yet pointedly rhetorical work of art, this statue stands testament to the American demand for Shakespeare as legitimate cultural capital and a firm foundation for nation building. Establishing Shakespeare in Central Park also allowed Americans to claim him as a cornerstone of national cultural identity. In so doing, the nineteenth-century businessmen and thespians who created this statue loudly proclaimed Shakespeare's worth and value as a commodity to the nineteenth-century American. They also asserted his place in an American canon, claiming his body in a vital act of cultural mythmaking.

Chapter Six

Erasing the Lines

Editing the Wallack Benefit

On May 21, 1888, a powerhouse roster of nineteenth-century theatrical stars gathered at the Metropolitan Opera House to pay tribute to ailing theatrical impresario Lester Wallack. In a one-night-only benefit performance of *Hamlet*, the time's best-known actors took the stage to raise money for their retired colleague. Edwin Booth played the eponymous hero, Polish-born actress Helena Modjeska was Ophelia, the great comedian Joseph Jefferson played the First Gravedigger, and Booth's acting partner Lawrence Barrett played the Ghost. Outside of the named parts, one hundred prominent actors and actresses volunteered to play supernumeraries in the Danish court.[1] This theatrical object, drafted for the purpose of deriving a hefty profit, was measurably successful: tickets for the coveted event were oversold and producer Augustin Daly was obliged to return $5,000 to would-be patrons.[2] The house was packed, festivities went on until past midnight, and the benefit raised over $20,000 for its beneficiary.[3] This success-by-the-numbers also echoed in qualitative indicators. In reviews of the evening's theatrical fare, the production was called the "ideal" *Hamlet*, "a magnificent testimonial in every respect," "the most notable performance ever given upon any stage," "the most remarkable performance of *Hamlet* known to the chroniclers of the stage."[4]

This chapter follows the development of a commercially successful theatrical object by commercially successful theatrical businesspeople in the tail end of New York's nineteenth century. In many ways, this chapter is about backsolving success based on what producers Augustin Daly and

Albert Marshman Palmer felt would sell. Considering Daly and Palmer's production process with the Wallack benefit shows how these producers leveraged their combined knowledge regarding theatrical success in order to create something that was successful. The Wallack benefit has a significant archival footprint—including personal correspondence, diaries, publicity materials, souvenir materials, and so on. In addition to affirming the event as it happened, these materials also reveal many avenues of pursuit that never came to fruition—dead ends that were part of the story but never made it onstage. As with any archival history, the public documents and private documents tell different pieces of the story and (perhaps predictably) the edges don't always match.

The variances between history as documented by formal published accounts and by more private writings are what I call "witness marks" to the way that the story of this benefit was changed in order to package and sell both the benefit itself and narratives about the benefit. I derive the term "witness marks" from horology and carpentry—a "witness mark" in those fields is a marking generally not made purposefully but rather a by-product of assembly such as a scratch, hand mark, or punch that helps to reverse engineer where parts fit in relation to each other. When a clock, for instance, is taken apart, witness marks that line up can help show how the pieces fit back together. Witness marks are physical remnants of something that is no longer present but whose absence leaves tangible evidence with the things that are. Witness marks are useful in constructing a dramaturgy of value since they reveal the places in a story where producers attempted to edit the historical record. They show a producer's understanding of how to interface with audiences—and when dealing with knowledgeable producers this understanding is telling of the market in general. The dialogue between producer and audience is in direct relationship with marketing, capitalism, audience, and profitability (all aspects of deriving value). Spotting and deconstructing witness marks shows what a producer's expert gaze from their vantage point "on the ground" told them about the possibilities of profit on their market.

When considering Daly and Palmer's perspectives about deriving profit via theatrical commodities, two neatly packaged histories of the Wallack benefit are worth particular note—an account published in 1893 by Palmer relating a narrative of how the benefit came to be, and a souvenir program that was printed with some pomp and circumstance to be sold in conjunction with the event. The 1893 account was printed by New York printer and typographer Theodore L. De Vinne and the bound volume (held by the Folger Shakespeare library) notes that it is "one of three copies printed."[5] This note indicates that the account was likely intended as more of a collector's item than as a mass public sale object. Still, Palmer's willingness to compile and print the piece suggests a desire to document a formal history. The program is an object I found in several archives, often with multiple copies in a single location.[6] Printed on heavy cream paper (and, in one instance I found, on silk), this document offers a full cast list (including the many supernumeraries), a signature page with autographs from the actors, a list of planning committee members, and also a compilation of letters that tell the story of the benefit coming together. Included are letters from the most notable players accepting their roles with delight, but these letters (as I will discuss) seem to be polished-for-publication versions of the history, if not outright fabrications. As a souvenir object, the program is a very clean and neat presentation of what eventually came to be, but that in itself should be suspect. Since this program was an object generated to be sold as part of the historical package on offer the night of the benefit, it best behooved the editors of this document (Daly and Palmer) to present something publication-ready. The fact that the document is so prolific in the archive suggests its success on two fronts: first as a marketing object (enough were sold and kept in relatively pristine condition that so many copies *do* exist in archival memory) and second as an attempt to record the history of this moment. Daly and Palmer created success not only with the ephemeral theatrical object they drafted but also with the story they told about this object and their ability to take control of this narrative.

Spotting the trick, then, is here about lining up the witness marks and uncovering the pieces of this story omitted from formal histories in order to determine what was valued (as Smith would argue) through this editing. In this regard, the dramaturgy of value is as much about what is absent as it is about what is present.

Because the story of the Wallack benefit is deeply entwined with Daly/Palmer and Wallack's personal and professional networks, there are many fringe characters in this story who play small roles, but whose mention adds to the picture of how success came to be generated in the commodity at hand. In this chapter, I have chosen to highlight smaller characters with short explanations between longer quotations of archival evidence. Understanding a network of profit is critical to deriving a dramaturgy of value, and I have chosen not to relegate these characters to footnotes in order to highlight these networks.

164 | Theatres of Value

"Be the players ready."

—Hamlet, *Hamlet*, III.ii

The success described earlier isn't surprising given the prestige of the benefit's chief players, old hats to the New York theatre industry both on and off the stage. Wallack himself inherited a theatrical career from his father and made a name in New York as an actor and manager.[7] Wallack's theatrical reputation is evident in newspaper writings about his person, brand, and career. Wallack clippings often highlight the features of this brand: its roots, its quality, and the reliability of its integrity in presenting those sources of value. For example: "Lester Wallack, with the single exception of Edwin Booth, was the best known American actor of this time. He inherited the management of a theatre bearing the family name, that for a long term of years represented the best that there was in the English drama."[8] A second clipping directly describes Wallack's relationship with an American audience: "As a manager he came to be looked upon as in a certain sense the guardian of the old comedies . . . Mr. Wallack sustained a unique relation to his audiences, and the bond which existed between them was one of mutual and affectionate regard."[9]

Wallack's name was thus a powerful brand that assured both theatrical quality and a connection to a certain traditional aesthetic. An 1868 article announcing a performance at Wallack's highlights the strength of this brand: "It seems only necessary to announce the name of Lester Wallack and the house is crowded. . . . The public seem to go to Wallack's as they go to Stewart's or Delmonico's; they know they are dealing with a responsible house, and even if the moon should fall they would get the worth of their money."[10] This passage explicitly links the name "Wallack" to profit, worth, value, and other nineteenth-century branding titans. "Stewart's" was one of the city's premier shopping destinations—Alexander Turney Stewart's dry goods empire crowned by its jewel the "marble palace" on Broadway and Tenth Street.[11] Stewart was the first dry goods seller in the city to establish a "one-price policy" where customers did not need to haggle over dry goods—there was one price, as advertised, which everyone paid. Stewart's later became known for selling luxuries like fur and imported kid gloves. "Delmonico's" was one of the city's top restaurants from its opening in March 1830 to its closing in 1923.[12] Owned by a pair of Swiss brothers (Giovanni and Pietro, anglicized to John and

Peter), the restaurant was largely responsible for introducing American audiences to *haute* French cuisine. Classic dishes such as lobster Newburg, baked Alaska, and the eponymous Delmonico steak and Delmonico potatoes originated in the kitchen at Delmonico's. Placing Wallack alongside Stewart's and Delmonico's recognizes that these names are more than just family monikers—they symbolize a value invested with assurances about quality and prestige—and here all three brands are explicitly linked to the worth of a dollar. Placing these three brands in the same sphere also depicts how this value transcends industry and preserves itself as identifiable beyond the stage—elevating Wallack's brand to a household object. Wallack's place in this elevated space meant that his retirement in 1886 due to illness had caused great sorrow to his friends (audiences and theatremakers alike).[13]

Because of this, Wallack's name on the benefit held a certain draw in and of itself—a draw the producers Daly and Palmer were acutely aware of. Palmer was old hat at producing theatre in New York and became the heir apparent of Wallack's success when he acquired Wallack's theatre following the actor's death in 1888.[14] As for Daly, his reputation as the "first American regisseur" was earned through many years of theatrical management innovation.[15] Daly's theatre on Broadway and Thirtieth Street (opened 1879) was primarily a house for comedy and Daly used the business as a platform from which to launch his extremely successful ideas about how theatre should work.[16] Daly's model was that a company should have no stars, but rather function as a strong ensemble company—a stock company, but with equal attention paid to all performers.[17] As I will detail, this model was likely a large contributing factor toward the Wallack benefit's success.[18] In addition to his achievements as a manager, Daly was also a playwright and produced some of the era's most sensational melodramas.[19] These two producers combined their years of experience in New York City show business and their networks gained therein to draft and sell the theatrical commodity that was the Wallack benefit.

The eventual benefit was the work of years. The 1888 *Hamlet* was at least the second if not the third time that Daly and Palmer had approached Wallack with the idea that they might produce something in his honor or that machinations were being made for such a performance. The earliest evidence I have found of these plans is a letter from Edwin Booth to Augustin Daly dated December 16, 1886: "Having heard favorably from Mr. Jefferson regarding the proposed testimonial to Mr. Wallack on May 18, I see no obstacle in my way, unless, indeed, Mr. Barrett has arranged

166 | THEATRES OF VALUE

for me to act anywhere on my way homeward from Kansas City—where my season, according to our original plan, terminates April 30th. . . . I have written to Mr. Barrett, and took the liberty of suggesting that he should take part in the benefit performance."[20] "Mr. Barrett" was actor Lawrence Barrett—Edwin Booth's then business partner both on and off the stage.[21] "Mr. Jefferson" was comic actor Joseph Jefferson who was most famed for his portrayal of Rip Van Winkle.[22] This letter indicates that by December of 1886, Daly and Palmer had already lined up some of their key players (Jefferson and Booth, and were well on the way to securing Barrett by way of Booth) as well as a potential date—March 18, 1887.

The earliest word I have found from the producers directly about this project is a letter written to Augustin Daly by A. M. Palmer on Friday December 31, 1886:

> I am with you, of course, if you determine to carry out the Benefit and think that Barrett will prove a strong help. There are reasons why I think Mrs. Langtry would not join us, but I will take steps to find out whether I am right or not before we meet. A newspaper man asked me yesterday if a Benefit to Wallack was in contemplation, and, a day or two since, Judge Dittenhoefer asked me the same question. It seems, despite our precautions (I have not mentioned it even to my wife) the matter is leaking out.[23]

"Mrs. Langtry" was Lillie Langtry, the British American "professional beauty" and fashion plate famed for her friendship with Oscar Wilde and investment in a stable of American racehorses.[24] "Judge Dittenhoefer" was Abram Jesse Dittenhoefer: one of the then-directors of the Metropolitan Opera House (where the eventual benefit would take place). Dittenhoefer was also a collaborator of Palmer's; the two filed initial incorporation and chartered bylaws for the still-extant charity the Actors Fund in 1882.[25] Langtry and Barrett were heavy-hitting names to secure at this early phase, though only one of these names (Barrett) would remain with the project. Perhaps most crucially, this letter confirms that by December of 1886, Daly and Palmer had discussed a potential benefit in enough depth that they had already sketched out several important details (including a cast), and enough public note had been made of these plans that questions were being asked despite Palmer's insistence that the matter be kept discrete.

*"When we mean to build, we first survey the plot,
then draw the model."*

—Lord Bardolph, *Henry IV, Part 2*, I.iii

In his account of the benefit of 1888, Palmer describes these early efforts:

> In the winter of 1886–87, Mr. Daly and myself had a conversation, in the course of which the subject of arranging a testimonial benefit to Mr. Wallack was broached by Mr. Daly. . . . Wallack, we both knew, was on his last legs. We felt that the day of his final retirement was near, and we thought that we both owed him, as his juniors associated in metropolitan management, our best services in making the occasion of his retirement as pleasant, as profitable, and as notable as possible. After much thought, and after receiving Wallack's assent, we determined upon a plan of operations. It was, in brief, to give a great play, with a great cast, at the greatest theatre in America. *Hamlet* was selected as the play, the Metropolitan Opera House as the place, the middle of May as the time, and the cast we set about procuring. Daly wrote to Booth and Barrett to secure their cooperation, and I wrote to Mrs. Langtry asking her to play the part of Ophelia. Jefferson being in town we, in the course of time, had an interview with him.[26]

This formal history indicates that Palmer and Daly had conceived the entire affair as early as spring of 1887 and had received Wallack's permission to proceed with their plans. That said, this note from Palmer was published in his official account of the testimonial printed in 1893 (five years after the benefit) so it's difficult to read with anything but rosy-colored glasses. The narrative does seem to corroborate the aforementioned private letter including the details of Langtry, Barrett, and Jefferson as potential cast members.

Despite this seemingly simple narrative of the benefit's inception, Palmer himself admits that Wallack's permission did not come easily. Palmer continues:

Some of the newspapers had got hold of the fact that a "benefit for Wallack" was being talked about, and instantly tongues were set wagging about his impecuniosity, his failures in management, etc. etc. One day Mr. Daly and myself received a request from Mr. Wallack that we should call at his theatre, and confer with him upon the subject. . . . Mr. Wallack opened the conversation by saying how "kind, and lovely, and thought-ful" we had been in proposing the testimonial, and in pushing the preparations for the same; but he feared the scheme was one of dubious propriety. . . . Mr. Moss was present at his request—would we listen to him? Daly and I turned to Moss, who spoke up promptly enough, and said: "Gentlemen, I have told Mr. Wallack he ought not to take a benefit; it would be a confession of weakness and of failure in the theatre I would not care to see him make. He should not forget that this is Wallack's Theatre, and that he is still its manager. Already it is being given out in the papers that he is poor, that he has failed in management, and that you have had to come to his rescue. I am emphatically opposed to the whole thing."[27]

"Mr. Moss" is Theodore Moss, the treasurer of Wallack's business and longtime friend and business partner.[28] Parsing the preceding conversation: Wallack appears gracious and kind, truly flattered by the offer of the benefit. He employs his friend, Moss, to be the heavy and enforce the fact that the benefit is a bad idea—allowing Moss to tell Daly and Palmer why such generosity would be detrimental.

While Palmer doesn't put a specific date on this conversation, context places it in later winter/early spring of 1887—early March or so. Palmer mentions that the rumor mills were already working at the prospect of the benefit (a fact that he had touched upon in his December 1886 letter cited earlier). Further evidence implies that by February of 1887 this rumor had made a wider sweep. That month saw a rush of newspapers as far away as New Orleans, Louisiana, and Cleveland, Ohio, print advertisements that Wallack had graciously refused the proposed benefit. One piece printed in several different papers reads:

The production of *Hamlet* had been considered, and if this play was decided on Messrs. Palmer & Daly were authorized to say that Mr. Booth would, no matter at what sacrifice of existing engagements, come to New York and play Hamlet. Mr. Barrett sent a cordial message with an offer to play Laertes on the same occasion. Joseph Jefferson would play the First Grave Digger and Mrs. Langtry would study Ophelia to appear in that character for the first time. . . . Mr. Wallack said that he was profoundly touched, but that he could not possibly accept the offer. He said that he had done what he could in his day to present honest dramatic work and to cater to cultivated tastes, and was glad to have this expression of appreciation from people whose approval he valued, but pointed out that while there was so much unrelieved poverty in the city and so many charitable organizations which found difficulty in securing the funds necessary for the prosecution of their work, he could not consent to a benefit by the proposed performance.[29]

Despite Wallack's articulated fears about the public portrayal of his financial situation, this notice spins Wallack's refusal as a charitable act to others who are most in need. A note along the same lines was printed in *The Times* of Owosso, Michigan: "Lester Wallack gratefully declined a benefit tendered by Booth, Barrett, Jefferson, and Mrs. Langtry, in the production of 'Hamlet,' which might have realized $25,000."[30] This shorter missive makes first mention of a projected monetary take—and does a fair job at estimating it (the benefit's eventual profit was $20,000), though it's unclear where either of these estimates came from.[31] These reports all seem to concur that Palmer's feelings were correct: the papers had gotten the story, but they did not seem to be reacting negatively to it or Wallack. Instead, they bolstered a national excitement about this benefit's possibilities.

Though Wallack shut down talk of a benefit at this early date, the idea did not die. Mrs. John D. Townsend (Margaret Townsend Tagliapietra) approached Daly and Palmer about the notion later that year.[32] A letter written on December 7, 1887, from Townsend to Daly and Palmer states:

I believe it is a popular sentiment among the ladies of New York that Mr. John Lester Wallack has well earned a public testimonial in recognition of his long and earnest efforts as a manager and actor. At all events I am sure that the ladies deserve to aid in any undertaking of that kind in order that they may manifest their appreciation of his efforts. In an interview I had with Mr. Wallack a few nights since he was much pleased with my suggestion but said that the first offer he had of a public testimonial in his behalf came from you gentlemen and he could not assent to any more in which you as his brother managers were not to take a leading part. Mr. Wallack seemed to feel pleased with the idea that the ladies had taken an interest in the matter.[33]

Mrs. Townsend's report regarding Wallack's feelings and how they had so drastically shifted might seem odd. Though he had been embarrassed about a public fundraiser earlier that year, Townsend portrays Wallack as enthusiastic when discussing the idea in 1887. This shift might have been due to optics (accepting a benefit from a group of women perhaps seemed different from accepting a benefit from two businessmen) but was also undoubtedly linked to events that had occurred over the interim. In the spring of 1887, Wallack had fallen ill and was forced to turn over management of his house to Henry E. Abbey, a successful manager who along with his firm of Abbey, Shoeffel & Grau owned the lease to the Metropolitan Opera House.[34] In May of 1887, the parties signed a contract that gave Abbey full artistic control of Wallack's theatrical house, and Wallack/Moss as a joint enterprise retained half interest in the business.[35] This arrangement would begin at the opening of the regular season on October 10th of 1887.[36]

Palmer recalls Wallack's change of heart, though he recounts a different source for first hearing of it:

> One day, in the winter of 1887–88, Mr. Daly sent for me and said he had come from an interview with Wallack, in the course of which the latter had told him he was now ready to accept the proposed testimonial. I was quite prepared for this, for in the course of the previous summer I had met Mrs. Wallack once or twice . . . and in conversation with her I had learned that the "Governor" had changed his mind completely in regard to the propriety of our scheme, and that he would be glad of its possible benefits.[37]

Palmer's account fails to mention Townsend and instead notes that Mrs. Wallack was the first to alert him of Wallack's new thinking. It is unclear why Palmer would omit Townsend from his recollection. Speculatively, the December letter from Townsend was full of "old news"—if Palmer's account is to be taken at its word, Palmer already knew of Wallack's readiness to accept a benefit from his summertime conversations with Mrs. Wallack. Perhaps Townsend's letter was a bit too late to be significant. In any case, Townsend's role in the final benefit (if she had any) does not appear in any accounts of the occasion, formal or otherwise.

By early January of 1888, the papers had the story again. The *New York Herald* published a letter to the editor on January 9, 1888, written in response to advertisements the paper had been running earlier that month: "I see in your admirable and carefully edited dramatic column this morning that the Wallack benefit *Hamlet* will be played, with Booth as Hamlet; Barrett as Laertes, and Jefferson as the First Gravedigger. This is a step toward what I want to see before I die—a great play with a fine actor in each part. *Hamlet* is the first of our tragedies, and every part a creation. Why should all interest in a dramatic cast centre around Hamlet?"[38] The *Herald* letter goes on to suggest an all-star cast to supplement the headliners mentioned earlier who had been publicly attached to the project since the benefit's origins a year earlier. This proposed cast included:

- Philadelphia-born actor James E. Murdoch (best known for his Hamlet) as the Ghost.[39]

- Wallack company actor and stage director of Wallack's theatre John Gilbert as Polonius.[40]

- Charles Coghlan, an Irish American playwright whom Daly brought to the United States in 1876, as Laertes.[41] The *Herald* author recast Barrett as King Claudius, presumably looking to see more of Barrett than the part of Laertes would allow (or looking for more novelty in Barrett's casting).

- American theatrical jack-of-all-trades and (as readers of chapter 5 of this book will note) the Central Park statue's body model Steele MacKaye as Horatio.[42]

- Ada Rehan, one of Daly's leading ladies, as Ophelia.[43]

- Agnes Booth, actress and wife of J. B. Booth Jr., as Queen Gertrude.[44]

This *Herald* letter and its fantasy draft expresses audience buy-in for the type of project Daly and Palmer were looking to produce. The author's

172 | Theatres of Value

note that such a theatrical object would be an important thing to see in his lifetime suggests impact beyond money for something theatrical of this caliber. To the author, there was value in the artistic artifact of a starring ensemble even in a play as well-worn as *Hamlet*. Additionally, the author suggests that such an artifact would derive value from its position as a historical event. This audience member's opinion shows that Daly/Palmer's instincts regarding audience hunger for their commodity were on point.

Thirteen days after the publication of this letter, the *Herald* printed a response from Palmer:

> Whoever suggested that cast knew what he was about, too . . . for he has included all the people that Mr. Daly and myself had planned and hoped for. . . . It has been our intention to secure such a cast of players that the performance would be made remarkable in the dramatic history of our time. . . . The only trouble I can see in such a performance of *Hamlet* with this cast suggested is that attending a lack of rehearsals. It is a mistake to suppose that because you have famous actors in the cast that *Hamlet* or any other play could be done without adequate preparations.[45]

Palmer's concerns regarding the possibilities of rehearsals were, perhaps, informed by the recruiting he and Daly had already done—at this point they had definitely secured Booth, Barrett, and Jefferson, and were likely negotiating this very issue with other potentials.

By late January of 1888, the benefit was fleshed out enough and widely enough talked about that a paper in Edenton, North Carolina (*Fisherman and Farmer*), published nearly an identical notice on January 20th and February 3rd. The January 20th piece held a bit more hesitance: "It is said that Lester Wallack's benefit will be given at the Metropolitan Opera House, New York, next May. *Hamlet* will be presented, with Edwin Booth as Hamlet, Lawrence Barrett as Laertes and Joseph Jefferson as the First Gravedigger."[46] On February 3rd the same paper was much more certain of these details: "At Lester Wallack's benefit in the Metropolitan Opera House, New York, next May, *Hamlet* will be played, with Booth in the title part, Barrett as Laertes, and Jefferson as the first grave digger."[47] It's worth noting that the paper got most of the details correct both times—Booth, Barrett, and Jefferson were all in the final cast—though the final benefit saw Barrett cast as the Ghost rather than Laertes. It is also worth noting that this is the first public mention of the benefit that doesn't also include Langtry.

Turning back to formal published versions of the history described here, the narrative of the benefit's inception as told by the commemorative program is very different. Knowing the struggle that went into getting Wallack to accept a benefit, it's almost comical to read the program's printed correspondence from Daly/Palmer to Wallack dated March 19, 1888:

> A year ago we proposed that you permit us to inaugurate some public demonstration in your honor but you did not seem to think it timely; we feel now like insisting upon your acceptance of the expression of regard which we are sure that all your managerial co-laborers, your professional brethren, your journalistic admirers and your social friends are but waiting for a word from you to utter in the fullness of their hearts. We have thought of some exceptional play, with a unique cast, as giving the most fitting outlet for this sentiment, and as affording the best opportunity to unite every element of friendly interest in your behalf and we now beg that you will favorably consider the spirit in which we urge your present acceptance of our proposal.[48]

Wallack's return letter (again, as printed in the commemorative program) is dated March 24, 1888: "The reception of your letter of the 19th is the most valued and gratifying incident of a long and somewhat eventful professional life. . . . All I can say is that the spirit and tone of the letter are so kind—so considerate and so flattering—that I should deem it ungracious in me did I make any reply but one of a willing and grateful acceptance."[49] It's strange to think that the *Herald* might print ads for a benefit as early as January 1888, but that the benefit's recipient wouldn't formally accept the gesture until the end of March. Even if the *Herald's* ads (which I have yet to find due to the rarity of extant *Herald* copies from this time period—though they are referenced in the January 9th letter) hadn't published a formal connection between the performance and Wallack, the preceding *Fisherman and Farmer* notices did. This witness mark casts aspersions on the authenticity of these program letters. Daly and Palmer almost certainly edited the dates on them—if not fabricated their contents entirely, rewrote them from memory, or asked the senders to produce these letters with a wink and a nudge. Another convenient

174 | THEATRES OF VALUE

fact of these letters that supports the hypothesis that they were written for the program is how neatly packaged they are—Daly/Palmer's letter succinctly and cleanly presents the narrative of what they propose, when they have previously proposed it, and what they next need from Wallack. These elements are presented breathlessly and floridly with great pomp and circumstance—and it's easy to imagine that Daly/Palmer might have so written for a wide audience such as they intended for the program.

Dating these letters middle or end of March 1888 for a May benefit must, then, be a rhetorical move. The story Daly and Palmer drafted in the program was that the entire benefit from conception to execution took two months (a pithy period considering factors theatrical and non). In so shaping the story, Daly and Palmer also drafted a narrative that theatrical production was a speedy process, and/or that this benefit was almost "meant to be" since so many highly billed theatrical stars could so swiftly be assembled. It created a fantasy about how quickly and smoothly theatrical labor can be gathered and deployed. This fantasy was a simplification of the complex machinations that went into the event, machinations that—as every thespian can attest—might derail the final product at any turn.

"Now name the rest of the players."

—Bottom, *A Midsummer Night's Dream*, I.ii

As I've discussed in previous chapters, Edwin Booth as Hamlet was an extremely marketable commodity and it's not a far leap to suggest that the inclusion of Booth and the decision to act *Hamlet* went hand in hand given his fame in the role. The first inkling I have found of correspondence between Daly/Palmer and Booth on this matter is the letter from Edwin Booth to Augustin Daly dated December 16, 1886, which I have cited previously. Despite Booth's initial agreement to give his Hamlet for the occasion, he soon had second thoughts. On January 27, 1887, Booth wrote to Daly: "As I am to play Hamlet for the Couldock benefit, I prefer to give Richelieu for Mr. Wallack's and would advise by all means to have a varied bill for the occasion—it would allow a larger audience."[50] Booth here references British-born actor Charles Walter Couldock who became a well-beloved sentimental actor on the American stage and who, by way of proof as to how small the nineteenth-century theatrical world was, played in the original cast of *Our American Cousin*.[51] Booth's suggestion for a change in bill can be taken at face value—it is plausible to believe that Booth truly thought it would raise more money to act a varied bill. Despite the economic implications that Booth cites, Daly/Palmer did not find Booth's new proposal to be a good one. While Daly/Palmer's insistence upon *Hamlet* might have partially been due to the marketability of Shakespeare, this is likely only a piece of the puzzle. *Richelieu* offered fewer plum parts in which to cast other star actors.

Booth's proposal also hints at some degree of ignorance about Daly/Palmer's plans. Standard practice for benefits would have included a single star actor in a role he was famous for—hence Booth's assumption that he could slot in any of his canonical plays just as handily as any other. This is a strange conjecture given the fact that Booth had already mentioned Jefferson in the 1886 letter but hints that Daly/Palmer might not have yet revealed the full extent of their plans to Booth.

The close association of Booth and Barrett in relation to the Wallack benefit taps into an already-successful brand merger that was relatively contemporary to the benefit's performance. In early 1887, Booth and Barrett were beginning to solidify a professional relationship that would prove extremely lucrative. Barrett biographer Elwyn Barron romantically insists that Booth was getting older and growing tired of touring, but Barrett's upbeat spirit and *joie de vivre* made him an invigorating companion for the aging actor (then fifty-four).[52] By September of 1887, the two had set off on tour together—a tour that would last nearly two years playing Shakespearean roles in opposition to each other (Othello and Iago, Brutus and Cassius, Hamlet and Laertes, Macbeth and Macduff, etc.)[53] It is almost certainly because of this tour that Palmer positions Booth and Barrett together in his account of the benefit, cited previously. Palmer notes that Daly wrote Booth/Barrett in early 1887 to secure them for the benefit.[54] These Booth letters, then, are likely part of the correspondence Palmer is recounting. The witness mark here is the erasure of a proposal about the change in bill—from *Hamlet* to *Richelieu* (notably, *Richelieu* was one of the plays Booth and Barrett performed on joint tour, which made it a logical choice for the two stars). This erasure suggests a few things: 1) that Daly/Palmer did not too long dwell on Booth's proposal, 2) that perhaps Palmer didn't want to paint Booth as someone who would be difficult to work with, and 3) that the picture Daly/Palmer wished to paint of the benefit even in hindsight was rosy and cleaner than reality.

176 | THEATRES OF VALUE

Returning to the souvenir program shows even more casting witness marks. There, a letter is printed from Booth and Barrett (presumably sent from the road of their 1887/1888 joint star tour). This letter, dated April 2, 1888, confirms the pair's involvement in the benefit:

> Sirs, we have copies of your correspondence with Mr. Wallack regarding the mark of respect which it is intended to offer him, as arranged when we met in New York in January. We assure yourselves and Mr. Wallack of our sincere anxiety to do all in our power to make the event worthy of the public endorsement. The selection of *Hamlet* as the play will be agreeable to us. . . . We would suggest that the night selected be the 21st of May.[55]

This letter, with its formal acceptance and ready summation of the details reeks of fabrication for publication. The date that Booth/Barrett propose here is also key because it directly contradicts a private and unpublished letter from Palmer to Daly dated April 6, 1888:

> I have a letter from Barrett suggesting that the Wallack benefit should take place on Monday evening, the 21st, instead of on Wednesday evening the 23rd, as we had arranged. He says this will be more convenient to Mr. Booth and himself. Speaking of the matter yesterday to some other managers, and suggesting to them the propriety of their closing up their houses on the night of the benefit, they said that it would be more convenient for them to close up on Monday night than on any other night.[56]

The switch from Wednesday to Monday is notably anachronistic with the program letter. It is possible that the letter Palmer is referencing is some version of the program letter, but the program letter only outlines May 21st as a potential date and fails to mention May 23rd at all. Again, the Booth/Barrett program letter presents the most straightforward version of the story written in ornamental prose, and this shifted detail casts aspersions on its truth.

Another noteworthy item to come from Palmer's letter here is the assurance of other business owners that they would be willing to close their theatres the night of the benefit in support of it. This suggests the depths of Daly/Palmer/Wallack's networks professionally, the goodwill all three had secured from the greater theatrical community, and the span of this buy-in. Other theatres were willing to sacrifice their bottom line for an evening to secure this benefit's success and that is no small mark of comradery from the New York theatre industry. The benefit would, by these assurances, be a literal showstopper.

Negotiations with Booth over the evening's bill were only the beginning of Daly/Palmer's casting woes. While the benefit's headlining men were (seemingly) easy to enlist, filling the parts of Ophelia and Gertrude were entirely different matters.

Initially, Palmer had hoped to cast Lillie Langtry in the part of Ophelia. Though he had doubts regarding whether she would acquiesce, he pursued the matter. On January 28, 1887, at least two letters were written from Palmer to Daly regarding the issue. One says: "I have a letter from Mrs. Langtry in which she promises to play Ophelia for the Wallack Testimonial."[57] A second dated that same day indicates that perhaps Langtry's first letter was not as firm a commitment as Palmer had thought, "I am sorry there is such a change in the plan of the proposed performance as I detailed the cast of *Hamlet* to Mrs. Langtry, and judged she was induced to consent to act for the sake of the association with so many distinguished names. However, I will try again. We could spare Barrett and I cannot understand why, if there is to be any performance shown by Booth, it should not be for Wallack."[58] This letter hints at some potential trouble—though it is unclear whether the trouble sits with Langtry, Booth, Barrett, or some permutation of the three. Additionally, it's unclear which letter was sent first—though here I have presented them as acquiescence followed by revocation, these just as easily could have occurred as precarity followed by affirmation.

Either way, unfortunately for Daly and Palmer, Lillie Langtry responded by inaction. On February 10, 1887, Palmer writes to Daly: "I have heard nothing further from Mrs. Langtry."[59] If there were any lingering Langtry longings after this, they were set to rest by timing. Langtry had committed to being on a California tour in the spring of 1888 and thus could not accept the role when the benefit finally did occur.[60] The part passed to Polish-born actress Madame Helena Modjeska.[61]

The role of Gertrude proved monumentally more difficult for producers to cast. A letter from Palmer to Daly in May of 1888 recapping the benefit (Daly had departed for London in the final weeks beforehand to manage the Gaiety Theatre and needed this after-action report) indicates

178 | Theatres of Value

that the part had been offered to Ada Rehan, then for reasons unknown passed to Rose Eytinge: "This cast underwent several changes before it was finally arranged . . . Rose Eytinge (who was substituted for Rehan) and several others backed out; but I really think the performance gained by their doing so."[62] Rose Eytinge was an actress who worked steadily at Wallack's from 1865 onward. She had previously appeared onstage with Booth and was known for her power as well as her defiance of the traditional nineteenth-century casting in strict lines of business.[63]

Despite Palmer's fairly smooth narrative, that doesn't seem to be the full story here. Curiously, a fourth name is mentioned in the role of the Queen in advertisements printed on March 21st and April 19th. On April 19th the *Evening World* reports the cast as: "Mr. Booth will appear as Hamlet, Mr. Barrett as Laertes, Joseph Jefferson as the first grave-digger, Modjeska as Ophelia and Mrs. Bowers as the Queen."[64] Elizabeth (née Crocker) Bowers was an actress, theatre manager, and playwright. She performed in New York after her debut at the Park Theatre in 1846, but had since moved on to manage both the Walnut Street Theatre and Philadelphia Academy of Music.[65] Bowers had previously played Gertrude to Booth's Hamlet, making her a logical choice for the part.[66] The letter from Booth/Barrett in the souvenir program (dated, as a reminder, April 2, 1888) also mentions the inclusion of Bowers in the cast.[67] Despite Palmer's omission of Bowers in his letter to Daly, he does include her in the casting chain in his account of the testimonial. He says that "Miss Eytinge was to have played the Queen-Mother, Mrs. E.B. Bowers having declined."[68] It seems, then, that the aforementioned newspaper ads (and the Booth/Barrett program letter) were written in the short window between Bowers' and Eytinge's castings, but before Bowers had declined formally. This leaves the question: Why would Bowers' involvement be left in the souvenir program at all? I have previously shown that many details of the letters reprinted in that document are suspect; why would this have been left when others were likely changed? It's a strange oversight, but perhaps a relic of how difficult the part of Gertrude was to cast, or perhaps a testament to how rushed the program was in its composition (a story I will relate in more depth later).

So, after a great deal of passing to and fro, the role of Gertrude came to rest on the shoulders of Rose Eytinge. Eytinge seems to have accepted the role but (much to everyone's chagrin) withdrew at the last minute. Palmer relates:

She accepted the part, when I offered it to her, with a great deal of effusiveness. The program as first printed contained her name. The first rehearsal was called for Friday, May 18th, on Wallack's stage. When I arrived, most of the cast had assembled. I looked about for Miss Eytinge. She was not there. We waited; her scenes were passed; she did not come. I sent a messenger to her house. He returned with word that Miss Eytinge had gone downtown. By this time rehearsal was over. On my return to my office I found a note which revealed to me what I had already suspected—the lady had tricked me. The note said she had suddenly been called to Chicago on business, and she was obliged to give up the part. The truth was she never went out of town at all. I think she "funked" (as we say when one is afraid to play a part) at the last moment.[69]

The letter that Eytinge wrote to Palmer on May 18, 1888, certainly hints at insincerity:

I am grieved and distressed beyond measure to tell you I cannot take part in the testimonial to Mr. Wallack next Monday Evening: I am called to Chicago on business so urgent and impressive as to admit no delay. And, as the timing of my detentions there is dependent upon business complications entirely beyond my control, I dare not promise to be able to return in time for Monday night. I therefore, most reluctantly, resign the part of the Queen, and my only relief in this dilemma is the thought that you will have no difficulty in obtaining a substitute for me. My summons to Chicago at this time is most unexpected.[70]

Whatever was at the heart of the matter, Eytinge's absence from rehearsal was noted by the public. An article appeared in New York paper *The Sun* on May 19: "The first rehearsal of the principals for the Wallack testimonial performance of 'Hamlet' was held at Wallack's Theatre yesterday noon. Rose Eytinge, who is to play queen Gertrude, was the only one of the principals absent."[71]

True to Eytinge's supposition, Palmer and Daly quickly replaced her. Working through Barrett, they enlisted the help of an actress by the name

180 | THEATRES OF VALUE

of Gertrude Kellogg, the daughter of Brooklyn businessman and spiritualist Charles Kellogg White.[72] Kellogg recounts May 18, 1888, in her diary:

> Late in the Afternoon had a telegram from Mr. Barrett crying that I am to play the Queen in *Hamlet* at the great Wallack Benefit at the Metropolitan Opera House next Monday night and asking me to see him at the theatre tonight. Of course I went over. It seems that Miss Eytinge threw them over at the last moment and Mr. Barrett said if they would destroy all the printing with her name in it and get out now with my name, I could play the part. Of course I am delighted.[73]

At long last, Daly/Palmer had found their Gertrude.

"Report is changeable."

—Earl of Kent, *King Lear*, IV.vii

It is already fairly clear that the Wallack benefit was successful by several different measures. Because of this success, a great deal of care was necessary in handling reports of the benefit's monetary outcomes. At this point, Daly/Palmer's editing of the souvenir program is evident. The fact that editing was happening is not the relevant magician's hand to watch since the act of editing isn't extraordinary. Rather the ways in which Daly/Palmer edited, how information about the benefit was processed and sold, is the trick. What was mentioned in accounts of the benefit, who/what was omitted, and what scrambling was relevant to these stories? All of these tensions were evident in the care that went into public discourse surrounding the fate of the benefit's profits. A March 1888 letter from Palmer to Daly discusses the details. Palmer writes:

> The other night at the Irony-Inman I had a brief conversation with Wallack in regards to Mrs. Wallack's having the money. He said that, while he was glad that the money was to be given to her, both of them felt that no announcement of that intention should be made. He seemed to fear it would, in some way, reflect upon him. I have, therefore, omitted all allusions

to it in the circular. Please change anything you do not like or add anything you please.[74]

Wallack's sensitivity in guarding his financial need is a topic that the benefit producers circle back to again and again. While the preceding notes mention Wallack's pride, this issue also extends to Wallack's fear of his debtors. Despite finally acquiescing to the benefit, Wallack remained uncomfortable with soliciting the public (even indirectly) for funds on his behalf, likely with a mind to how such solicitations might look to those whom Wallack owed money. Palmer's account elucidates:

> Our design was to raise as large an amount of money as possible, and, in order to keep it out of the hands of Wallack's creditors, Daly suggested that Wallack should decline to receive it himself, but ask us to give it to his wife. All our correspondence with him, intended for publication, was prepared with this end in view. . . . We calculated that, with what would be taken at the doors, we should realize $30,000, or perhaps $40,000 . . . "I want her [Mrs. Wallack] to have it, every dollar of it," said the veteran; "but bless my soul! I owe something to my own dignity and I mustn't give it out that I am afraid to have anything in my own name." So the letter about Mrs. Wallack was suppressed, and the note published in the program, in which the disposition of the money is referred to in rather ambiguous terms, was substituted in its place.[75]

It is again noteworthy how carefully Daly/Palmer presented their story to the public, as well as Palmer's casual reference to letters "intended for publication." This remembrance from Palmer also indicates the rhetoric that went into selecting letters for the program—suppressing some and publishing only those that would tell the story intended. Since Wallack had died in September of 1888, Palmer's frank 1893 account was able to reveal more details than anything released at the time of the benefit as the need for discretion had passed.

Another item of note is the inflated benefit take. The February 1887 *Times* article (cited earlier) published early estimates about prospective profit that hovered closer to $20,000. Here, suddenly, Palmer inflates that number by 150 to 200 percent. It is unclear what back-end number-crunching yielded either estimate, but a second letter from Palmer to Daly written

182 | THEATRES OF VALUE

on April 10, 1888, explicitly addresses the fate of the receipts, as well as some clues about how money was made via the benefit.

> [Both Mr. Wallack] and Mrs. Wallack are rather afraid that they will be placed in an embarrassing position if too much is said regarding the disposition of the receipts, and they prefer to leave the matter wholly in our hands without any expression of a wish on Mrs. Wallack's part. Wallack also prefers that we should rely wholly on the receipts of the performance, and not solicit subscriptions. He says that the subscriptions, besides being a little hurtful to his pride, will, he fears, interfere with the receipts of the performance.[76]

Wallack's hesitance to include subscription in the benefit's take is here presented as both a shyness about accepting charity and also as a strategy about how best to make money. Given the success of Daly, Palmer, and Wallack in the New York theatrical world, this strategy is well worth note. First: the notion of soliciting "subscriptions" might have held several different connotations to the trio of managers. The modern sense of subscribing to a theatrical season for which one might receive choice seats to all shows contained therein was an activated meaning of the term during Wallack's time. During the nineteenth century, such subscriber-only tickets might be provided either to public events or private shows held only for subscribers.[77] In another context, subscription lists were donor lists for moneys given to charitable and civic causes.[78] Here, Wallack and Daly/Palmer seem to be discussing a subscription list that would bolster the benefit's take but perhaps would damage ticket sales as subscribers opted to forego the box office in favor of simply giving whatever sum of money they felt best. Whether this agreement about subscriptions stood in the way of profit-making is difficult to say. Was Daly/Palmer's inflated projection reliant on subscription lists? Since the benefit sold out, the gap between expected ($30,000–$40,000) and actual profits ($20,000) was certainly not the result of empty seats. It is also possible that Palmer misremembered this detail (again, the narrative was published several years after the benefit and substantially longer since such an estimate would have been calculated), but why would he publish a number so distant from the final benefit take in an account largely intended to document the benefit's success? This witness mark remains a strange discrepancy in the story.

Erasing the Lines | 183

While Daly/Palmer did not take up subscriptions (on Wallack's request), they did hold an auction for boxes that inflated the final take. Palmer recounts:

> The boxes were sold at auction in the Madison Square Theatre. . . . The upstart price of the boxes was $60 each, but they averaged, with premiums, $160 each. The highest premium paid was $500—by Wallack's old friend and leading lady, Mrs. John Hoey. The next highest was $250 by that charming woman, Agnes Ethel Tracy. James Gordon Bennett, whom Daly and I (and Wallack too) had expected would pay a very large premium for a box, waited until the premiums got down below $200, and took a box at $150. . . . Before the curtain rose on the first act of *Hamlet* the receipts were exactly $21,558.57.[79]

Mrs. John Hoey née Josephine Shaw succeeded Laura Keene as the leading lady at Wallack's and, in the early 1860s, was considered "the best dressed actress in New York."[80] James Gordon Bennett was James Gordon Bennett Jr., heir to his father's newspaper the *Herald*.[81] Agnes Ethel Tracy was an actress in Daly's company in the late 1860s and managed by Palmer in 1872. She was moderately well known in her heyday but faded into some obscurity after her retirement in 1890.[82] Palmer's comments about the auction draw clear parallels between the social class commodity of a prime space in New York City theatrical networks and the product Daly/Palmer were selling. Additionally, the cutting comment about Bennett shows a connection between the health of network connections and Daly/Palmer's commodity. Daly/Palmer sold an experience, but they were relying on social status to imbue a sense of value into higher premium boxes and the social commodity translated directly to Daly/Palmer's bottom line.

Outside the theatrical elite, the hoi polloi were also eager to secure tickets. While perhaps this comes as no surprise to the reader given the general levels of excitement expressed in public facing sources quoted earlier, ticket sales were not a given—especially in light of elevated ticket prices. Palmer recalls:

> Observing early that there was the greatest interest excited concerning the performance, I determined to adopt the highest scale of prices ever asked for a dramatic entertainment

184 | THEATRES OF VALUE

> in America. It was as follows: Boxes to be sold by auction. Orchestra chairs, $10. Dress-circle, $5 and $4. Balcony seats, $2. Top gallery, $1. Admission, $2. Consulting with the treasurer of the Metropolitan Opera House, the late Mr. Chipman, in regard to these prices, he was very incredulous about my being able to fill the house. He said such prices would stagger the most inveterate amusement-seeker. "You had better halve them, Mr. Palmer. You will get more money." But I had made up my mind and, hit or miss, I was determined to go ahead. The result was beyond my most sanguine expectations.[83]

Mr. Chipman was George R. Chipman, who died in 1888 and was then-treasurer of the Metropolitan Opera House.[84] In spite of Chipman's warning, Palmer's instincts seem to have served him well: all of the more expensive tickets sold out quite early in the box office process: "Before tickets were ready to be delivered I had in my hands money enough not only to pay for every seat in the house, but $5,000 besides, which I was obliged to return to the senders. Not a seat for this entertainment was sold except in this way. The only things ever sold at the box office of the Metropolitan Opera House were the admission tickets of $2 and $1."[85]

Ticket sales had been so robust that the producer had had a hard time keeping up with them. Many were shocked at how quickly the benefit sold out. Palmer describes:

> People were glad to sit or stand anywhere, so long as they could catch a glimpse of the stage. Just before the doors were opened I had occasion to go to the front of the house, and I was pointed out by an elderly man and woman, as the manager. They told me they had come five hundred miles to see the performance and that the man in the box office refused to sell them even an admission ticket (by this time we had been notified by the police to stop the sale). I took it upon myself to sell just two more tickets.[86]

In reports of the benefit, it wasn't just the number of audience members that signaled success but also the quality of those audience members. This is made explicit by a note in the *Post* printed the morning of the benefit:

> Everything is now in readiness for the Wallack Testimonial performance of *Hamlet* in the Metropolitan Opera-house this

evening, and there can be no doubt that the occasion will prove to be one of the most brilliant theatrical events that have ever occurred in this city. . . . Every seat in the house, as has been announced before, has been sold, and twice as many could have been disposed of. After the third act of the tragedy, Mr. Wallack himself will appear upon the stage and address the audience, which will probably be the largest and most distinguished he has ever faced in his long and honorable career.[87]

The *Post* article not only indicates Daly/Palmer's success in attracting audience members but also praises how "distinguished" this assembly is as a mark of favor toward Wallack and, by extension, his benefit.

A second clipping, a review of the production, notes similar dynamics at play: "In the social significance of the audience, in the number and individual rank and hearty co-operation of his fellow actors, and in the magnitude of the financial result, the benefit cannot be paralleled in our history."[88] Here, the social capital generated by the audience as aggregate connected directly to the benefit's value as both a cultural object and an economic success. In this testament of the object's value, Mirowski's social theory of value (that value is defined socially rather than individually) reflects directly in the community of consumers who came together to behold Daly/Palmer's commodity.[89] By these papers' accountings, value can be calculated in direct proportion to the relative prestige of an item's consumers—a remixed conception of Perry's theory of value (that the value of a thing is directly proportionate to how much personal esteem or interest is held in it).[90] Daly/Palmer's commodity, then, reflected its value in and by the audience assembly—and as such can be called successful because of these metrics.

Hints of this success can also be found in the attitudes of those involved with the benefit even before the critics' reviews were in. Gertrude Kellogg recorded in her diary: "The rehearsal was fun but the evening was funner. Such crowds before and behind the curtain! Mrs. Wallack gave Madame Modjeska, Rose Coghlann, and myself large bouquets of pink and white roses. Madam Modjeska's Ophelia was a lovely performance. I think I held my own with the others."[91] Kellogg's impressions of success couched in the experience of performing are also anchored in her impression of the merits of her own (and her colleagues') performances, impressions influenced heavily by audience reception. To Kellogg, success was evidenced by the crowds, the accolades, and the feeling of a great show.

> "Come, let's see the event."
>
> —Fabian, *Twelfth Night*, III.iv

Anticipation was rife for the Wallack benefit and both audiences and performers were excited for the product—but what was the product on sale actually like? I have argued that Daly/Palmer used a "strong ensemble" method of fusing star actors' cultural capital to make a product worth selling. The anchor of this product was Booth's Hamlet. In 1888, Edwin Booth was fifty-five years old and nearing the end of his stage career. His Hamlet was well known to audiences—a tried-and-true commodity. But Booth was the anomaly that evening; every cast member besides was asked to present a novelty—slotted into a role they had never before played for a New York audience.

The logical conclusion of a Booth/Barrett *Hamlet* would have been to see Barrett in the part of Laertes—a part he played to Booth's Hamlet often during their joint tour. As I have previously mentioned, Barrett was originally slated for this role but was shifted into the much smaller role of the Ghost (though when this shift occurred is unclear). While Barrett had played the Ghost before, he had never played it in New York.[92] Barrett's name was a clear draw, particularly in opposition to Booth, though Daly/Palmer would certainly have made the over-under calculation when substituting the long-forgotten Eben Plympton in the role. Plympton was a popular leading man at Wallack's, though he remains all-but-absent from contemporary scholarship.[93] While I can find no direct indications from Daly/Palmer about why this change was made, one hint comes from an article in the *Tribune*, which reports: "Great interest attached to Mr. Barrett's performance of the Ghost, a part in which he had not previously been seen here."[94] The novelty of Barrett's ghost in New York was, perhaps, more of a draw than seeing him duel Booth yet again. In a model they would replicate with other cast members, Daly and Palmer remixed well-known cultural capital to find new bankable value within it.

Modjeska's Ophelia was another novel performance in the mélange. Though Modjeska was widely known as an actress, she had only played Ophelia once before at the very beginning of her American career, on August 25, 1877, at the California Theatre in San Francisco.[95] While some papers praised her Ophelia at that time, others found that her declamatory acting style was better fit for non-Shakespearean roles.[96] One notable difference in Modjeska's early acting that might have influenced this opinion was her speech: early in her career Modjeska's accent was very heavy. While it softened through the years, it never disappeared and returned most heavily when she was anxious or dealing with "foreign-sounding speech."[97] This in mind, Modjeska's Ophelia of 1888 was likely still accented but boasted clearer diction than her Ophelia of eleven years prior.

Perhaps this mellowing of Modjeska's accent might account for some of the shifted opinions Modjeska received from her critics. Pages upon pages of glowing reviews of Modjeska's performance in the Wallack benefit can be found in a scrapbook held by the New York Public Library. One clipping claims that Modjeska brought out something in Booth's Hamlet that had not yet been seen by audiences: "Having Mme. Modjeska for an Ophelia it can hardly be seen that some of the subtlest and tenderest lines met with a stimulating object not always encountered in Mr. Booth's performance of Hamlet."[98] A second clipping from this collection focuses more specifically upon Modjeska's performance. This one claims: "Her mad scenes were exceedingly pathetic, and wonderful in their variety. Her love for Hamlet in the early scenes is marked very strongly, and her conception of the charac-ter is generally stronger and more sounding in contrasts than that adopted by most actresses. The personality in her hands acquires greater tragic significance, without losing anything in the way of gentleness of charm."[99] Modjeska's mad scenes were said to "touch the audience more closely than any other incident of the evening. It was beautifully done."[100] It's safe to say that Modjeska's Ophelia the night of the Wallack benefit was a hit.

Yet another Wallack benefit novelty was Joseph Jefferson III in the part of the gravedigger. Having made his name by performing Rip Van Winkle, Jefferson was a staple of American comedy. The part of the gravedigger was a rare late-career role debut for the comedian. At the time of the testimonial, Jefferson was acting two roles almost exclusively: Bob Acres in *The Rivals*, and Rip Van Winkle.[101] Audiences appreciated the change of pace; his gravedigger was hailed as "deliciously humorous—a gem of artistic low comedy."[102] Much like Modjeska, Jefferson's name proved an audience draw; but more than just his name, the opportunity to see this actor act in a part unfamiliar to his fans was a rare treat.

In general, critics were generous with their praise (as, it seems, was the audience). It was reported that "there were storms of applause from the time that the curtain was raised until it fell. . . . Every one was cheered."[103] Even after the final curtain, the audience was unwilling to disband. Palmer recalls the aftermath:

188 | THEATRES OF VALUE

> After the performance was finished, there was more enthusiasm, and there were more calls. Booth had a tremendous demonstration, as had Barrett, Jefferson, Modjeska, and Florence. At last, after all these had retired and as the audience kept calling, I went forward, and was received with great kindness, the entire audience apparently being on their feet, waving handkerchiefs and shouting. When silence was restored I told them in as few words as possible how proud and happy I was that partly through my humble efforts so good a result had been achieved for the chief of our American managerial guild, and that, in point of fact, I should always regard that as one of the proudest days of my life. . . . I retired amidst more cheering and applause, and the audience slowly dispersed.[104]

The ovations show the audience's enthusiasm for the event they had just witnessed. The waiting, the cost, the crowds, and the hype (it seems) had all been worthwhile to them and they were more than willing to demonstrate how worthwhile.

Palmer was similarly pleased with the results of his and Daly's efforts. In his remembrances of the event, he reports, "The performance was in all respects a fine one. It was generally conceded that all the disappointment there was in it was of an agreeable nature; everything and everybody was better than the most sanguine had hoped."[105] This public documentation of the producer's satisfaction was matched by privately documented satisfaction. Just moments after the benefit's grand finale, Palmer sent the following telegraph to Daly: "Think we may congratulate each other with reason everything has passed off without a hitch and to the great satisfaction of everybody the money result is 21,550 and I shall hand Mrs. Wallack tomorrow in your name and my own 20,000."[106] On May 22, Palmer had the time to write a longer letter to Daly detailing the event:

> Our grand benefit is over—thank God! As you can imagine I am thoroughly worn out with the attention to petty details which it has required from me during the past two weeks. The performance was really a splendid one, Booth, Jefferson, and Modjeska covering themselves with glory. . . . I think he [Wallack] feels very grateful. . . . You will probably be disappointed, as I was, in the programme. I took every pain to get something very striking and unique and, with the usual

result. . . . However there is always consolation in the thought that they might have been much worse, and, as everybody appears to be satisfied with them, I should not mourn long over this. . . . P.S.: I have just handed Mrs. Wallack a certified cheque for $20,000; the expense was about $1,700.[107]

Palmer's dissatisfaction with the program, that document that keeps resurfacing as an unreliable narrator in this tale, is notable in light of one seemingly albeit curiously unanticipated by-product of the benefit's success—the birth of a feverish market for mementos of the evening, including the souvenir program. These booklets seem to have been one of the evening's hottest commodities. Supply of these programs apparently ran short early, which led to a scramble for purchasing them and a sliding scale of pricing on the spontaneous aftermarket. The *Sun* reports: "Perhaps not enough were printed to supply a demand that was of necessity voracious, because this was a souvenir event entirely out of the common. It is certain, however, that some of the distributors of them saw a dollar in sight, for they disappeared with remarkable celerity. After the first act had begun they were to be had at a sliding scale of prices. On the lower floor it was possible to possess one at the outlay of $1.50. A *Sun* reporter climbed up to the fifth tier and bought two for half a dollar."[108] This location-specific cost inflation did not end inside the theatre. The *Evening News* recalls, "Even the programs could have been sold last night for $5 each. I was offered that amount for mine by an energetic corridor fiend."[109] Even despite Palmer's dissatisfaction with this particular commodity, it was successful in that it sold (and sold well).

This demonstration of audience voracity for consumption of the formal history is in some ways Daly/Palmer's last laugh. Audiences bought and preserved these souvenir programs assuring that this official history is (by and large) what would last not just in popular but also archival memory; in my hunt for documentary evidence of the Wallack benefit I encountered this souvenir program frequently preserved in multiple archives (sometimes with multiple copies even in a single archive).[110] In drafting a tangible commodity that preserved a sense of the benefit's history, Daly/Palmer ensured that they maintained control over the benefit's narrative—and this control was reaffirmed by Palmer's published account some years later. This act of editing and the market demand it reflected creates a lasting memory of Daly/Palmer's impressions of the New York theatrical market. In so documenting their benefit's success, Daly and

Palmer were able to use their own voices to narrate the terms of their success, and to ensure the story was packaged in a way that felt (to them) correct. In analyzing the benefit's dramaturgy of value, this story speaks both in words and in silence—in the things it says and (just as loudly) in the things it tries not to say. But even those items omitted from Daly/Palmer's official story have not been completely expunged from historical record and the witness marks of their editing shows footprints of the path Daly/Palmer took to create this successful theatrical object.

Conclusion

The Dramaturgy of Value at Large

It's December 2021 and I'm at the Union Square Holiday Market. It's a fairly mild winter day; a light jacket and some half-mitts are all I need to keep warm. To me, this is perfect New York City walking weather. I've opted to mask because the threat of COVID-19 looms ever-present in packed communal spaces. I'm not the only one. All around me, masked New Yorkers bustle between adorable semi-permanent chalet stalls to browse wares of sundry varieties: jewelry, art prints, tchotchkes (both festive and non), artisanal chocolate, seasonal outerwear, soaps, candles, spices . . . there's precious little by way of casual gifting that can't be found at the Union Square Holiday Market. I'm entranced by a booth selling antique prints and clippings, particularly a page out of *Frank Leslie's Illustrated Newspaper* with a large image depicting the 1865 fire at Barnum's American Museum, though ultimately I decide that the $195 price tag is a little too rich for my blood. I *do* spend $25 on a replica print of Theodore Muller's 1850 lithograph *New York et Brooklyn—Vue prise au dessus dela batterie* (Bird's-eye view of the battery), which now hangs outside my home office.

Around the corner is another booth, a booth I know well due to my literary proclivities. The Unemployed Philosophers Guild is a Brooklyn-based tongue-in-cheek dispensary of intellectual-adjacent paraphernalia: finger puppets based on literary figures, "secular saint" candles featuring Ruth Bader Ginsburg and Jane Austen, a mug with Henry VIII and wives (the wives vanish when you pour hot liquid into it), and so on. Of course, there's a hearty section of Shakespeareana: Shakespearemints to freshen your breath, Lady Macbeth's guest soap (actual soap wrapped in tartan

192 | THEATRES OF VALUE

emblazoned with "out damn spot!" and a blood spot), the Much Ado about Nothings noting set with various sizes of sticky notes, among others. Over the years, many a gift has been procured for me here (what do you gift an acquaintance whose most salient features include a lifelong interest in Shakespeare and a quirky sense of humor?) I have a small stack of the note-taking sets, a felted Shakespeare Christmas tree ornament, a William Shakespeare secular saint candle, and (perhaps my favorite) a Shakespearean Insults mug that were all acquired (no doubt) from this very stand.

The mental jugglings that go into any purchase are everyday expressions of the dramaturgy of value. What is this item for? Why am I purchasing it? How much do I like the person I'm gifting this to? Is the occasion fit for the magnitude of the gift? Will *where* I bought the gift make a difference? Can I get the same thing cheaper online? Does the cost difference matter to me more than supporting local businesses? These questions, and many others like them, create a mental flow-chart that eventually leads to the decision: to buy or not to buy.

About a third of a mile north of the market is Edwin Booth's The Players club and, just in front of it, Gramercy Park. Inside Gramercy is one of the most publicly prevalent and lasting images of Edwin Booth: a statue of the actor in the character of Hamlet unveiled on November 13, 1918, to memorialize Booth on his birthday twenty-five years after his death.

Getting into this gated park is one of the most closely guarded privileges of New York City real estate. Keys to Gramercy Park are numbered, nearly impossible to duplicate, and the locks on the gated property are changed annually.[1] To enter Gramercy and thus have the elite privilege of a visit with Booth from beyond the gate, you could (perhaps) own property in one of the thirty-nine buildings surrounding the park that pay an annual $7,500 fee per lot for the privilege of having park keys to sign out to residents. You could be a member in good standing of one of the four clubs or religious organizations on Gramercy Park with key privileges (The Players is one of these clubs), or you might be a guest of some such person (key holders are entitled to five guests per visit). Lastly, you could be a guest of the Gramercy Park Hotel, and then you would need to be escorted both to and from the park by staff (a means taken to prevent guests from pilfering signed-out keys—which had been a large problem until this policy was instated). Once a year on Christmas Eve the park is open to the public for a single hour of Christmas caroling. This event is generally coordinated via Facebook and has been canceled multiple times during pandemic years due to cautiousness about large gatherings.

One such canceled year was 2021. Outside of these memberships and one elusive event, you have precious little chance of setting foot in Gramercy Park. The doors are double locked to discourage vigilante visitors (they lock behind you after you close them so you will require your key to exit as well as enter). The park has been gated since the mid-1830s when it was first built by lawyer and politician Samuel B. Ruggles who wanted an ornamental park on his property in Manhattan. The gates have been locked since 1844. Placing Booth, the great American Hamlet, in one of Manhattan's most exclusive outdoor locations is a clear articulation of Booth's value but also a statement about who can/should access this value. I have not yet set foot in Gramercy Park, though I have wandered past its wrought iron gates many times.

The statements about cultural capital this statue embodies, particularly when considered alongside the municipal Central Park statue, are highlighted by these two objects' dramaturgies of value. In 2023, Shakespeare as a concept might be freely available to a wide audience, but the layered dramaturgies that connect Booth, and by that token *Hamlet*, to this capital are locked behind an iron gate only accessibly to those with privilege. Offhand Shakespeare references abound in popular culture and, generally, are readily identified as a signifier of highbrow literature or thespianism. Consider, for instance, the inclusion of Shakespeare in the 2014 *LEGO Movie* as one of the film's so-called "master builders," beings who have the ability to create anything they want out of LEGO bricks without using any instructions and who, thus, have authorial agency over the LEGO world.[2] Shakespeare is seen in this film for a grand total of about five seconds in three separate bit-part background appearances, and he has one line ("Rubbish!"), but his presence among other historical and imaginary figures of influence (other master builders include Abraham Lincoln, Gandalf, Dumbledore, and Batman) paints a clear image of established cultural authority. On the other hand, consider the layered dramaturgies innate to understanding a film like *Shakespeare in Love* (1998) or the 2007 *Doctor Who* episode "The Shakespeare Code."[3] Both these pieces offer surface readings of Shakespeare's cultural capital for those who may walk past the gates and peer through the bars to get a sense of the image, but unlocking these gates to gain a full unincumbered picture requires deeper historical inquiry or base knowledge.

Of course, no piece of Shakespearean cultural capital is more wellworn than *Hamlet*. This play is so deeply connected to the idea of reified cultural capital that the connection itself is effectively a cliché. Over the

194 | THEATRES OF VALUE

course of writing this book, I returned to this question multiple times: Why *Hamlet* rather than any other work of literature? What makes the actor kneeling holding a skull while wearing "ye olde clothing" such an iconic and aggressively present Shakespearean reference—to say the least of *Hamlet*'s place as a highbrow intellectual referent?

The question "why *Hamlet*?" is too large for this conclusion to tackle exhaustively, but I can offer some breadcrumbs engaged with this book's study of America's nineteenth century as revealed by the dramaturgy of value. In this book's introduction, I promised the reader that I would use the dramaturgy of value to help answer several questions about Shakespeare's cultural capital in the United States, including how Shakespeare's value was used, accepted, communicated, and invested. Booth's brand marriage to Hamlet invested his authority-as-capital into the character, an investment that caused audiences to reevaluate *Hamlet*'s worth as a cultural artifact. This evaluation manifested in audience interest, which created a market interest in the commodity of *Hamlet*, a market interest that remains valuable to this day. As I discussed in chapter 4, Booth became America's quintessential Hamlet. This fact remains true: as of July 2023, Wikipedia's first image on the *Hamlet* landing page is of Booth in the same costume he wears in the Gramercy statue, seated upon the same chair he poses with.[4] In chapter 4 I discussed how the Booth brand's rehabilitation was innately entwined with American national identity in the wake of the Civil War, and how Edwin's ability to return to the stage was bolstered by his association with Northern intellectual sensibilities and his triumph through survival over the Southern sensibilities of his brother John Wilkes. Edwin's carefully cultivated association with Hamlet and with the rebuilding of American national identity in the postbellum era meant that *Hamlet* became equally entwined with this development. In addition to being an ideal star vehicle, *Hamlet* thus stood also as a reminder of the values that Edwin Booth represented, how those values triumphed in the face of adversity, and what they meant to the American nation. Edwin Booth made *Hamlet Hamlet* and, once he did, the Shakespeare brand reabsorbed this value expression.

To plot this process, let's return to chapter 5. In 1864, about seven months before debuting the hundred nights' *Hamlet*, Booth worked with Hackett, Wheatley, and Daly to try and assemble the monetary capital on the fly for a Shakespeare memorial statue in Central Park. While they did pull together some of the eventual $35,000 needed, they could not finalize the necessary resources until much later. In November of 1864, the Booth brothers used their collective capital to generate the most successful benefit the Shakespeare statue fund received: their one-night-only production of *Julius Caesar*. Directly after this, Booth debuted what would became the hundred nights' *Hamlet* (November 25, 1864–March 22, 1865). On April 15, 1865, Abraham Lincoln was assassinated, and on January 3, 1866, Booth returned to the stage as Hamlet.

The Shakespeare statue wasn't installed until May 23, 1872—long after Booth cemented himself as Hamlet in the American zeitgeist. And, of course, 1888 saw the Wallack benefit create massive commercial success on the back of Booth's Hamlet. While Brown and even Barnum were unable to generate slam dunks with their Shakespearean iterations, the ability to remix the cultural capital that was Shakespeare became available to theatremakers after Booth transformed Shakespeare into a cornerstone of American identity.

Understanding cultural capital means understanding economics and purposefully diving into the specifics of exchange. The dramaturgy of value offers the opportunity and vocabulary to do just this. The calculations of buying and selling are personal. They entail private knowledge of one's finances, a deep connection to one's interest and values, and an emotional "x" factor that can be linked to any node in the aforementioned flow chart for any number of anecdotal or manufactured reasons. Even so, the calculations of buying and selling are intensely public (particularly in eras before electronic transactions were commonplace). The demand for a physically embodied sales experience mandates that the market be a public space. Exchanging cash for items requires the presence of buyer, seller, items, and cash, all things that can be noted by passersby and fellow market participants. Theatrical markets are even more public since their commodities are necessarily embodied experiences; the purchaser enjoys the commodity only through presence in a specific time and place.

Theatre is commerce. The creation of art is a necessarily economic act and the creation of a collaborative artform like theatre doubly so. The act of buying and selling tickets is only the most obvious manifestation of this economy; an equal amount of value calculation goes into selection of venue, season selection, hiring artists to work on a show, costuming, the manufacture of stage properties, the degree of intricacy and design of each set element weighed against the cost to make it, choices made about the type and number of lighting instruments utilized for a show, the music rights procured for a show (and, for small theatres, whether to procure those rights at all or simply tiptoe through the gray areas of fair use). Every show is the product of a seemingly infinite number of value calculations. The dramaturgy of value can be relied upon as a tool to ask deeper questions about these calculations and the people who make them.

Engaging with a market means understanding what drives the sale of something. Why does a product exist? Who made it and who did they think would buy it? Who did buy it and why? What did they pay for it? In asking these questions, one engages with the networks of value that I have highlighted in this book. Highlighting these networks can continue to produce deeper understandings about the human x factors that go into the deeply personal act of opening one's wallet and that such understandings can continue to aid explorations of history.

Notes

Introduction. Deriving a Dramaturgy of Value

1. Edwin G. Burrows and Mike Wallace, *Gotham* (Oxford: Oxford University Press, 1999), 762. An account of this rivalry specifically can be found in: Jill Lepore, *The Name of War: King Philip's War and the Origins of American Identity* (New York: Alfred A. Knopf, 1998), 199–200.

2. Burrows and Wallace, *Gotham*, 762.

3. Burrows and Wallace, 761.

4. A popular but very thorough account of the riot can be found in: Nigel Cliff, *The Shakespeare Riots: Revenge, Drama, and Death in Nineteenth-Century America* (New York: Random House, 2007), 209–31. A second popular account written by a scholar can be found in: James Shapiro, *Shakespeare in a Divided America: What His Plays Tell Us about Our Past and Future*, digital ed. (New York: Penguin, 2020).

5. A historical account of the riots is contained in: William Toynbee, *The Diaries of William Charles Macready 1833–1851* (New York: G. P. Putnam's Sons, 1912). A discussion of the riots as class division, especially as this pertains to literature, can be found in: Dennis Berthold, "Class Acts: The Astor Place Riots and Melville's 'The Two Temples,'" *American Literature* 71, no. 3 (September 1999): 429–61.

6. Over the course of this volume, I will use the term "American" specifically to denote "US American." There is a rich history of nineteenth-century Shakespeare in performance outside the United States, and for studies on that see (as a small sampling): Bernice W. Kilman and Rick Santos, eds., *Latin American Shakespeares* (Madison: Farleigh Dickinson University Press, 2005); Jill L. Levenson and Robert Ormsby, eds., *The Shakespearean World* (London: Routledge, 2017). Since Hawaii wasn't annexed until 1898 and didn't become a state until 1959, throughout most of the nineteenth century it was still an entity unto its own: Laura Lehua Yim, "Reading Hawaiian Shakespeare: Indigenous Residue Haunting Settler Colonial Racism," *Journal of American Studies* 54, no. 1 (2019): 36–43.

198 | NOTES TO INTRODUCTION

7. See, for instance: Anne Cattaneo, "Dramaturgy: An Overview," in *Dramaturgy in American Theater: A Sourcebook*, ed. Susan Jonas, Geoffrey S. Proehl, and Michael Lupu (New York: Harcourt, Brace, 1997), 3–15; Michael Mark Chemers, *Ghost Light: An Introductory Handbook for Dramaturgy* (Carbondale: Southern Illinois University Press, 2010); Scott R. Irelan, Anne Fletcher, and Julie Felise Dubiner, *The Process of Dramaturgy: A Handbook* (Indianapolis: Hackett, 2010).

8. *The Hamburg Dramaturgy* is a series of essays written by Lessing between 1767 and 1769. It was first translated into English, in excerpts, in 1890 and wasn't translated fully until 2019. Gotthold Ephraim Lessing, *The Hamburg Dramaturgy: A New and Complete Translation*, ed. Natalya Baldyga, trans. Wendy Arone and Sara Figal (New York: Routledge, 2019), https://mcpress.media-commons.org/hamburg.

9. Mark Bly, "Bristling with Multiple Possibilities," in *Dramaturgy in American Theater: A Sourcebook*, ed. Susan Jonas, Geoffrey S. Proehl, and Michael Lupu (New York: Harcourt, Brace, 1997), 49.

10. Social performances also enact dramaturgy, as elucidated by the social theories of Erving Goffman: Erving Goffman, *The Presentation of Self in Everyday Life* (New York: Doubleday, 1959).

11. The concept of "conspicuous consumption" was drafted by Thorstein Veblen in 1899 and describes the phenomenon of those on the class line participating in outward shows of leisure/consumption in order to establish their place in a higher social class. I will explore this theory more deeply in chapter 2. Thorstein Veblen, *The Theory of the Leisure Class*, ed. Martha Banta (Oxford: Oxford University Press, 2007).

12. Phineas Taylor Barnum, "Mr. Barnum on Museums," *The Nation*, August 10, 1865.

13. Edwin's account of this incident is quoted in full in: Albert Furtwangler, *Assassin on Stage: Brutus, Hamlet, and the Death of Lincoln* (Urbana: University of Illinois Press, 1991), 49.

14. An account of this evening can be found in: "Mr. Booth's Appearance: A Magnificent Return to the Winter Garden," January 3, 1866, Harvard Theater Collection, Houghton Library, Harvard University.

15. This idea of a *lieu de mémoire* was created by Pierre Nora, and I will discuss it in further depth in chapter 5. Pierre Nora, "Between Memory and History: *Les Lieux de Mémoire*," *Representations* 26 (Spring 1989): 7–24.

16. For more on Seneca Village, see: Roy Rosenzweig and Elizabeth Blackmar, *The Park and the People: A History of Central Park* (Ithaca: Cornell University Press, 1992), 64–73. Of course, the island of Manhattan is the traditional territory of the Lenape people. My book will not deal with the seventeenth-century colonization of this territory by Dutch settlers, but it is important to acknowledge that white "ownership" of any land in the United States is a problematic construction that ignores crucial histories and peoples. A fantastic resource for determining

land provenance is: "NativeLand.Ca," Native-land.ca—Our home on native land, https://native-land.ca/, accessed January 25, 2021.

17. Robin Bernstein, *Racial Innocence: Performing American Childhood from Slavery to Civil Rights* (New York: New York University Press, 2011), 14.

18. It is because of this expansiveness that Valerie Fazel and Louise Geddes suggest we might best refer to the oeuvre of Shakespearean-related fan-created cultural output as a "multiverse." Valerie M. Fazel and Louise Geddes, *The Shakespeare Multiverse Fandom as Literary Praxis* (New York: Routledge, 2021).

19. A useful history of the theory of value and economists' evolving perceptions on it can be found in: David Throsby, *Economics and Culture* (Cambridge: Cambridge University Press, 2004), 19–23.

20. L. M. Fraser, *Economic Thought and Language* (London: Adam and Charles Black, 1947), 56–60.

21. Lawrence W. Levine, *Highbrow/Lowbrow: The Emergence of Cultural Hierarchy in America* (Cambridge: Harvard University Press, 1988).

22. Karl Marx, *Capital: A Critique of Political Economy*, ed. Frederick Engels, trans. Samuel Moore and Edward Aveling (Chicago: Charles H. Kerr, 1912), 42.

23. Marx, 42.

24. Karl Marx, *The Grundrisse*, ed. David McLellan (New York: Harper and Row, 1971), 27.

25. Tracy Davis, *The Economics of the British Stage 1800–1914* (Cambridge: Cambridge University Press, 2000), 334.

26. Ralph Barton Perry, *General Theory of Value* (Cambridge: Harvard University Press, 1967), 115–16.

27. Philip Mirowski, "Learning the Meaning of a Dollar: Conservation Principles and the Social Theory of Value in Economic Theory," *Social Research* 57, no. 3 (Fall 1990): 703.

28. John Laird, *The Idea of Value* (Cambridge: Cambridge University Press, 1929), 4.

29. Barbara Herrnstein Smith, *Contingencies of Value* (Cambridge: Harvard University Press, 1988), 9.

30. Smith, 16.

31. Smith, 30.

32. Smith, 52. For a deeper dive into the history of value and culture from an economic standpoint, see: Michael Hutter and David Throsby, eds., *Beyond Price: Value in Culture, Economics, and the Arts* (Cambridge: Cambridge University Press, 2008).

33. Pierre Bourdieu, *The Field of Cultural Production*, ed. Randal Johnson (New York: Columbia University Press, 1993), 37.

34. Pierre Bourdieu, *Outline of a Theory of Practice*, trans. Richard Nice (Cambridge: Cambridge University Press, 1977), 72.

200 | Notes to Introduction

35. Bourdieu, 72.

36. Bourdieu, *The Field of Cultural Production*, 40.

37. Levine, *Highbrow/Lowbrow: The Emergence of Cultural Hierarchy in America*.

38. John Frow, *Cultural Studies and Cultural Value* (Oxford: Clarendon, 1995), 144.

39. Frow, 5–6.

40. Fraser, *Economic Thought and Language*, 124.

41. Marx, *Capital*, 41.

42. For one account of this, see: Gary Taylor, *Reinventing Shakespeare: A Cultural History from the Restoration to the Present* (New York: Weidenfeld and Nicolson, 1989).

43. A large assortment of such items is held at the Folger Shakespeare Library in their realia collection.

44. Michael D. Bristol, *Big-Time Shakespeare* (London: Routledge, 1996), 233.

45. Pramod Nayar, "Branding Bill: The Shakespearean Commons," *Economic and Political Weekly* 50, no. 12 (March 21, 2015): 42.

46. Nayar, 42.

47. Kate Rumbold, "Brand Shakespeare?," *Shakespeare Survey* 64, no. 1 (2011): 25–37.

48. Rumbold, 26.

49. Douglas B. Holt, *How Brands Become Icons: The Principles of Cultural Branding* (Boston: Harvard School of Business, 2004), 3.

50. Derek Miller, *Copyright and the Value of Performance, 1770–1911* (Cambridge: Cambridge University Press, 2018), 5.

51. Jean-Christophe Agnew, *Worlds Apart: The Market and the Theater in Anglo-American Thought, 1550–1750* (Cambridge: Cambridge University Press, 1986), 42.

52. Marx's explanation can be found in: Marx, *Capital*, 164.

53. Agnew, *Worlds Apart: The Market and the Theater in Anglo-American Thought, 1550–1750*, 56.

54. Ronald T. Takaki, *Iron Cages: Race and Culture in Nineteenth-Century America* (New York: Alfred A. Knopf, 1979), 76.

55. Takaki, 75–127.

56. Marx, *Capital*, 164. Marx enters into a long description of the circulation of commodities, involving the transformation of commodities into money then back to commodities or C-M-C, alongside the M-C-M model, which symbolizes the transformation of money into commodities then back into money, or buying in order to sell.

57. Fraser, *Economic Thought and Language*, 237–38.

58. Pierre Bourdieu, *Distinction: A Social Critique of the Judgement of Taste*, trans. Richard Nice (Cambridge: Harvard University Press, 1984).

59. Miller, *Copyright and the Value of Performance, 1770–1911*, 10.

NOTES TO INTRODUCTION | 201

60. Pierre Bourdieu, *Pascalian Meditations*, trans. Richard Nice (Stanford: Stanford University Press, 2000), 241.

61. Bourdieu, 242.

62. Bourdieu, 242.

63. Some work has already been done on this topic. For an introduction to it, see: Kim Sturgess, *Shakespeare and the American Nation*, paperback reissue (Cambridge: Cambridge University Press, 2004); Virginia Mason Vaughan and Alden T. Vaughan, *Shakespeare in America* (Oxford: Oxford University Press, 2012).

64. For instance, throughout their history, Americans used theatre to articulate and clarify their identity as Americans—as Raymond Knapp argues Americans did in developing the form of the American musical, Andrea Most argues Jews did in the golden age Broadway Musical, and Jeffrey Richards argues early American thespians did by Americanizing British-import plays. Raymond Knapp, *The American Musical and the Formation of National Identity* (Princeton: Princeton University Press, 2005); Andrea Most, *Making Americans: Jews and the Broadway Musical* (Cambridge: Harvard University Press, 2004); Jeffrey H. Richards, *Drama, Theatre, and Identity in the American New Republic* (Cambridge: Cambridge University Press, 2009). See also: J. Ellen Gainor, Introduction to *Performing America: Cultural Nationalism in American Theater*, by Jeffrey D. Mason and J. Ellen Gainor (Ann Arbor: University of Michigan Press, 1999), 7–15.

65. For more on this, see: Heather Nathans, *Early American Theatre from the Revolution to Thomas Jefferson: Into the Hands of the People* (Cambridge: Cambridge University Press, 2003).

66. Diana Taylor, *The Archive and the Repertoire: Performing Cultural Memory in the Americas* (Durham: Duke University Press, 2003), 143.

67. Benedict Anderson, *Imagined Communities: Reflections on the Origin and Spread of Nationalism* (London: Verso, 2006), 6.

68. Anderson, 7.

69. Anthony D. Smith, *National Identity* (Reno: University of Nevada Press, 1991), 14.

70. For more on the history of America's federal currency, see: Robert Craig West, *Banking Reform and the Federal Reserve, 1863–1923* (Ithaca: Cornell University Press, 1977).

71. "The Celebration of Shakespeare's Birthday," *New York Herald*, January 31, 1864.

72. Thomas Cartelli, *Repositioning Shakespeare: National Formation, Postcolonial Appropriations* (New York: Routledge, 1999).

73. I use the term "branding" harmonizing most closely with its economic connotations, but its alternate meaning as a way to physically mark property is not unfounded here.

74. While I will discuss this in chapters 1 and 3, further reading can be done on immigrants' constructions of American identity via Shakespeare in: Elisabeth H. Kinsley, *Here in This Island We Arrived: Shakespeare and Belonging*

in Immigrant New York (University Park: Pennsylvania State University Press, 2019). Additionally, further discussion about the commodification of American national identity (particularly in relation to the commodification of otherness and savagery in the freak show) can be found in: Linda Frost, *Never One Nation: Freaks, Savages, and Whiteness in U.S. Popular Culture 1850–1877* (Minneapolis: University of Minnesota Press, 2005).

75. Bourdieu, *Distinction: A Social Critique of the Judgement of Taste*, 117.

76. Bourdieu, 131.

77. Bourdieu, *Pascalian Meditations*, 76–77.

78. I borrow the term "Shakespeare user" from Valerie Fazel and Louise Geddes, who argue that those who seek to do things with Shakespeare and his cultural capital can be called such. See: Valerie M. Fazel and Louise Geddes, eds., *The Shakespeare User* (New York: Palgrave Macmillan, 2017).

Chapter One. What William Brown Knew: The African Theatre and the Growing Threat of Legitimacy

1. Michael Warner et al., "A Soliloquy 'Lately Spoken at the African Theatre': Race and the Public Sphere in New York City, 1821," *American Literature* 73, no. 1 (2001): 17.

2. Leo H. Hirsch Jr., "The Free Negro in New York," *Journal of Negro History* 16, no. 4 (1931): 417. New York State was one of four states at the time that had any proviso for free Black voters. They were joined by Connecticut, New Jersey, and Pennsylvania in securing any sort of rights for Black voters at the time. Brainerd Dyer, "One Hundred Years of Negro Suffrage," *Pacific Historical Review* 37, no. 1 (February 1968): 1.

3. Hirsch, "The Free Negro in New York," 418.

4. Hirsch, 420.

5. "African Amusements," *National Advocate*, September 25, 1821.

6. The story of the African Theatre has been previously explored by: Marvin McAllister, *White People Do Not Know How to Behave at Entertainments Designed for Ladies and Gentlemen of Color* (Chapel Hill: University of North Carolina Press, 2003); George A. Thompson Jr., *A Documentary History of the African Theatre* (Evanston: Northwestern University Press, 1998); Warner et al., "A Soliloquy 'Lately Spoken at the African Theatre': Race and the Public Sphere in New York City, 1821."

7. Graham Russell Hodges observes: "By 1810, free blacks outnumbered slaves by 8,137 to 1,686 in New York City . . . the black pulsation of New York City was overwhelmingly young. In 1820, free black males under forty-five years of age outnumbered their elders by 3,588 to 606 while females under forty-five outnumbered some above that age by 5,340 to 834. . . . By 1820, nearly two-

thirds of New York City's blacks lived in independent households." Graham Russell Hodges, *Root and Branch: African Americans in New York and East Jersey 1613–1863* (Chapel Hill: University of North Carolina Press, 1999), 193.

8. See: Heather Nathans, "A Much Maligned People: Jews on and off the Stage in the Early American Republic," *Early American Studies* 2, no. 2 (2004): 310–42; Heather Nathans, *Hideous Characters and Beautiful Pagans: Performing Jewish Identity on the Antebellum American Stage* (Ann Arbor: University of Michigan Press, 2017). For a discussion of Noah's racism particularly dealing with the African Theatre, see: Jacob Crane, " 'One Day Our Warmest Friend; the Next Our Bitterest Enemy': Mordecai Manuel Noah and the Black-Jewish Imaginary," *Studies in American Jewish Literature* 39, no. 2 (September 2020): 182–95.

9. Levine, *Highbrow/Lowbrow: The Emergence of Cultural Hierarchy in America*, 74–75.

10. Mark Hodin, "The Disavowal of Ethnicity: Legitimate Theatre and the Social Construction of Literary Value in Turn-of-the-Century America," *Theatre Journal* 52, no. 2 (2000): 212.

11. To Marx, a "universal equivalent" is a commodity against which all other commodities uniformly express their value. See: Marx, *Capital*, 78.

12. For more on Perry's theory of Value, see my discussion in the introduction to this volume or: Perry, *General Theory of Value*, 115–16.

13. McAllister, *White People Do Not Know How to Behave at Entertainments Designed for Ladies and Gentlemen of Color*, 41.

14. For more on pleasure gardens, see: Naomi J. Stubbs, *Cultivating National Identity through Performance: American Pleasure Gardens and Entertainment* (New York: Palgrave Macmillan, 2013).

15. Thompson, *A Documentary History of the African Theatre*, specifically 5–6.

16. Thompson, 5.

17. "African Amusements," *National Advocate*, September 21, 1821.

18. Neither George Thompson nor myself could locate these records. Thompson discusses this in: Thompson, *A Documentary History of the African Theatre*, 6–7.

19. For accounts of this vandalism, see: Hodges, *Root and Branch: African Americans in New York and East Jersey 1613–1863*, 197; Thompson, *A Documentary History of the African Theatre*, 15, 32.

20. George Clinton Odell, *Annals of the New York Stage*, vol. 3 (New York: Columbia University Press, 1928), 36. This playbill is also reprinted in: Eileen Southern, "The Origin and Development of the Black Musical Theater: A Preliminary Report," *Black Music Research Journal* 2 (1982–1981): 1–14.

21. "African Amusements," September 25, 1821.

22. This is the conclusion that Marvin McAllister comes to as well: McAllister, *White People Do Not Know How to Behave at Entertainments Designed for Ladies and Gentlemen of Color*, 48.

204 | Notes to Chapter One

23. McAllister, 45.

24. Odell, *Annals of the New York Stage*, 3: 36.

25. For more details about emancipation in New York City, see: Hodges, *Root and Branch: African Americans in New York and East Jersey 1613–1863*; Shane White, *Stories of Freedom in Black New York* (Cambridge: Harvard University Press, 2002); Shane White, *Somewhat More Independent: The End of Slavery in New York City, 1770–1810* (Athens: University of Georgia Press, 1991). For a broader overview of emancipation in context, see: W. E. B. Dubois, *Black Reconstruction in America* (Oxford: Oxford University Press, 2007), 154–97.

26. For specifics about some of these arrangements as well as the violence that accompanied them, see: White, *Stories of Freedom in Black New York*, 14–16.

27. All of these laws may be found in the Minutes of the Common Council; the ordinances specifically referenced are the "Law for Regulating Negroes and Slaves in the Night Time," a 1731 revision of a 1712 ordinance (revised law can be found in *Minutes of the Common Council of the City of New York 1675–1776*, vol. 4 [New York: Dodd, Mead, 1905], 86, and the original in *Minutes of the Common Council of the City of New York 1675–1776*, vol. 3 [New York: Dodd, Mead, 1905], 30); the "Law Restraining slaves, negroes, and Indians from Gaming with Moneys or for Moneys," a 1731 revision of a 1721 law (revision: *Minutes of the Common Council of the City of New York 1675–1776*, 4: 87; original: *Minutes of the Common Council of the City of New York 1675–1776*, 3: 275.), and "A Law Giving A Reward to any Person or Persons who Shall Apprehend any Negro or Indian Slaves Offending against any of the Acts of General Assembly of this Colony," a 1731 revision of a 1726 law (original: *Minutes of the Common Council of the City of New York 1675–1776*, 3: 400; revision: *Minutes of the Common Council of the City of New York 1675–1776*, 4: 90.). Other laws remained on the books to govern the behavior of Slaves, but those did not pertain to free Black peoples.

28. Likely, many of these anxieties were roiling from the knowledge of slave revolts brewing in the South, as well as the memory of the 1741 slave conspiracy that resulted in several devastating fires and a purported attempt to level New York City. Jill Lepore discusses this event in depth, as well as its social and legislative ripples, in: Jill Lepore, *New York Burning* (New York: Alfred A. Knopf, 2005). More information on slave revolts can be found in: Herbert Aptheker, *American Negro Slave Revolts*, new edition (New York: International, 1969).

29. Edwin Olson, "The Slave Code in Colonial New York," *Journal of Negro History* 29, no. 2 (April 1944): 147.

30. Olson, 147.

31. I have preserved the nonstandard capitalization from the original text; *Minutes of the Common Council of the City of New York 1675–1776*, 4: 240.

32. Among these sources, see: Errol Hill, *Shakespeare in Sable: A History of Black Shakespearean Actors* (Amherst: University of Massachusetts Press, 1984), 12; Hodges, *Root and Branch: African Americans in New York and East*

Jersey 1613–1863, 197; McAllister, *White People Do Not Know How to Behave at Entertainments Designed for Ladies and Gentlemen of Color*, 28; Yvonne Shafer, "Black Actors in the Nineteenth-Century American Theatre," *CLA Journal* 20, no. 3 (1977): 391; Thompson, *A Documentary History of the African Theatre*, 31; Warner et al., "A Soliloquy 'Lately Spoken at the African Theatre': Race and the Public Sphere in New York City, 1821," 20.

33. See the advertisements in: *Commercial Advertiser*, July 31, 1820; *New York Daily Advertiser*, January 4, 1821; *Mercantile Advertiser*, September 4, 1818.

34. David Longworth and Andrew Beers, *Longworth's American Almanac, New York Register, and City Directory* (New York: Published at the old established directory office, Shakespeare-Gallery, by David Longworth, 1819).

35. David Longworth and Andrew Beers, *Longworth's American Almanac, New York Register, and City Directory* (New York: Published at the old established directory office, Shakespeare-Gallery, by David Longworth, 1823).

36. "Record of Assessed Valuation of Real Estate (Ward 2)," 1821, New York Municipal Archive.

37. Quoted in Odell, *Annals of the New York Stage*, 1928, 3: 36.

38. January 4, 1821; *New York Daily Advertiser*, January 6, 1821.

39. *Commercial Advertiser*, January 16, 1822. Found in: Thompson, *A Documentary History of the African Theatre*, 87.

40. McAllister, *White People Do Not Know How to Behave at Entertainments Designed for Ladies and Gentlemen of Color*, 41.

41. Samuel A. Hay, *African American Theatre: An Historical and Critical Analysis* (Cambridge: University of Cambridge Press, 1994), 238.

42. Thompson, *A Documentary History of the African Theatre*, 8.

43. McAllister, *White People Do Not Know How to Behave at Entertainments Designed for Ladies and Gentlemen of Color*, 48.

44. Hay presumes a six-performance week, and corroborating with Odell it seems likely that this was the schedule at Price's theatre at the time. See: Hay, *African American Theatre: An Historical and Critical Analysis*, 238.

45. This assumption is still a broad one as it is optimistic to presume that a back room of a tavern would have the space to accommodate a play in addition to fifty audience members.

46. White, *Somewhat More Independent: The End of Slavery in New York City, 1770–1810*, 178.

47. Please note: There is a tolerance in my figure of a few blocks in either direction, but it still shows the general feel of each neighborhood. Each black dot represents a free Black household in the year 1810. White's original map can be found in: White, *Stories of Freedom in Black New York*, 176. The historical map I've used is: S. G. Goodrich and Thomas G. Bradford, *New York (City). Engraved by G. W. Boynton, 1841*, 36 cm. x 29 cm., 1841, David Rumsey Map Collection.

48. Warner et al., "A Soliloquy 'Lately Spoken at the African Theatre': Race and the Public Sphere in New York City, 1821."

49. Cartelli, *Repositioning Shakespeare: National Formation, Postcolonial Appropriations*, 2.

50. Cartelli, 2.

51. Frantz Fanon, *Black Skin, White Masks*, trans. Richard Philcox (New York: Grove, 2008), 2.

52. "African Amusements," September 21, 1821.

53. "Literary blackface" is a term coined by David Waldstreicher to describe when a white writer personifies a Black speaker in writing in an effort to convince the reader that they are (in fact) Black for other rhetorical purposes. Generally, the writer would adopt a similar affect to Noah's in his descriptions of Hewlett's speech. In my usage, the term "literary blackface" is describing a white writer discussing a Black performer's speech. This differs slightly from Waldstreicher's coinage. Still, I believe it is a relevant term because of its connotations of harm to the imitated, as well as its connections to the performative nature of Noah's public writings. David Waldstreicher, *In the Midst of Perpetual Fetes: The Making of American Nationalism, 1776–1820* (Chapel Hill: University of North Carolina Press, 1997), 209. A more general history of blackface can be found in: Ayanna Thompson, *Blackface* (London: Bloomsbury, 2021).

54. For more on Bobalition literature and its harmful impact on Black expression, see: Shane White and Graham White, *Stylin': African-American Expressive Culture from Its Beginnings to the Zoot Suit* (Ithaca: Cornell University Press, 1999), 108–14.

55. For more on this dynamic at work in nineteenth-century America, see: Kenneth Cmiel, *Democratic Eloquence: The Fight over Popular Speech in Nineteenth-Century America* (New York: William Morrow, 1990).

56. Todd Vogel, *Rewriting White: Race, Class, and Cultural Capital in Nineteenth-Century America* (New Brunswick: Rutgers University Press, 2004), 17–23.

57. Vogel, 18.

58. Literacy is difficult to determine at this point in American history, especially among nonwhite populations. The US Census did not include a question about literacy until 1840, and even then Black people were not accounted for in this question (it specifically asked about "white" household members who could read and write, and it asked the head of the household to self-identify who could, and who could not). Still, analyses of records from Philadelphia merchant seamen can capture a glimpse of projected literacy rates—about three in ten nonwhite merchant seamen were literate between 1810 and 1820, and about two in ten between 1830 and 1831. While it is impossible to say if Welsh, a Black woman in New York likely working as a domestic servant, was literate, it's a fair guess that she might not have been. Statistics taken from: Lee Soltow and Edward Stevens, *The Rise of Literacy and the Common School in the United States: A Socioeconomic Analysis to 1870* (Chicago: University of Chicago Press, 1981), 50.

NOTES TO CHAPTER ONE | 207

59. A popular account of this anecdote can be found in: Gene Smith, *American Gothic: The Story of America's Legendary Theatrical Family Junius, Edwin, and John Wilkes Booth* (New York: Simon and Schuster, 1992), 54.

60. "African Amusements," September 21, 1821.

61. Peter Neilson, *Recollections of a Six Years' Residence in the United States of America* (Glasgow: David Robertson, 1830), 20.

62. This account is quoted in: Hodges, *Root and Branch: African Americans in New York and East Jersey 1613-1863*, 197.

63. The cast lists posted on various playbills indicate that either the play was very deeply cut, or performed in excerpt. A notice posted in the National Advocate advertises Brown's cast list: "King Henry, Mr. Hutchington—Prince of Wales, Miss Welsh—Richard, Mr. Hewlett—Buckingham, Hutchington—Lord Stanley, Stewart—Richmond, Wathews—Lady Ann, Miss Welsh—Queen Elizabeth, Miss Welsh"; this total of four named actors necessitated a dramatically pared-down text. "African Amusements," September 25, 1821; Warner posits that perhaps merely scenes were performed from the play. Warner et al., "A Soliloquy 'Lately Spoken at the African Theatre'; Race and the Public Sphere in New York City, 1821," 8.

64. "African Amusements," September 21, 1821.

65. White, *Stories of Freedom in Black New York*, 6.

66. Stubbs, *Cultivating National Identity through Performance: American Pleasure Gardens and Entertainment.*

67. Stubbs.

68. While Black people were permitted to enter the pleasure gardens as waiters, they were not allowed as patrons until theatres were built within the pleasure gardens with segregated areas for patrons of color. This occured as early as 1819 but still did not guarantee Black people admission to the pleasure garden as a whole. Stubbs, 88.

69. This attitude was prevalent during the theatre's lifetime and eventually cumulated in writings such as: Nathaniel Southgate Shaler, *The Negro Problem* (Boston: Atlantic Monthly, 1884); Nathaniel Southgate Shaler, *The Neighbor; the Natural History of Human Contacts* (Boston: Houghton, Mifflin, 1904).

70. *Commercial Advertiser*, January 16, 1822, found in: Thompson, *A Documentary History of the African Theatre*, 88.

71. Thompson, *A Documentary History of the African Theatre*, 8.

72. Details about this math and my conclusions can be found in: Rosvally, "'Off with His Head! . . . So Much for Hewlett/Brown': The African Grove Theatre Presents *Richard III*."

73. White, *Stories of Freedom in Black New York*, 190–98.

74. McAllister, *White People Do Not Know How to Behave at Entertainments Designed for Ladies and Gentlemen of Color*, 3.

75. Hay, *African American Theatre: An Historical and Critical Analysis*, 16–17. The examination of minstrelsy as a performance form has its own vast literature, but a few canonical titles are: Eric Lott, *Love and Theft: Blackface Minstrelsy and*

208 | NOTES TO CHAPTER TWO

the American Working Class, 20th anniversary edition (Oxford: Oxford University Press, 2013); Robert C. Toll, *Blacking Up: The Minstrel Show in Nineteenth-Century America* (Oxford: Oxford University Press, 1977).

76. The incident, and Mathews's career, is well documented in sources such as: Tracy Davis, "Acting Black, 1824: Charles Mathews's Trip to America," *Theatre Journal* 63 (2011): 163–89; Hay, *African American Theatre: An Historical and Critical Analysis*, 170; Hill, *Shakespeare in Sable: A History of Black Shakespearean Actors*, 11; Robert Michael Lewis, "Speaking Black, 1824: Charles Mathews's Trip to America Revisited," *Nineteenth Century Theatre and Film* 43, no. 1 (May 2016): 43–66; Herbert Marshall and Mildred Stock, *Ira Aldridge: The Negro Tragedian* (Carbondale: Southern Illinois University Press, 1958), 40; Joyce Green MacDonald, "Acting Black: 'Othello,' 'Othello' Burlesques, and the Performance of Blackness," *Theatre Journal* 46, no. 2 (May 1994): 232; McAllister, *White People Do Not Know How to Behave at Entertainments Designed for Ladies and Gentlemen of Color*, 40; Over, "New York's African Theatre: Shakespeare Reinterpreted," 76; Thompson, *A Documentary History of the African Theatre*, 34; Warner et al., "A Soliloquy 'Lately Spoken at the African Theatre': Race and the Public Sphere in New York City, 1821," 11.

77. Hewlett was quite upset at Mathews's representation of his act and wrote a scathing reply to it that was published in the *National Advocate*. Still, Hewlett's words are framed by Noah's paper, and a foreword from Noah that appeared before the letter allowing Noah to have the ultimate position of interlocutor despite Hewlett's direct words being published. For a copy of the letter and Noah's introduction, see: Thompson, *A Documentary History of the African Theatre*, 147–48.

78. Odell, *Annals of the New York Stage*, 3: 36.

79. Thompson, *A Documentary History of the African Theatre*, 6; Warner et al., "A Soliloquy 'Lately Spoken at the African Theatre': Race and the Public Sphere in New York City, 1821," 13.

80. Hay seems to corroborate Warner's thoughts, see: Hay, *African American Theatre: An Historical and Critical Analysis*, 8.

81. White, *Somewhat More Independent: The End of Slavery in New York City, 1770–1810*, 173–75.

Chapter Two. The Value of a Name: P. T. Barnum's American Dream

1. "Disastrous Fire," *New York Times*, July 14, 1865; Barnum was serving in the Connecticut state legislature at the time and received word of the fire while addressing the assembly in Hartford. He wrapped up his business and returned to New York posthaste, which is why it took him a day and a half to visit the

NOTES TO CHAPTER TWO | 209

ashes of his museum. Phineas Taylor Barnum, *The Life of P. T. Barnum Written by Himself Including His Golden Rules for Money-Making Brought Up to 1888* (Buffalo: Courier, 1888), 241.

2. "A Word about Museums," *The Nation*, July 27, 1865.

3. Phineas Taylor Barnum, "Mr. Barnum on Museums," *The Nation*, August 10, 1865.

4. See: Levine, *Highbrow/Lowbrow: The Emergence of Cultural Hierarchy in America*. For a discussion of the term "user" in regard to Shakespearean interactions, see: Fazel and Geddes, *The Shakespeare User*.

5. Bruce A. McConachie, "Museum Theatre and the Problem of Respectability for Mid-century Urban Americans," in *The American Stage: Social and Economic Issues from the Colonial Period to the Present*, ed. Ron Engle and Tice L. Miller (Cambridge: Cambridge University Press, 1993), 65–80.

6. Rumbold, "Brand Shakespeare?," 26.

7. Rumbold, 29.

8. This story has been propagated in such sources as: Harvey W. Root, *The Unknown Barnum* (New York: Harper and Brothers, 1927), 211; Irving Wallace, *The Fabulous Showman: The Life and Times of P. T. Barnum* (New York: Alfred A. Knopf, 1959), 132; M. R. Werner, *Barnum* (New York: Harcourt, Brace, 1923), 95; "What Is Talked About," *Literary World*, November 17, 1849; John Perry, "P. T. Barnum's American Museum," *Early American Life* 7, no. 56 (June 1976): 16. Perhaps the most informative and least sensational account of this event can be found in: Sturgess, *Shakespeare and the American Nation*.

9. Barnum relates the story of his visit to Shakespeare's house in his 1888 autobiography: Barnum, *The Life of P. T. Barnum Written by Himself Including His Golden Rules for Money-Making Brought Up to 1888*, 93.

10. Julia Thomas, "Bidding for the Bard: Shakespeare, the Victorians, and the Auction of the Birthplace," *Nineteenth-Century Contexts* 30, no. 2 (2008): 215–28.

11. Phineas Taylor Barnum, *Struggles and Triumphs* (Buffalo: Warren, Johnson, 1872), 365.

12. I discussed these theories in some depth in the introduction to this volume, but see also: Laird, *The Idea of Value*; Smith, *Contingencies of Value*.

13. "Barnum's American Museum Illustrated" (New York: Norden and Leslie Illustrated Book Printers, 1850), New-York Historical Society.

14. Nayar, "Branding Bill, 45; Douglas Lanier, "Recent Shakespeare Adaptation and the Mutations of Cultural Capital," *Shakespeare Studies (0582-9399)* 38 (January 2010): 104.

15. Lanier, "Recent Shakespeare Adaptation and the Mutations of Cultural Capital," 104.

16. Phineas Taylor Barnum, *The Life of Barnum* (Philadelphia: H. J. Smith, 1900), 90.

210 | Notes to Chapter Two

17. Perry, "P. T. Barnum's American Museum," 14–15.

18. An account of the second museum's opening can be found in: "Classified Ads 18," *New York Times*, September 5, 1865. Accounts of the museum's closing can be found in volume 7 of: Odell, *Annals of the New York Stage*, 318.

19. A. H. Saxon, *P. T. Barnum: The Legend and the Man* (New York: Columbia University Press, 1989), 107–08.

20. There are several detailed accounts of the museum's holdings, including: "Barnum's American Museum Illustrated"; "Disastrous Fire," *New York Times*; *Catalogue or Guide Book of Barnum's American Museum New York: Containing Descriptions and Illustrations of the Various Wonders and Curiosities of This Immense Establishment* (New York: Wynkoop, Hellenbeck and Thomas, Steam Book and Job Printers, 1863), New-York Historical Society. Additionally, a digital recreation of the museum and repository of primary source documentation about it can be found courtesy of: "The Lost Museum," https://lostmuseum.cuny.edu/, accessed April 14, 2021.

21. For Barnum's admission prices before 1865, see: Bluford Adams, *E. Pluribus Barnum: The Great Showman and the Making of U.S. Popular Culture* (Minneapolis: University of Minnesota Press, 1996), 75. It is also discussed in: Andrea Stulman Dennett, *Weird and Wonderful: The Dime Museum in America* (New York: New York University Press, 1997), 8. Barnum writes about the admission price hike in a letter to Bayard Taylor dated July 16, 1865, anthologized in: A. H. Saxon, ed., *Selected Letters of P. T. Barnum* (New York: Columbia University Press, 1983), 137.

22. McConachie, "Museum Theatre and the Problem of Respectability for Mid-century Urban Americans." The democratization of the museum, particularly how Barnum played a role in it, is also discussed in: Dennett, *Weird and Wonderful: The Dime Museum in America*.

23. Barnum's show schedule is documented in many places, including: Barnum, *The Life of Barnum*, 82–85; "Disastrous Fire," *New York Times*; Werner, *Barnum*, 65.

24. Stubbs, *Cultivating National Identity through Performance: American Pleasure Gardens and Entertainment*.

25. That is, at least, until 1865. In his second museum, Barnum charged an extra thirty cents for reserved seats and sixty cents for private boxes. Dennett, *Weird and Wonderful: The Dime Museum in America*, 38.

26. "Disastrous Fire," *New York Times*.

27. Barnum describes the availability of ice water at his museum in: Barnum, "Mr. Barnum on Museums." While ice wasn't an extreme luxury at the time due to New York City's profuse ice-harvesting industry and proximity to the Hudson River, it was certainly a novelty. For more on the availability of ice and its acquisition during New York's nineteenth century, see: Wendy Elizabeth

Harris and Arnold Pickman, "Towards an Archaeology of the Hudson River Ice Harvesting Industry," *Northeast Historical Archaeology* 29 (2000): 51.

28. Phineas Taylor Barnum, *The Life of P. T. Barnum, Written by Himself* (London: Sampson, Low & Son, 1855).

29. Barnum, *The Life of P.T. Barnum Written by Himself Including His Golden Rules for Money-Making Brought Up to 1888*, 1.

30. William Cowper, *The Task: A Poem, in Six Books. By William Cowper . . .* (London: J. Johnson, 1785), 140.

31. William Shakespeare, *As You Like It*, ed. Juliet Dusinberre, Arden third series (London: Thompson Learning, 2006), 2292.7.165.

32. Veblen, *The Theory of the Leisure Class*. Marx's theory of consumption can be found in: Marx, *Capital*, 42.

33. Adams, *E. Pluribus Barnum: The Great Showman and the Making of U.S. Popular Culture*, 80.

34. Barnum, *The Life of P. T. Barnum Written by Himself Including His Golden Rules for Money-Making Brought Up to 1888*, 245.

35. James W. Cook, ed., *The Colossal P. T. Barnum Reader: Nothing Else Like It in the World* (Urbana: University of Illinois Press, 2005), 6.

36. Quoted in: Cook, 6.

37. Frost, *Never One Nation: Freaks, Savages, and Whiteness in U.S. Popular Culture 1850–1877*.

38. Barnum relates the story of Heth in: Barnum, *The Life of P. T. Barnum Written by Himself Including His Golden Rules for Money-Making Brought Up to 1888*, 149. More about Barnum and Heth can be found in: Benjamin Reiss, *The Showman and the Slave: Race, Death and Memory in Barnum's America* (Cambridge: Harvard University Press, 2001).

39. I will go into more depth about this dynamic in chapter 4 of this book.

40. For a deeper dive into the role of theatre, specifically, in the supposed degradation of society as portrayed by its inclusion in nineteenth-century advice manuals, see: Karen Halttunen, *Confidence Men and Painted Women* (New Haven: Yale University Press, 1982), 4. For more on women's place in nineteenth-century museum theatres: Nan Mullenneaux, *Staging Family: Domestic Deceptions of Mid-Nineteenth-Century American Actresses* (Lincoln: University of Nebraska Press, 2018), 8.

41. "New York Theatre and the Moral Drama," *United States Magazine of Science, Art, Manufactures, Agriculture, Commerce, and Trade*, May 15, 1854.

42. Barnum, *The Life of P. T. Barnum Written by Himself Including His Golden Rules for Money-Making Brought Up to 1888*, 196.

43. "Barnum's Museum," *New York Tribune*, June 19, 1850.

44. Adams, *E. Pluribus Barnum: The Great Showman and the Making of U.S. Popular Culture*, 118.

212 | NOTES TO CHAPTER TWO

45. Barnum, *The Life of P. T. Barnum Written by Himself Including His Golden Rules for Money-Making Brought Up to 1888*, 199.

46. "Disastrous Fire."

47. "Barnum's Museum."

48. Frick claims that "by late 1847, Barnum was consuming a full bottle of champagne each day and, as a consequence, was unable to work after noon. In 1848, evidently swayed by a particularly persuasive temperance lecture directed at 'moderate' drinking delivered by Universalist minister Edwin Chapin, Barnum went to his wine cellar and destroyed sixty to seventy bottles of champagne. Shortly thereafter, Barnum sought the Rev. Chapin, asked for a copy of the tee-totalers' pledge, signed it, and for the remainder of his life, both swore off drink and dedicated himself to the temperance cause." John W. Frick, *Theatre, Culture and Temperance Reform in Nineteenth-Century America* (Cambridge: Cambridge University Press, 2003), 119.

49. Frick, 52.

50. Tyler Anbinder, *Five Points* (New York: Free Press, 2001), 191.

51. Frick, *Theatre, Culture and Temperance Reform in Nineteenth-Century America*, 24.

52. George Catlin, *Five Points*, 1827, oil, 1827, WikiCommons, http://en.wikipedia.org/wiki/File:Five_Points_-_George_Catlin_-_1827.jpg.

53. Anbinder, *Five Points*, 26.

54. "New York Theatre and the Moral Drama," 22–23.

55. McConachie, "Museum Theatre and the Problem of Respectability for Mid-century Urban Americans," 68.

56. Paul Boyer, *Urban Masses and Moral Order in America, 1820–1920* (Cambridge: Harvard University Press, 1978), 1.

57. For more on the popularization of speech, see: Cmiel, *Democratic Eloquence: The Fight over Popular Speech in Nineteenth-Century America*.

58. This is discussed in greater depth in: Halttunen, *Confidence Men and Painted Women*, 35–40.

59. There are several good discussions of this phenomenon in relation to the times including: Halttunen, 59; Jackson Lears, *Fables of Abundance: A Cultural History of Advertising in America* (New York: Basic Books, 1994), 75–76; McConachie, "Museum Theatre and the Problem of Respectability for Mid-century Urban Americans."

60. Halttunen, *Confidence Men and Painted Women*, 58; Mullenneaux, *Staging Family: Domestic Deceptions of Mid-Nineteenth-Century American Actresses*.

61. For a deeper examination of this, see: Halttunen, *Confidence Men and Painted Women*, 1.

62. "Guide Book to Barnum's American Museum," n.d., Harvard Theater Collection, Houghton Library, Harvard University.

63. "Guide Book to Barnum's American Museum."

NOTES TO CHAPTER TWO | 213

64. The outfitting of the museum like a parlor is discussed in: McConachie, "Museum Theatre and the Problem of Respectability for Mid-century Urban Americans," 70. The ice cream garden is related in: Perry, "P. T. Barnum's American Museum," 16. The "good taste" with which Barnum decorated the museum is a quotation from: "Barnum's American Museum Illustrated."

65. Amy G. Richter, *At Home in Nineteenth-Century America: A Documentary History* (New York: New York University Press, 2015), 6.

66. Richter, 12.

67. Halttunen, *Confidence Men and Painted Women*, 59.

68. Barnum, "Mr. Barnum on Museums," August 10, 1865; Dennett, *Weird and Wonderful: The Dime Museum in America*, 36; Philip B. Kunhardt Jr., Philip B. Kunhardt III, and Peter W. Kunhardt, *P. T. Barnum: America's Greatest Showman* (New York: Alfred A. Knopf, 1995), 107.

69. Dennett, *Weird and Wonderful: The Dime Museum in America*, 36.

70. This advertisement can be found in the pamphlet: "A Guide to Rapid and Accurate Computation by Professor Hutchings," n.d., Bridgeport Public Library.

71. A good source for investigating what Barnum produced is: Odell, *Annals of the New York Stage*.

72. "Barnum's American Museum Illustrated," 2.

73. "Broadside: Barnum's American Museum," August 19, 1853, New-York Historical Society.

74. In addition to the archival resources of institutions such as the Harvard Theater Collection, American Antiquarian Society, New York Public Library, Museum of the City of New York, and New-York Historical Society, I also mined: T. Allston Brown, *A History of the New York Stage*, vol. 1, 3 vols. (New York: Benjamin Blom, 1903); Odell, *Annals of the New York Stage*. To view this data in its entirety, visit my website: http://www.daniellerosvally.com.

75. The frequency of *The Merchant of Venice* in performance at Wallack's is likely due to James Wallack's famous portrayal of Shylock.

76. "Barnum's American Museum Illustrated," 6.

77. Nathaniel Hawthorne, "Recollections of a Gifted Woman," *Atlantic Monthly*, January 1863.

78. The original story of the theft is attributed to Nicholas Rowe and was printed in: Nicholas Rowe, *Some Account of the Life of Mr. William Shakespear* (Samuel H. Monk, 1709). A literary analysis of deer poaching as a plot device in Shakespeare's works, as well as a survey of modern scholarship debunking the tale, can be found in: Jeffrey Theis, "The 'Ill Kill'd' Deer: Poaching and Social Order in *The Merry Wives of Windsor*," *Texas Studies in Literature and Language* 43, no. 1 (2001 Spring 2001): 46–73.

79. Douglas Lanier, "Shakespeare : Myth and Biographical Fiction," in *The Cambridge Companion to Shakespeare and Popular Culture*, ed. Robert Shaughnessy (Cambridge: Cambridge University Press, 2007), 93–113.

214 | Notes to Chapter Three

80. A lengthy explanation of the acquisition and marketing of the mermaid is detailed in: P. T. Barnum, *The Life of P. T. Barnum Written by Himself*, ed. Terence Whalen (Urbana: University of Illinois Press, 2000), 230–37; while a more scholarly account of the mermaid can be found in: William T. Anderson, ed., *Mermaids, Mummies, and Mastodons: The Emergence of the American Museum* (Washington, DC: American Association of Museums, 1992). For more on mermaids generally, see: Jennifer A. Kokai, *Swim Pretty: Aquatic Spectacles and the Performance of Race, Gender, and Nature*. Carbondale: Southern Illinois University Press, 2017.

Chapter Three. Taking the Reins: The American Reading Career of Mrs. Fanny Kemble

1. This letter to George Combe of Edinburgh, held by the National Library of Scotland in Edinburgh, is reprinted in: Fanny Kemble Wister, *Fanny: The American Kemble* (Tallahassee: South Pass Press, 1972), 134.

2. Gerald Kahan, "Fanny Kemble Reads Shakespeare: Her First American Tour, 1849–50," *Theatre Survey* 24, no. 1–2 (1983): 88. The Lyceum was on 178–186 Washington Street in Brooklyn but later removed to 192–204 Washington Street in order to accommodate the Brooklyn Bridge. In 1893, the Lyceum merged with the Brooklyn Apprentice's Library and formed the Brooklyn Institute (later renamed the Brooklyn Institute of Arts and Sciences). Wallace Goold Levison, Copyright Claimant, "Brooklyn Institute and Adjoining Houses, 192–204 Washington St., Brooklyn, New York," June 10, 1891, Library of Congress, https://www.loc.gov/item/2010648520/.

3. Deirdre David, *Fanny Kemble: A Performed Life* (Philadelphia: University of Pennsylvania Press, 2007), 130; Mullenneaux, *Staging Family: Domestic Deceptions of Mid-Nineteenth-Century American Actresses*, 243; Wister, *Fanny: The American Kemble*, 140.

4. Kemble was the daughter of English actor Charles Kemble and niece to the great Sarah Siddons and John Philip Kemble.

5. Fanny Kemble, *The Journal of Frances Anne Butler*, 1970 reprint (New York: Benjamin Blom, 1970), 27.

6. Frances Anne Kemble, *Far Away and Long Ago* (New York: H. Holt, 1889); Frances Anne Kemble, *Further Records* (New York: Henry Holt, 1891); Frances Anne Kemble, *Records of a Girlhood*, 3 vols. (London: H. Holt, 1879); Frances Anne Kemble, *Records of Later Life*, 3 vols. (New York: H. Holt, 1882; Frances Anne Kemble, *Journal of a Residence on a Georgia Plantation* (New York: Harper, 1863); Frances Anne Kemble, *A Year of Consolation* (London: Moxon, 1847). For more on the editing process of these volumes, see: David, *Fanny Kemble: A Performed Life*, xv. Kemble was also a prolific writer of plays and poems and she published several volumes of her more creative writings.

NOTES TO CHAPTER THREE | 215

7. Pierce Butler, *Mr. Butler's Statement: Originally Prepared in Aid of His Professional Council* (Philadelphia: J. C. Clark, 1850), 23.

8. Rebecca Schneider, *Performing Remains: Art and War in Times of Theatrical Reenactment* (Florence: Taylor & Francis, 2011), 10.

9. Ciaran B. Trace, "What Is Recorded Is Never Simply 'What Happened': Record Keeping in Modern Organizational Culture," *Archival Science* 2, no. 1–2 (March 2002): 137–59.

10. Kemble family patriarch Charles Kemble (Fanny Kemble's grandfather) was an outspoken opponent of the actress-as-courtesan stereotype. Catherine Clinton, *Fanny Kemble's Civil War* (Oxford: Oxford University Press, 2000), 15.

11. Kemble's friends and correspondents certainly agreed. A letter dated August 28, 1840, to Barbarina Brand, "Lady Dacre," indicates that Brand had noted as much. Kemble begins her correspondence with a retaliation, "You say I am ungrateful to [the stage]." Frances Anne Kemble, *Records of Later Life*, 2nd ed., vol. 2 (London: R. Bentley, 1882), 35.

12. Wister, *Fanny: The American Kemble*, 106.

13. Frances Anne Kemble, *Records of Later Life*, 2nd ed., vol. 3 (London: R. Bentley, 1882), 371.

14. Faye E. Dudden, *Women in the American Theatre: Actresses and Audiences, 1790–1870* (New Haven: Yale University Press, 1994), 40.

15. Clinton, *Fanny Kemble's Civil War*, 54.

16. Pierce Butler and Fanny Kemble, "Pierce Butler vs. Frances Anne Butler: Libel for Divorce with Answer and Exhibits" (Court of Common Pleas of Philadelphia County, 1848); Butler, *Mr. Butler's Statement: Originally Prepared in Aid of His Professional Council.*

17. Butler and Kemble, "Pierce Butler vs. Frances Anne Butler: Libel for Divorce with Answer and Exhibits."

18. Pierce Butler, *Mr. Butler's Statement : Originally Prepared in Aid of His Professional Council*, 5.

19. Egbert S. Oliver, "Melville's Goneril and Fanny Kemble," *New England Quarterly* 18, no. 4 (December 1945): 498.

20. J. C. Furnas, *Fanny Kemble: Leading Lady of the Nineteenth-Century Stage* (New York: Dial, 1982), 350.

21. Gail Marshall, *Shakespeare and the Victorian Woman* (Cambridge: Cambridge University Press, 2009), 75.

22. Philip Hone, *The Diary of Philip Hone*, vol. 1 (New York: Dodd, Mead, 1889), 357.

23. Dudden, *Women in the American Theatre: Actresses and Audiences, 1790–1870*, 3.

24. Nancy Isenberg, *Sex and Citizenship in Antebellum America* (Chapel Hill: University of North Carolina Press, 1998), 156.

216 | NOTES TO CHAPTER THREE

25. A chronology of the divorce can be found in: David, *Fanny Kemble: A Performed Life*; Anne Russell, " 'Playing the Men': Ellen Tree, Fanny Kemble, and Theatrical Constructions of Gender," *Borrowers and Lenders* 7, no. 1 (April 2013): 6.

26. Mullenneaux, *Staging Family: Domestic Deceptions of Mid-Nineteenth-Century American Actresses*, 244–45.

27. Kemble, *Records of a Girlhood*, 1: 437.

28. Kemble, *Records of Later Life*, 3: 332, emphasis original.

29. Kahan, "Fanny Kemble Reads Shakespeare: Her First American Tour, 1849–50," 78.

30. Furnas, *Fanny Kemble: Leading Lady of the Nineteenth-Century Stage*, 338.

31. Kemble, *Records of Later Life*, 3: 633.

32. Kemble, *Records of Later Life*, 3: 534–35.

33. Jacky Bratton, "Frances Anne Kemble," in *Great Shakespeareans: Jameson, Cowden Clarke, Kemble, Cushman*, by Gail Marshall, vol. 7 (London: Continuum, 2011), 126.

34. "Mrs. Kemble's Reading in Aid of the Hungarian Exiles," *New York Daily Tribune*, January 25, 1850; *Daily Richmond Times*, January 30, 1850; *Daily Crescent*, February 7, 1850; *Alexandria Gazette*, January 29, 1850.

35. David, *Fanny Kemble: A Performed Life*, 224.

36. Butler and Kemble, "Pierce Butler vs. Frances Anne Butler: Libel for Divorce with Answer and Exhibits," 30.

37. Mullenneaux, *Staging Family: Domestic Deceptions of Mid-Nineteenth-Century American Actresses*, 275.

38. Wister, *Fanny: The American Kemble*, 207. Wister's account is corroborated in newspaper reviews of Kemble's Boston readings such as: "Mrs. Butler in Boston," *Alexandria Gazette*, February 1, 1849.

39. Sara M. Evans, *Born for Liberty: A History of Women in America* (New York: Free Press, 1989), 62.

40. Evans, 67.

41. Clinton, *Fanny Kemble's Civil War*, 146.

42. This idea, especially in regard to Kemble's thinking on *The Tempest*, is explored in further depth by Alison Booth, "From Miranda to Prospero: The Works of Fanny Kemble," *Victorian Studies* 38, no. 2 (Winter 1995): 228.

43. Mullenneaux, *Staging Family: Domestic Deceptions of Mid-Nineteenth-Century American Actresses*, xv–xvi.

44. Amy G. Richter, *At Home in Nineteenth-Century America: A Documentary History* (New York: New York University Press, 2015).

45. Kemble, *Records of Later Life*, 3: 371.

46. Clinton, *Fanny Kemble's Civil War*, 145; David, *Fanny Kemble: A Performed Life*, 229; Claudia D. Johnson, *American Actress: Perspective on the Nineteenth Century* (Chicago: Nelson-Hall, 1984), 105; Kahan, "Fanny Kemble Reads Shakespeare: Her First American Tour, 1849–50," 80; Marshall, *Shakespeare and*

the Victorian Woman, 117; Mullenneaux, *Staging Family: Domestic Deceptions of Mid-Nineteenth-Century American Actresses*, 148.

47. Kahan, "Fanny Kemble Reads Shakespeare: Her First American Tour, 1849–50."

48. Maria Chappell, "Taking Note, Fanny Kemble's Shakespeare," PhD dissertation, University of Georgia, 2018.

49. Kemble, *Records of Later Life*, 3: 371.

50. Chappell, "Taking Note, Fanny Kemble's Shakespeare," 22–27. While I had intended to travel to the UGA archive to examine these volumes in person, the COVID-19 pandemic made such a trip dangerous and, ultimately, impossible.

51. Chappell, 27.

52. Kemble, *Records of Later Life*, 2: 632.

53. Kemble, 2: 371–72.

54. Furnas, *Fanny Kemble: Leading Lady of the Nineteenth-Century Stage*, 346.

55. For more on this, see: Mullenneaux, *Staging Family: Domestic Deceptions of Mid-Nineteenth-Century American Actresses*, 272.

56. Mullenneaux, 219.

57. "From the Editor," *Wilmington Journal*, October 12, 1849.

58. *Herald of the Times*, October 11, 1849.

59. *Herald of the Times*, June 21, 1849; *Herald of the Times*, October 11, 1849.

60. "Mrs. Butler," *Staunton Spectator and General Advertiser*, October 17, 1849; "Mrs. Butler in Boston," *Alexandria Gazette*.

61. See, for instance: "Mrs. Butler," *Staunton Spectator and General Advertiser*; *Herald of the Times*, June 21, 1849; "Mrs. Butler—Her Appearance—Dress—Stoutness," *Minnesota Pioneer*, March 20, 1850.

62. *Daily Union*, November 6, 1849, 6.

63. David, *Fanny Kemble: A Performed Life*, 234; Kahan, "Fanny Kemble Reads Shakespeare: Her First American Tour, 1849–50," 89; Wister, *Fanny: The American Kemble*, 207.

64. *The Republic*, October 8, 1849.

65. "Mrs. Butler—Her Appearance—Dress—Stoutness," *Minnesota Pioneer*.

66. Furnas, *Fanny Kemble: Leading Lady of the Nineteenth-Century Stage*, 324. Catherine Clinton also makes this argument: "In her new guise, she drew an entirely new audience: those who might never have considered attending the theater because of religious or moral scruples, but were willing to be entertained by an evening of Shakespeare read aloud." Clinton, *Fanny Kemble's Civil War*, 145.

67. Clinton, *Fanny Kemble's Civil War*, 145.

68. Kemble, *Records of Later Life*, 2: 632.

69. David L. Rinear, *Stage, Page, Scandals, and Vandals: William E. Burton and Nineteenth-Century American Theatre* (Carbondale: Southern Illinois University Press, 2004), 104.

218 | Notes to Chapter Four

70. The emphasis here is from Tree's original. This letter is quoted in full without further bibliographic information in: William G. B. Carson, *Letters of Mr. and Mrs. Charles Kean Relating to Their American Tours* (St. Louis: Washington University Press, 1945), 38.

71. Merrell R. Davis and William H. Gilman, eds., *The Letters of Herman Melville* (New Haven: Yale University Press, 1960), 78.

72. Isenberg, *Sex and Citizenship in Antebellum America*, 44.

73. Isenberg, 47.

74. Davis and Gilman, *The Letters of Herman Melville*, 78.

75. Elizabeth Reitz Mullenix, "So Unfemininely Masculine: Discourse, True/False, Womanhood, and the American Career of Fanny Kemble," *Theatre Survey* 40, no. 2 (November 1999): 37.

76. "Mrs. Butler," *Staunton Spectator and General Advertiser*.

77. See, for instance: "Revolution among the Petticoats," *Athens Post*, May 23, 1851.

78. "Mrs. Butler—Her Appearance—Dress—Stoutness," *Minnesota Pioneer*.

79. *Litchfield Enquirer*, November 29, 1849.

80. "Mrs. Kemble and Her New Costume," *The Lily*, December 1, 1849.

81. "Mrs. Kemble's Macbeth," *Lynchburg Virginian*, April 4, 1850.

82. "Mrs. Butler," *Staunton Spectator and General Advertiser*.

83. *Columbia Democrat*, May 12, 1849.

84. Johnson, *American Actress: Perspective on the Nineteenth Century*, 56.

85. Johnson, 56.

86. Nicholas B. Wainwright, ed., *A Philadelphia Perspective: The Diary of Sidney George Fisher Covering the Years 1834–1871* (Philadelphia: Historical Society of Pennsylvania, 1967), 226.

87. "Letter from New York," *Alexandria Gazette*, March 21, 1849.

88. Clinton, *Fanny Kemble's Civil War*, 145.

89. Hone, *The Diary of Philip Hone*, 1: 357.

Chapter Four. Both Booth's Brothers: The Bulletproof Brand

1. Booth's writings can be found in: John Rhodehamel and Louise Taper, eds., *"Right or Wrong, God Judge Me": The Writings of John Wilkes Booth* (Urbana: University of Illinois Press, 1997), 154. The Booth production of *Caesar* will be discussed in greater depth in the next chapter. Its archival documentation is expansive, but perhaps the best remembrance of it can be found in: "Clippings: The Booth Family," August 2, 1934, New York Public Library Billy Rose Theatre Collection.

2. Rhodehamel and Taper, *"Right or Wrong, God Judge Me": The Writings of John Wilkes Booth*, 154–55.

Notes to Chapter Four | 219

3. Both references are to *Macbeth* rather than *Caesar*, but the language they use is salient. "A Deed without a Name," *Union Vedette*, April 17, 1865; "'Murder Most Foul!': Remembering Lincoln," *Daily Intelligencer*, April 17, 1865.

4. Here, the word "brand" doesn't carry Rumbold's connotations, discussed in this book's introduction. The Booths were purposefully building a sellable product connected to their family name, so the notion of a "Booth brand" is completely palpable in a more traditional sense of "branding." Rumbold, "Brand Shakespeare?"

5. Michael Anderegg, *Lincoln and Shakespeare* (Lawrenceville: University Press of Kansas, 2015); Furtwangler, *Assassin on Stage: Brutus, Hamlet, and the Death of Lincoln*; Thomas Goodrich, *The Darkest Dawn: Lincoln, Booth, and the Great American Tragedy* (Bloomington: Indiana University Press, 2005); Bethany Schneider, "Thus, Always: Julius Caesar and Abraham Lincoln," in *Shakesqueer: A Queer Companion to the Complete Works of William Shakespeare*, ed. Madhavi Menon (Durham: Duke University Press, 2011), 152–62; Stephen Sondheim and John Weidman, *Assassins* (New York: Theatre Communications Group, 1991). More on the assassination, with a focus on the theatrical laborers in Ford's that night as well as the theatre itself, can be found in: Thomas A. Bogart, *Backstage at the Lincoln Assassination* (Washington, DC: Regnery History, 2013).

6. Newspaper stories indicate that audiences were keen to see the man who rivaled Kean, and many reports of Booth's coming to America as well as early American reviews stress audience opinion about how well he measured up to his London rival. See: "Mr. Booth," *Washington Gazette*, November 9, 1821; "New York October 7," *Washington Gazette*, October 9, 1821; "Mr. Booth; Attend; Theatre; Witness; Present," *National Advocate*, October 8, 1821; *Gazette*, November 29, 1821; "Communication," *Evening Post*, October 8, 1821; "Excellent Theatrical," *Commercial Gazette*, July 19, 1821; "From the Richmond Daily Advertiser," *Evening Post*, July 10, 1821. For general details about this early performance, see: Gordon Samples, *Lust for Fame: The Stage Career of John Wilkes Booth* (Jefferson: McFarland, 1982), 59.

7. A full examination of Booth Sr. and his career can be found in: Stephen M. Archer, *Junius Brutus Booth: Theatrical Prometheus* (Carbondale: Southern Illinois University Press, 1992).

8. Philip C. Lewis, *Trouping: How the Show Came to Town* (New York: Harper and Row, 1973), 136.

9. Asia Booth Clarke, *The Elder and the Younger Booth* (Boston: James R. Osgood, 1882), 106.

10. Of Edwin Booth's Hamlet, much has been written and it is outside the scope of this project to describe the entire performance in detail. The chief published source on this is, of course, Charles H. Shattuck, *The Hamlet of Edwin Booth* (Urbana: University of Illinois Press, 1969).

220 | NOTES TO CHAPTER FOUR

11. Mary Isabella Stone, "Mary Isabella Stone Notes on Edwin Booth, 1879–1884," n.d. Mary Isabella Stone saw Booth's Hamlet about a half-dozen times between November 1879 and February 1884. Stone's work is held by the Harvard Theater Collection and has been examined and published by Daniel Watermeier, ed., *Edwin Booth's Performances: The Mary Isabella Stone Commentaries* (Ann Arbor: University of Michigan Press, 1990), 38.

12. Edwina Booth Grossman, *Edwin Booth: Recollections by His Daughter Edwina Booth Grossman and Letters to Her and His Friends* (New York: Century, 1894), 2–3.

13. Clara Morris, *Life on the Stage* (New York City: McClure, Phillips, 1902).

14. Gary Jay Williams, "Edwin Booth: What They Also Saw When They Saw Booth's Hamlet," in *Macready, Booth, Terry, Irving: Great Shakespeareans*, ed. Richard Schoch, vol. 6 (London: Bloomsbury, 2011), 62.

15. Williams, 62.

16. Asia Booth Clarke, *John Wilkes Booth: A Sister's Memoir*, ed. Terry Alford (Jackson: University Press of Mississippi, 1996), 77.

17. Stanley Kimmel, *The Mad Booths of Maryland*, 2nd revised and enlarged ed. (New York: Dover, 1969), 159.

18. Kimmel, 153.

19. Goodrich, *The Darkest Dawn: Lincoln, Booth, and the Great American Tragedy*, 35.

20. It is certain that J. B. Booth Sr. was an alcoholic and likely that he suffered from deeper mental illness throughout his lifetime. Incidents that point to this are well documented by Clarke, including Booth Sr.'s insistence on holding a funeral for his favorite horse and penchant for disappearing immediately before scheduled performances only to be found somewhere well away from the theatre very drunk. Clarke, *The Elder and the Younger Booth*.

21. Rhodehamel and Taper, *"Right or Wrong, God Judge Me": The Writings of John Wilkes Booth*, 5.

22. The speech is printed in full in: Rhodehamel and Taper, 48–67.

23. Rhodehamel and Taper, 50.

24. William Shakespeare, *Julius Caesar*, ed. David Daniell, The Arden Shakespeare (London: Thomson Learning, 2005), 257.

25. Rhodehamel and Taper, *"Right or Wrong, God Judge Me": The Writings of John Wilkes Booth*, 55.

26. An examination of Booth's motives for starting the club as well as a brief history of the club's founding can be found in: Benjamin McArthur, *Actors and American Culture, 1880–1920* (Philadelphia: Temple University Press, 1984), 76–83.

27. The Folger Shakespeare Library holds an impression of the seal, though the original seal is held in the papers of Frederick F. Hassam of Hyde Park Massachusetts "Impression from Edwin Booth's Fob Seal," 1893, Folger Shakespeare

NOTES TO CHAPTER FOUR | 221

Library. The Folger also houses a large collection of Booth's letters, in which one can see his propensity for quoting Shakespeare in his personal correspondence. Of particular note is letter 481, in which Booth consoles William Winter regarding the death of his son with lines from *Hamlet*, "Edwin Booth Letters," n.d., Folger Shakespeare Library.

28. *Booth Medal*, 1894, collection of the Folger Shakespeare Library.

29. *Teacup and Saucer Set*, circa 1895, collection of the Folger Shakespeare Library.

30. This is discussed at length in: Nina Silber, "Emancipation without Slavery: Remembering the Union Victory," in *In the Cause of Liberty: How the Civil War Redefined American Ideals*, by William J. Cooper Jr. and John M. McCardell Jr. (Baton Rouge: Louisiana State University Press, 2009). This is also discussed in: Du Bois, *Black Reconstruction in America*, 288–91.

31. This is also discussed at length in: Heather Cox Richardson, "North and West of Reconstruction: Studies in Political Economy," in *Reconstructions: New Perspectives on Postbellum America*, ed. Thomas J. Brown (Oxford: Oxford University Press, 2006), 66–90.

32. George M. Fredrickson, *The Inner Civil War: Northern Intellectuals and the Crisis of the Union* (New York: Harper and Row, 1965), 9–10.

33. Quoted in Fredrickson, 11.

34. Rose Eytinge, *The Memories of Rose Eytinge* (New York: Frederick A. Stokes, 1905), 32.

35. Sarah Blackwood, "Limbs: Postbellum Portraiture and the Mind-Body Problem," in *The Portrait's Subject: Inventing Inner Life in the Nineteenth-Century United States* (Chapel Hill: University of North Carolina Press, 2019), 79–106.

36. "Shakespeare at the Winter Garden," November 28, 1864, 63, Folger Shakespeare Library.

37. William Winter, *The Life and Art of Edwin Booth* (New York: Macmillan, 1894), 165.

38. For a deeper study of the construction of whiteness, see: Stephen Middleton, David R. Roediger, and Donald M. Shaffer, Introduction to *The Construction of Whiteness: An Interdisciplinary Analysis of Race Formation and the Meaning of a White Identity* (Jackson: University Press of Mississippi, 2016).

39. For a more in-depth analysis of nonwhite race as otherness in nineteenth-century America, see: Frost, *Never One Nation: Freaks, Savages, and Whiteness in U.S. Popular Culture 1850–1877*, 2005.

40. For more on this argument, see: Toni Morrison, *Playing in the Dark: Whiteness and the Literary Imagination* (Cambridge: Harvard University Press, 1992); Thomas Ross, "The Rhetorical Tapestry of Race," in *Critical White Studies*, ed. Richard Delgado and Jean Stefancic (Philadelphia: Temple University Press, 1997), 89–97.

222 | NOTES TO CHAPTER FOUR

41. Du Bois, *Black Reconstruction in America*, 3.

42. David R. Roediger, *The Wages of Whiteness: Race and the Making of the American Working Class* (London: Verso, 1991), see especially 20 and 49.

43. Cheryl I. Harris, "Whiteness as Property," *Harvard Law Review* 106, no. 8 (1993): 1707–91.

44. Harris, 1720–21.

45. Harris, 1734.

46. I discuss the concept of esteem-value in this book's introduction, but more information can be found in: Fraser, *Economic Thought and Language*.

47. Again, I explore utility's equation with value in the introduction to this book, but for deeper explorations of use-value and utility, see: Fraser; Laird, *The Idea of Value*; Marx, *Capital*.

48. Nell Irvin Painter, *The History of White People* (New York: W. W. Norton, 2010).

49. James Deetz, "Material Culture and Worldview in Colonial Anglo-America," in *The Recovery of Meaning: Historical Archaeology in the Eastern United States*, by Mark P. Leone and Parker B. Potter Jr. (Washington, DC: Smithsonian Institution Press, 1988), 219–34.

50. Bridget T. Heneghan, *Whitewashing America: Material Culture and Race in the Antebellum Imagination* (Jackson: University Press of Mississippi, 2003), 10.

51. Heneghan, 10.

52. This document was the basis for Charles Shattuck's reproduction of Booth in the part and is held by the Folger Shakespeare Library. Charles Clarke, "On Booth's Hamlet," n.d., Folger Shakespeare Library; Shattuck, *The Hamlet of Edwin Booth*.

53. Clarke, "On Booth's Hamlet," 6–7.

54. Philip Lawrence, "Edwin Booth as Hamlet," November 20, 1876, Folger Shakespeare Library.

55. *Hamlet* critics have long engaged with debates about Hamlet's mental state and nineteenth-century critics are no exception. While I will not enter into an analysis of Hamlet's melancholy and its signification as a market value to nineteenth-century audiences, I do think it worth mentioning that this ailment triggered medical and nonmedical conversations about masculinity, mental illness, and the relationship between the two. For more on this, see: Meredith Conti, *Playing Sick: Performances of Illness in the Age of Victorian Medicine* (London: Routledge, 2018).

56. Elise Lemire, *"Miscegenation": Making Race in America* (Philadelphia: University of Pennsylvania Press, 2002), 21.

57. Thomas Jefferson, *Notes on the State of Virginia* (Chicago: University of Chicago Press, 1784), 200–04.

58. R. Meade Bache, "Reaction Time with Reference to Race," *Psychological Review* 2, no. 5 (September 1895): 475–86.

NOTES TO CHAPTER FOUR | 223

59. Bache, 481.

60. Johnson's address as well as its reflection of the historical moment in which it was delivered is discussed in: Du Bois, *Black Reconstruction in America*, 281. A full copy of the address can be found on: "Third Annual Message: The American Presidency Project," https://www.presidency.ucsb.edu/documents/third-annual-message-10, accessed March 29, 2021.

61. I discussed the harm of minstrelsy in chapter 1 of this book, but more information can be found in: Marvin McAllister, *Whiting Up: Whiteface Minstrels and Stage Europeans in African American Performance* (Chapel Hill: University of North Carolina Press, 2011); Lott, *Love and Theft: Blackface Minstrelsy and the American Working Class*; Yuval Taylor and Jake Austen, *Darkest America: Black Minstrelsy from Slavery to Hip-Hop* (New York: W. W. Norton, 2012); Toll, *Blacking Up: The Minstrel Show in Nineteenth-Century America*. For more on the freak show, see: Rachel Adams, *Sideshow USA: Freaks and the American Cultural Imagination* (Chicago: University of Chicago Press, 2001); Rosemarie Garland-Thomson, *Freakery: Cultural Spectacles of the Extraordinary Body* (New York: New York University Press, 1996).

62. Lott, *Love and Theft: Blackface Minstrelsy and the American Working Class*, 41.

63. Frost, *Never One Nation: Freaks, Savages, and Whiteness in U.S. Popular Culture 1850–1877*, 3.

64. Clarke, *John Wilkes Booth: A Sister's Memoir*, 77.

65. The letter is printed in full in: Clarke, 116. It is also quoted in full in: Furtwangler, *Assassin on Stage: Brutus, Hamlet, and the Death of Lincoln*, 49.

66. Rhodehamel and Taper, *"Right or Wrong, God Judge Me": The Writings of John Wilkes Booth*, 11.

67. Asia Booth Clarke, *The Unlocked Book: A Memoir of John Wilkes Booth*, ed. Eleanor Farjeon (New York: G. P. Putnam's Sons, 1938), 111–12.

68. Winter, *The Life and Art of Edwin Booth*, 272.

69. "Booth Family Scrapbook," n.d., 87, Folger Shakespeare Library.

70. Winter, *The Life and Art of Edwin Booth*, 37.

71. The letter is mentioned in: "Edwin-Booth at the Winter Garden," *New-York Daily Tribune*, January 4, 1866.

72. James Gordon Bennet, *New York Herald*, December 24, 1865, vol. 30, no. 357.

73. See, as a small sampling: Charles Bailey (Figaro) Seymour, "Dramatic Feuilleton," *New York Saturday Press*, December 30, 1865; Charles Bailey (Figaro) Seymour, "Dramatic Feuilleton," *New York Saturday Press*, January 6, 1866; "Edwin-Booth at the Winter Garden," *New-York Daily Tribune*; "The Reappearance of Edwin Booth," *New-York Daily Tribune (1842–1866)*, January 3, 1866.

74. Seymour, "Dramatic Feuilleton," January 6, 1866.

75. "Mr. Booth's Appearance: A Magnificent Return to the Winter Garden."

224 | NOTES TO CHAPTER FIVE

76. "Edwin Booth Scrapbook," n.d., Folger Shakespeare Library.

77. "Mr. Booth's Appearance: A Magnificent Return to the Winter Garden."

78. Daniel J. Watermeier, ed., *Between Actor and Critic: Selected Letters of Edwin Booth and William Winter* (Princeton: Princeton University Press, 1971), 58–59.

Chapter Five. Our American Shakespeare: The Central Park Statue and National Identity

1. A firsthand account of the occasion of the cornerstone being laid appears in "Personal," *The Round Table: A Saturday Review of Politics, Finance, Literature, Society, and Art*, May 7, 1864. The statue is described in Dianne L. Durante, *Outdoor Monuments of Manhattan: A Historical Guide* (New York: New York University Press, 2007).

2. F. W. Bourdillon, "A Spring Evening," *The Galaxy*, April 1876, vol. 21, issue 4 ed., 542; Sadakichi Hartman finds that at the time of the Ward sculpture's unveiling there were five other sculptures of Shakespeare in the world: the Stratford memorial bust; the marble monument sculpted by Peter Scheemakers erected in 1740 at Westminster Abbey; a second Westminster-style statue gifted by David Garrick to the town of Stratford-upon-Avon and standing in the external niche on the north side of Town Hall; a sculpture made by Louis-François Roubiliac gifted by Garrick to the British Museum in 1779; and a sculpture by Giovanni Fontana adapted from the work of Scheemakers and Roubiliac gifted to stand in London's Leicester Square in 1879. Sadakichi Hartman, *Shakespeare in Art* (Boston: L. C. Page, 1901).

3. I discussed Smith's theory of value in this book's introduction. See: Smith, *Contingencies of Value.*

4. A complete history of the park, its construction, and the various political battles embroiled in its creation can be found in: Rosenzweig and Blackmar, *The Park and the People: A History of Central Park.*

5. Rosenzweig and Blackmar, 332.

6. Rosenzweig and Blackmar, 330.

7. Roy Rosenzweig and Elizabeth Blackmar, "Pig Keepers, the Story of Bone Boilers, and Central Park," *Humanities* (November 2003): 325–29.

8. This phenomenon was visible in non-English-language theatre in the United States at the time as well. Nineteenth-century US Spanish-language theatre, for instance, was almost entirely from Spain. Nicolás Kanellos, *A History of Hispanic Theatre in the United States: Origins to 1940* (Austin: University of Texas Press, 1990).

9. William Winter, "Drama," *The Albion, a Journal of News, Politics, and Literature* 42, no. 8 (February 20, 1864): 91.

NOTES TO CHAPTER FIVE | 225

10. More on English celebrations of the tercentenary can be found in: Richard Foulkes, "A Babel of Bardolaters: The 1864 Tercentenary," in *Performing Shakespeare in the Age of Empire* (Cambridge: Cambridge University Press, 2002), 58–81.

11. Two good volumes on this history are: John Keegan, *The American Civil War: A Military History* (New York: Alfred A. Knopf, 2009); Adam I. P. Smith, *The American Civil War* (New York: Palgrave Macmillan, 2007).

12. The figure can be found in: "Letters from New York," *Saturday Evening Gazette*, May 7, 1864, and this estimate regarding present-day currency was generated using the relative consumer price index provided by the US government and extrapolations from the CPI made by economists via the "Measuring Worth" project; http://www.measuringworth.com.

13. Anderson, *Imagined Communities: Reflections on the Origin and Spread of Nationalism*, 6–7.

14. Smith, *National Identity*, 14. I address these qualities point-by-point in this book's introduction, especially as indicators of how the United States had yet to develop its own sense of national identity at this time.

15. Nora, "Between Memory and History: *Les Lieux de Mémoire*."

16. Nora, 12.

17. Douglas M. Lanier, "Commemorating Shakespeare in America, 1864," in *Celebrating Shakespeare: Commemoration and Cultural Memory*, ed. Clara Calvo and Coppélia Kahn (Cambridge: Cambridge University Press, 2015), 156.

18. "The Three Hundredth Anniversary of Shakespeare's Birth," *New York Herald*, April 20, 1864.

19. Several good histories of Central Park have previously been written, including: Durante, *Outdoor Monuments of Manhattan*; Morrison H. Heckscher, "Creating Central Park," *Metropolitan Museum of Art Bulletin*, New Series 65, no. 3 (Winter 2008): 1–3, 5–74; Rosenzweig and Blackmar, *The Park and the People: A History of Central Park*; Rosenzweig and Blackmar, "Pig Keepers, the Story of Bone Boilers, and Central Park."

20. The term "democratic experiment" in this context is from: Lawrence W. Rosenfield, "Central Park and the Celebration of Civic Virtue," in *American Rhetoric: Context and Criticism* (Carbondale: Southern Illinois University Press, 1989), 222.

21. Rosenzweig and Blackmar, *The Park and the People: A History of Central Park*. Though of course the land that Manhattan is built upon is the traditional territory of the Lenape people who were displaced by Dutch settlers in 1626: Burrows and Wallace, *Gotham: A History of New York City to 1898*, 23–24.

22. Rosenzweig and Blackmar, *The Park and the People: A History of Central Park*, 61.

23. Diana diZerega, Nan A. Rothschild, and Meredith B. Linn, "Constructing Identity in Seneca Village," in *Archaeology of Identity and Dissonance*, ed. Diane F. George and Bernice Kurchin (Gainesville: University of Florida Press, 2019), 158.

226 | Notes to Chapter Five

24. Rosenzweig and Blackmar, *The Park and the People: A History of Central Park*, 61.

25. Rosenzweig and Blackmar, 62.

26. More about this fight can be found in: Burrows and Wallace, *Gotham: A History of New York City to 1898*, 791–92.

27. Burrows and Wallace, 792.

28. Rosenzweig and Blackmar, *The Park and the People: A History of Central Park*, 65.

29. Rosenzweig and Blackmar, 67.

30. Rosenzweig and Blackmar, 70.

31. Diana diZerega Wall, Nan A. Rothschild, and Cynthia Copeland, "Seneca Village and Little Africa: Two African American Communities in Antebellum New York City," *Historical Archaeology* 42, no. 1 (2008): 99–103. The 1821 Constitutional Convention discussed in chapter 1 introduced suffrage with the requirement of owning at least $250 worth of property—nine residents of Seneca Village so qualified. Wall, Rothschild, and Copeland, 101.

32. Rosenzweig and Blackmar, *The Park and the People: A History of Central Park*, 58–64.

33. Rosenzweig and Blackmar, 68.

34. See: diZerega, Rothschild, and Linn, "Constructing Identity in Seneca Village," 175.

35. New York City especially, argues Paul Boyer, was seen as a categorically immoral place to live. See: Boyer, *Urban Masses and Moral Order in America, 1820–1920*.

36. Report read by Olmsted to the Central Park Commissioners on October 13, 1857, and printed in part in the *New-York Tribune* on the following day. Excerpt found in: Frederick Law Olmsted Jr., *Frederick Law Olmsted, Landscape Architect, 1822–1903* (New York: B. Blom, 1970), 59.

37. For more on this, see: Rosenzweig and Blackmar, *The Park and the People: A History of Central Park*, 26.

38. The two most prominent examples, from different ends of the nineteenth century, are: Henrietta Maria Bowdler, *The Family Shakespeare in Four Volumes* (Bath: R. Cruttwell, 1807); Charles Lamb and Mary Lamb, *Tales from Shakespeare*, illustrated version with Walter Paget (New York: Nister Dutton, 1910).

39. Thomas Selzer finds: "In 1864, as many as 6,120,179 people visited the park and two years later . . . the Park visitors numbered 10,764,411." Thomas Seltzer, *Central Park* (New York: Central Park Association, 1926), 57.

40. Kevin Coffee, "The Material Significance of Carriage Drives to the Design of Central Park," *Journal of the Society for Industrial Archeology* 38, no. 1 (2012): 83.

41. Rosenzweig and Blackmar, *The Park and the People: A History of Central Park*, 232.

NOTES TO CHAPTER FIVE | 227

42. Bernstein, *Racial Innocence.*

43. An image of the statue at this time, and surrounding foliage, can be found in the archives of the Metropolitan Museum of Art, American Wing.

44. Bernstein, *Playing Innocent: Childhood, Race, Performance,* 77.

45. "The Shakespeare Statue Fund," *New-York Tribune,* April 23, 1864.

46. J. B. Booth Sr. had five children who lived past infancy: Junius Brutus Booth Jr. (1821–1883); Rosalie Ann Booth (1823–1889); Edwin Thomas Booth (1833–1893); Asia Sydney Booth (1835–1888); John Wilkes Booth (1838–1865); and Joseph Adrian Booth (1840–1902). Joseph became a physician and was generally uninvolved with the theatre. L. Terry Oggel, *Edwin Booth: A Bio-bibliography* (New York: Greenwood Press, 1992), 8.

47. Kimmel, *The Mad Booths of Maryland,* 191.

48. Clarke, *The Elder and the Younger Booth,* 159.

49. Samples, *Lust for Fame: The Stage Career of John Wilkes Booth,* 164.

50. The formation of this brand and its relationship to national identity that I discussed in the previous chapter should not go without note either.

51. "Booth Family Scrapbook," n.d., Folger Shakespeare Library, 53.

52. Michael W. Kauffman, *American Brutus* (New York: Random House, 2004); "Letters from New York," *Saturday Evening Gazette.*

53. Arthur W. Bloom, *Edwin Booth: A Biography and Performance History* (Jefferson: McFarland, 2013), 69.

54. "Diary of Junius Brutus Booth," n.d., Folger Shakespeare Library.

55. Winter Garden (Theater New York, N.Y. 1859–1867), "Broadside: Winter Garden, Farewell Benefit of Mrs. Barney Williams" (Herald Print, 1862), American Antiquarian Society.

56. Bloom, *Edwin Booth: A Biography and Performance History,* 70.

57. John Ripley, *Julius Caesar on Stage in England and America 1599–1973* (Cambridge: Cambridge University Press, 1980), 101–02.

58. "Booth Family Scrapbook," 53.

59. Kauffman, *American Brutus,* 149; Bloom, *Edwin Booth: A Biography and Performance History,* 80.

60. I use the term "ghosting" as Marvin Carlson coined it to indicate the things an audience sees present with an actor onstage alongside their performance of a given role in a given scenario. Marvin Carlson, *The Haunted Stage,* 2011 paperback reprint (Ann Arbor: University of Michigan Press, 2001).

61. "Rebel Plot Attempt to Burn City; All Principal Hotels Simultaneously Set Fire," *New York Times,* November 26, 1864.

62. Bloom, *Edwin Booth: A Biography and Performance History,* 70; Furtwangler, *Assassin on Stage: Brutus, Hamlet, and the Death of Lincoln,* viii; Kimmel, *The Mad Booths of Maryland,* 192; Kauffman, *American Brutus,* 150; Ora Titone, *My Thoughts Be Bloody: The Bitter Rivalry between Edwin and John Wilkes Booth That Led to an American Tragedy* (New York: Free Press, 2010), 338.

228 | NOTES TO CHAPTER SIX

63. Hecksecher, "Creating Central Park," 68. More on Ward's life and career can be found in: Lewis I. Sharp, *John Quincy Adams Ward: Dean of American Sculpture* (Newark: University of Delaware Press, 1985).

64. A good history of Shakespeare statuary can be found in: Balz Engler, "Shakespeare, Sculpture, and the Material Arts," in *The Edinburgh Companion to Shakespeare and the Arts*, ed. Mark Thornton Burnett, Adrian Streete, and Ramona Wray (Edinburgh: Edinburgh University Press, 2011), 435–44.

65. JQA Ward, March 1910, Box 4, Folder 7, JQA Ward Papers, Albany Institute of History.

66. The sources Ward turned to for Shakespeare's face remain, to this day, regarded as the best sources for understanding Shakespeare's appearance despite the fact that they were both posthumous. As for Shakespeare's body, there was a full-body statue of Shakespeare installed at Westminster in 1741, but this was over one hundred years after Shakespeare's death. It can hardly therefore be relied upon as "historically accurate."

67. Edwin Booth, "Edwin Booth to JQA Ward," typescript copy in research files, the American Wing, n.d., Metropolitan Museum of Art.

68. *The Aldine* 6, no. 10 (October 1873): 209.

69. Percy MacKaye, *Epoch: The Life of Steele MacKaye*, reprinted, vol. 1 (Grosse Pointe: Scholarly Press, 1968), 79.

70. Joseph Roach, *Cities of the Dead* (New York: Columbia University Press, 1996), 26.

71. Roach, 77.

72. "Ward's Statue of Shakespeare," *Christian Union*, May 29, 1872, sec. Literature and Arts.

Chapter Six. Erasing the Lines: Editing the Wallack Benefit

1. "Clippings Related to Lester Wallack," n.d., 5, Harvard Theater Collection, Houghton Library, Harvard University.

2. A. M. Palmer, "Palmer's Account of the Testimonial Benefit Performance to Mr. Lester Wallack," Thoe L. De Vinne, May 1893, 10, Folger Shakespeare Library.

3. "The Ideal Hamlet," *New York Herald*, May 22, 1888.

4. In order of appearance in my text, these quotations come from: "The Ideal Hamlet," *New York Herald*; *Alexandria Gazette*, May 22, 1888; *Fort Worth Daily Gazette*, May 28, 1888; Edward Robins, *Twelve Great Actors 1862–1943* (New York: Knickerbocker Press, 1900), 455.

5. Palmer, "Palmer's Account of the Testimonial Benefit Performance to Mr. Lester Wallack," May 1893.

6. I have found copies of the souvenir playbill at the New York Public Library: "Robinson Locke Collection of Theatrical Scrapbooks," n.d., New York

Notes to Chapter Six | 229

Public Library Billy Rose Theatre Collection. The Folger Shakespeare Library has at least three: "Lester Wallack Scrapbook Volume 2," n.d., Folger Shakespeare Library; "Lester Wallack Scrapbook Volume 3," n.d., Folger Shakespeare Library; and the Harvard Theater Collection has at least eight: "Metropolitan Opera House Playbills 1888," Harvard Theater Collection, Houghton Library, Harvard University.

7. Heather Nathans goes so far as to say, "No discussion of cosmopolitan theatrical family networks would be complete without the Wallack family." Nathans, *Hideous Characters and Beautiful Pagans: Performing Jewish Identity on the Antebellum American Stage*, 125.

8. "Scrapbook: Lester Wallack," n.d., Folger Shakespeare Library.

9. "Scrapbook: Lester Wallack."

10. "What the Theatres Are Doing," *Watson's Art Journal* 8, no. 15 (1868): 209.

11. For more on Stewart and his stores, see: Stephen N. Elias, *Alexander T. Stewart: The Forgotten Merchant Prince* (Westport: Praeger, 1992).

12. The story of Delmonico's and its impact on American cuisine can be found in: Andrew F. Smith, *Eating History: Arts and Traditions of the Table* (New York: Columbia University Press, 2009), 19–28.

13. For more information on Wallack's retirement and reactions to it, see: Robins, *Twelve Great Actors 1862–1943*, 454.

14. Horace Townsend, "Lester Wallack's Successor," *North American Review* 147, no. 385 (1888): 703–04.

15. Kim Marra, "Taming America as Actress: Augustin Daly, Ada Rehan, and the Discourse of Imperial Frontier Conquest," in *Performing America: Cultural Nationalism in American Theater*, ed. Jeffrey D. Mason and J. Ellen Gainor (Ann Arbor: University of Michigan Press, 1999), 52. Marra also discusses Daly's career in: Kim Marra, *Strange Duets: Impresarios and Actresses in the American Theatre, 1865–1914* (Iowa City: University of Iowa Press, 2006).

16. Marra, "Taming America as Actress: Augustin Daly, Ada Rehan, and the Discourse of Imperial Frontier Conquest," 61.

17. Marvin Felheim, *The Theater of Augustin Daly: An Account of the Late Nineteenth Century American Stage* (Cambridge: Harvard University Press, 1956), 16; Don Wilmeth and Rosemary Cullen, *Plays by Augustin Daly* (Cambridge: Cambridge University Press, 1984), 17.

18. This is a model that Don Wilmeth and Rosemary Cullen argue Daly learned from Wallack's father, and the model Daly and Palmer used to stitch together the Wallack benefit. Wilmeth and Cullen, *Plays by Augustin Daly*, 4.

19. For a few of these plays anthologized, see: Wilmeth and Cullen, *Plays by Augustin Daly*. For reflections on Daly's plays in their time, see: Bruce A. McConachie, *Melodramatic Formations* (Iowa City: University of Iowa Press, 1992), especially: 200, 205–10.

20. Edwin Booth, "Edwin Booth to Augustin Daly," December 16, 1886, Folger Shakespeare Library.

230 | Notes to Chapter Six

21. Two nineteenth-century biographies of Barrett can be found in: Elwyn A. Barron, *Lawrence Barrett: A Professional Sketch* (Chicago: Knight & Leonard, 1889); William Cartwright, *Biography of Lawrence Barrett (1838–1891)* (Paterson, NJ: Manuscript Club, 1847).

22. Arthur W. Bloom, *Joseph Jefferson: Dean of the American Theatre* (Savannah: Frederic C. Beil, 2000).

23. A. M. Palmer, "A. M. Palmer to Augustin Daly," December 31, 1886, Folger Shakespeare Library.

24. A brief biographical sketch of Langtry can be found in: Rebecca A. Umland, "Lillie Langtry: From 'Professional Beauty' to International Icon," in *Women in the Arts in the Belle Epoque*, ed. Paul Fryer (Jefferson: McFarland, 2021), 48–60; Langtry also published an autobiography: Lillie Langtry, *The Days I Knew* (New York: George H. Doran, 1925).

25. Dittenhoefer is listed as a member of the Met's board of directors in: "The Evening Telegram," May 21, 1888, Kellogg Family Papers, Box 11, Folder: Notices and Reviews, New-York Historical Society. A bio-sketch of Dittenhoefer is contained in: Michael Bennett Leavitt, *Fifty Years in Theatrical Management* (New York: Broadway, 1912), 594–95; Dittenhoefer was also a key player in theatrical copyright law, and this story is explored in: Zvi S. Rosen, "The Twilight of the Opera Pirates: A Prehistory of the Exclusive Right of Public Performance for Musical Compositions," *Cardozo Arts and Entertainment Law Journal* 24 (2007): 1157–1218. The Actors Fund is a 501(c)(3) that strives to help performing artists and entertainment professionals in moments of struggle by way of providing a safety net in an industry that often doesn't have such allocations. More information can be found on their website: "The Actors Fund: About Us," December 11, 2015, https://actorsfund.org/about-us.

26. Palmer, "Palmer's Account of the Testimonial Benefit Performance to Mr. Lester Wallack," May 1893, 3–4.

27. Palmer, 3–5.

28. W. J. Florence, "Lester Wallack," *North American Review* 147, no. 383 (October 1888): 544–45; T. Allston Brown, *A History of the New York Stage*, vol. 3 (New York: Dodd, Mead, 1903), 324.

29. "Wallack's Wish," *Daily Picayune*, February 19, 1887. This same story is printed identically in: "Lester Wallack Declines a Testimonial Performance of Brother Professionals," *Plain Dealer*, February 19, 1887.

30. *The Times*, February 25, 1887.

31. The projected take of the benefit is reported in several places: "Wallack's Wish," *Daily Picayune*; Palmer, "Palmer's Account of the Testimonial Benefit Performance to Mr. Lester Wallack," May 1893, 6.

32. While the Daly/Palmer letter doesn't include Mrs. Townsend's first name, cross-referencing the address from which the letter was written (343 W.

NOTES TO CHAPTER SIX | 231

Thirty-Fourth Street) yields confirmation of Townsend's full name. One key hint is the inscription of this copy of a photographic album to "Margaret Townsend Tagliapietra" at the same address: G. R. Fardon, "San Francisco Album : Photographs of the Most Beautiful Views and Public Buildings of San Francisco," 1856, New-York Historical Society, https://digitalcollections.nyhistory.org/islandora/object/nyhs%3A23971#page/2/mode/1up.

33. Mrs. John D. Townsend, "Mrs. John D. Townsend to A. M. Palmer and Augustin Daly," December 7, 1887, Folger Shakespeare Library.

34. "Death of Henry E. Abbey," *New York Times*, October 18, 1896.

35. "The Changes at Wallack's: Arrangements and Plans of the New Management," *New York Times*, May 11, 1887.

36. "Changes at Wallack's: Mr. Abbey's Assumption of the Management," *New York Times*, August 21, 1887.

37. Palmer, "Palmer's Account of the Testimonial Benefit Performance to Mr. Lester Wallack," May 1893, 6–7.

38. "A Herald Cast for 'Hamlet,'" *New York Herald*, January 9, 1888. I have hunted high and low for the referenced advertisements, but January 1888 issues of the *Herald* are all but vanished from archival holdings.

39. A biographical sketch of Murdoch is offered as preface to a reissued edition of his book: J. Bunting, "Biographical Sketch of the Author," in *The Stage*, by James Murdoch, reissued ed. (Bronx: Benjamin Blom, 1969), 13–24.

40. For more on Gilbert, see William Winter's brief biography: William Winter, *A Sketch of the Life of John Gilbert: Together with Extracts from His Letters and Souvenirs of His Career* (New York: The Dunlap Society, 1890).

41. A sketch of Coghlan's life can be found in his obituary: "Charles Coghlan Is Dead," *New York Times*, 1899. William Winter also briefly details Coghlan's performance as Macbeth (to Langtry's Lady Macbeth): William Winter, *Shakespeare on the Stage* (New York: Moffat Yard, 1911), 492–93.

42. For more on MacKaye's career, see the biography of him written by his son: MacKaye, *Epoch: The Life of Steele MacKaye*.

43. Rehan and her professional relationship with Daly is detailed in: Marra, "Taming America as Actress: Augustin Daly, Ada Rehan, and the Discourse of Imperial Frontier Conquest"; Marra, *Strange Duets*.

44. The Booth family tree and details on the Booth acting dynasty can be found in: Montrose Jonas Moses, *Famous Actor-Families in America* (New York: T. Y. Crowell, 1906), 49.

45. "Mr. Wallack's Benefit," *New York Herald*, January 22, 1888.

46. *Fisherman and Farmer*, January 20, 1888.

47. "Newsy Gleanings," *Fisherman and Farmer*, February 3, 1888.

48. "Lester Wallack Scrapbook," n.d., New York Public Library Billy Rose Theatre Collection.

232 | NOTES TO CHAPTER SIX

49. "Lester Wallack Scrapbook."

50. Edwin Booth, "Edwin Booth to Augustin Daly," January 27, 1887, Folger Shakespeare Library.

51. A summation of Couldock's career can be found in a *New York Times* article advertising a benefit on his behalf: "Couldock's Long Career," *New York Times*, May 12, 1895.

52. Barron, *Lawrence Barrett: A Professional Sketch*, 93.

53. Cartwright, *Biography of Lawrence Barrett (1838–1891)*, 15.

54. Palmer, "Palmer's Account of the Testimonial Benefit Performance to Mr. Lester Wallack," 4.

55. "Robinson Locke Collection of Theatrical Scrapbooks," n.d.

56. A. M. Palmer, "A. M. Palmer to Augustin Daly," April 6, 1888, Folger Shakespeare Library.

57. A. M. Palmer, "A. M. Palmer to Augustin Daly," January 28, 1887, Folger Shakespeare Library.

58. A. M. Palmer, "A. M. Palmer to Augustin Daly," January 28, 1887, Folger Shakespeare Library.

59. A. M. Palmer, "A. M. Palmer to Augustin Daly," February 10, 1887, Folger Shakespeare Library.

60. "Mr. Wallack's Benefit," *New York Herald*.

61. Several biographical accounts exist of Helena Modjeska, varying in publication date from her lifetime to the recent past: Jameson Torr Altemus, *Helena Modjeska* (New York: Benjamin Blom, 1971); Marion Moore Coleman, *Fair Rosalind: The American Career of Helena Modjeska* (Cheshire: Cherry Hill Books, 1969); Mabel Collins, *The Story of Helena Modjeska* (London: W. H. Allen, 1883); Antoni Gronowicz, *Modjeska: Her Life and Loves* (New York: Thomas Yoseloff, 1956); Beth Holmgren, *Starring Madame Modjeska* (Bloomington: Indiana University Press, 2012). Modjeska also published an autobiography: Helena Modjeska, *Memories and Impressions of Helena Modjeska: An Autobiography* (New York: Macmillan, 1910).

62. A. M. Palmer, "A. M. Palmer to Augustin Daly," May 22, 1888, Folger Shakespeare Library. For more on Ada Rehan, see: Marra, "Taming America as Actress: Augustin Daly, Ada Rehan, and the Discourse of Imperial Frontier Conquest."

63. Nan Mullenneaux, "Trials and Vicissitudes," in *Staging Family: Domestic Deceptions of Mid-Nineteenth-Century American Actresses*, 33–79. Eytinge's autobiography details her encounters with Booth as well as her general attitudes about stage work: Eytinge, *The Memories of Rose Eytinge*.

64. "5 O'clock Extra," *The Evening World*, April 19, 1888. The March 21st advert mentioning Mrs. Bowers is posted in: "Testimonial to Wallack," *Washington Critic*, March 21, 1888.

NOTES TO CHAPTER SIX | 233

65. For a precis of Bowers's career managing theatres in Philadelphia, see: Jane Kathleen Curry, "Women in Nineteenth Century American Theatre Management," PhD dissertation, City University of New York, New York, 1991, 77–82. For a brief biographical sketch of Bowers, see: Amelia Howe Kritzer, "Antebellum Plays by Women," in *The Oxford Handbook of American Drama*, ed. Jeffrey H. Richards and Heather S. Nathans (Oxford: Oxford University Press, 2014).

66. "Amusements: 'Hamlet' at the Academy," n.d., Museum of the City of New York, "Hamlet" Edwin Booth.

67. "Lester Wallack Scrapbook Volume 3," n.d.

68. Palmer, "Palmer's Account of the Testimonial Benefit Performance to Mr. Lester Wallack," May 1893, 14.

69. Palmer, 14–15.

70. Rose Eytinge, "Rose Eytinge to A. M. Palmer," May 18, 1888, Harvard Theater Collection, Houghton Library, Harvard University.

71. *The Sun*, May 19, 1888.

72. Kellogg was the daughter of Brooklyn businessman and spiritualist Charles White Kellogg. Charles and family's papers (including personal correspondence, diaries, financial records, etc.) can be found in the archive of the New-York Historical Society: "Papers of the Kellogg Family," n.d., New-York Historical Society, New York, New York.

73. Gertrude Kellogg, "Diary of Gertrude Kellogg," May 18, 1888, New-York Historical Society.

74. A. M. Palmer, "A. M. Palmer to Augustin Daly," March 1888, Y.C. 4689 47–51, Folger Shakespeare Library.

75. Palmer, "Palmer's Account of the Testimonial Benefit Performance to Mr. Lester Wallack," May 1893, 8–9.

76. A. M. Palmer, "A. M. Palmer to Augustin Daly," April 10, 1888, Y.C. 4689 57–62, Folger Shakespeare Library.

77. Matthew Franks, *Subscription Theater: Democracy and Drama in Britain and Ireland, 1880–1939* (Philadelphia: University of Pennsylvania Press, 2020), 17.

78. Franks, 83–90.

79. Palmer, "Palmer's Account of the Testimonial Benefit Performance to Mr. Lester Wallack," May 1893, 10–13.

80. Mullenix, "So Unfemininely Masculine: Discourse, True/False, Womanhood, and the American Career of Fanny Kemble," 332.

81. Don C. Seitz, *The James Gordon Bennetts, Father and Son, Proprietors of the New York Herald* (Indianapolis: Bobbs-Merrill, 1928).

82. "Once Well-Known Actress Succumbs to Heart Disease—Was Engaged to Be Married," *New York Times*, 1903.

83. Palmer, "Palmer's Account of the Testimonial Benefit Performance to Mr. Lester Wallack," May 1893, 9–10.

234 | NOTES TO CHAPTER SIX

84. Deshler Welch, "Necroloy of 1888," *The Theatre*, January 18, 1889, vol. 5, no. 3. ed.

85. Palmer, "Palmer's Account of the Testimonial Benefit Performance to Mr. Lester Wallack," May 1893, 10.

86. Palmer, 12–13.

87. "The Wallack Testimonial," *The Post*, May 21, 1888.

88. "A Nestor of the Stage" (*The Star*, n.d.), The Gen Ts 211.5.3 F, Harvard Theater Collection, Houghton Library, Harvard University.

89. I discuss this theory in greater depth in this book's introduction. Mirowski, "Learning the Meaning of a Dollar: Conservation Principles and the Social Theory of Value in Economic Theory," 703.

90. I discuss this theory of value, as well, in this book's introduction. Perry, *General Theory of Value*, 115–16.

91. Kellogg, "Diary of Gertrude Kellogg."

92. There are several late nineteenth-century biographies of Barrett and his work, including: Barron, *Lawrence Barrett: A Professional Sketch*; Cartwright, *Biography of Lawrence Barrett (1838–1891)*. William M. Laffan recounts a brief bio-sketch of Barrett in: Brander Matthews and Laurence Hutton, *The Life and Art of Edwin Booth and His Contemporaries* (Boston: L. C. Page, 1886), 37–54.

93. A brief biographical sketch of Plympton can be found in: Gerald Bordman and Thomas S. Hischak, *The Oxford Companion to American Theatre* (Oxford: Oxford University Press, 2004), 504.

94. "The Wallack Testimonial" (*Tribune*, n.d.), The Gen Ts 211.5.3 F, Harvard Theater Collection, Houghton Library, Harvard University.

95. Coleman, *Fair Rosalind: The American Career of Helena Modjeska*, 881. Other accounts of Modjeska's career can be found in: Altemus, *Helena Modjeska*; Collins, *The Story of Helena Modjeska*; Holmgren, *Starring Madame Modjeska*; Gronowicz, *Modjeska: Her Life and Loves*; Modjeska, *Memories and Impressions of Helena Modjeska: An Autobiography*.

96. Coleman, *Fair Rosalind: The American Career of Helena Modjeska*, 96.

97. Holmgren, *Starring Madame Modjeska*, 214.

98. "Modjeska Scrapbook," n.d., New York Public Library Billy Rose Theatre Collection.

99. "Modjeska Scrapbook."

100. "Modjeska Scrapbook."

101. A thorough account of Jefferson's career can be found in: Bloom, *Joseph Jefferson: Dean of the American Theatre*.

102. Bloom, 195.

103. "Clippings Related to Lester Wallack," 16.

104. Palmer, "Palmer's Account of the Testimonial Benefit Performance to Mr. Lester Wallack," May 1893, 22–23.

105. Palmer, 14.

NOTES TO CONCLUSION | 235

106. A. M. Palmer, "A. M. Palmer to Augustin Daly," May 1888, Y.C. 4689 57–62, Folger Shakespeare Library.

107. Palmer, "A. M. Palmer to Augustin Daly," May 22, 1888.

108. (*The Sun*, n.d.), The Gen Ts 211.5.3 F, Harvard Theater Collection, Houghton Library, Harvard University.

109. "Clippings Related to Lester Wallack," 16.

110. These souvenir programs can be found in: "Robinson Locke Collection of Theatrical Scrapbooks," n.d., New York Public Library Billy Rose Theatre Collection; "Hamlet Playbill," n.d., Folger Shakespeare Library; "Lester Wallack Scrapbook Volume 2," n.d., Folger Shakespeare Library; "Lester Wallack Scrapbook Volume 3," n.d., Folger Shakespeare Library; "Metropolitan Opera House Playbills 1888," Harvard Theater Collection, Houghton Library, Harvard University. This last collection has eight playbills from the benefit, including one in silk.

Conclusion. The Dramaturgy of Value at Large

1. Robin Finn, "That's Some Key," *New York Times*, September 30, 2012.

2. Phil Lord and Christopher Miller, directors, *The LEGO Movie*, Warner Bros. Pictures, 2014, 1hr., 40 mins.

3. Both cinematic explorations involve taking the audience to Shakespeare's London to cast modern sensibilities on things like production conditions, William Shakespeare's love life and proclivities, and his work habits. John Madden, director, *Shakespeare in Love*, Miramax, 1998, 2 hrs., 3 mins.; *Doctor Who*, 2007, season 3, episode 2, "The Shakespeare Code," directed by Charles Palmer, aired April 7, 2007, on BBC.

4. The statue was not made in this image but rather from an 1870 portrait done by William Wallace Scott owned by the Harvard Theater Collection, available through the National Portrait Gallery. William Wallace Scott, *Edwin Booth as Hamlet*, 1870, National Portrait Gallery, 83.2 cm. x 58.2 cm., 1870, https://npg.si.edu/object/npg_MA250730.

Bibliography

"The Actors Fund: About Us," December 11, 2015. https://actorsfund.org/about-us. Accessed December 13, 2022.

Adams, Bluford. *E. Pluribus Barnum: The Great Showman and the Making of U.S. Popular Culture*. Minneapolis: University of Minnesota Press, 1996.

Adams, Rachel. *Sideshow USA: Freaks and the American Cultural Imagination*. Chicago: University of Chicago Press, 2001.

Agnew, Jean-Christophe. *Worlds Apart: The Market and the Theater in Anglo-American Thought, 1550–1750*. Cambridge: Cambridge University Press, 1986.

The Aldine 6, no. 10 (October 1873): 209.

Alexandria Gazette. January 29, 1850.

———. "Letter from New York," March 21, 1849.

———. May 22, 1888.

———. "Mrs. Butler in Boston," February 1, 1849.

Altemus, Jameson Torr. *Helena Modjeska*. New York: Benjamin Blom, 1971.

"Amusements: 'Hamlet' at the Academy," n.d. Museum of the City of New York, "Hamlet" Edwin Booth.

Anbinder, Tyler. *Five Points*. New York: Free Press, 2001.

Anderegg, Michael. *Lincoln and Shakespeare*. Lawrenceville: University Press of Kansas, 2015.

Anderson, Benedict. *Imagined Communities: Reflections on the Origin and Spread of Nationalism*. London: Verso, 2006.

Anderson, William T., ed. *Mermaids, Mummies, and Mastodons: The Emergence of the American Museum*. Washington, DC: American Association of Museums, 1992.

Aptheker, Herbert. *American Negro Slave Revolts*. New ed. New York: International, 1969.

Archer, Stephen M. *Junius Brutus Booth: Theatrical Prometheus*. Carbondale: Southern Illinois University Press, 1992.

Athens Post. "Revolution among the Petticoats," May 23, 1851.

238 | Bibliography

Bache, R. Meade. "Reaction Time with Reference to Race." *Psychological Review* 2, no. 5 (September 1895): 475–86.

Barnum, Phineas Taylor. "Mr. Barnum on Museums." *The Nation.* August 10, 1865.

———. *The Life of Barnum.* Philadelphia: H. J. Smith, 1900.

———. *The Life of P. T. Barnum, Written by Himself.* London: Sampson, Low and Son, 1855.

———. *The Life of P. T. Barnum Written by Himself.* Edited by Terence Whalen. Urbana: University of Illinois Press, 2000.

———. *The Life of P. T. Barnum Written by Himself Including His Golden Rules for Money-Making Brought Up to 1888.* Buffalo: Courier Company Printers, 1888.

———. *Struggles and Triumphs.* Buffalo: Warren, Johnson, 1872.

"Barnum's American Museum Illustrated." Norden and Leslie Illustrated Book Printers, 1850. New-York Historical Society.

Barron, Elwyn A. *Lawrence Barrett: A Professional Sketch.* Chicago: Knight and Leonard, 1889.

Bennet, James Gordon. *New York Herald.* December 24, 1865, vol. 30, no. 357 ed.

Bernstein, Robin. *Racial Innocence: Performing American Childhood from Slavery to Civil Rights.* New York: New York University Press, 2011.

Berthold, Dennis. "Class Acts: The Astor Place Riots and Melville's 'The Two Temples.'" *American Literature* 71, no. 3 (September 1999): 429–61.

Blackwood, Sarah. "Limbs: Postbellum Portraiture and the Mind-Body Problem." In *The Portrait's Subject: Inventing Inner Life in the Nineteenth-Century United States*, 79–106. Chapel Hill: University of North Carolina Press, 2019.

Bloom, Arthur W. *Edwin Booth: A Biography and Performance History.* Jefferson: McFarland, 2013.

———. *Joseph Jefferson: Dean of the American Theatre.* Savannah: Frederic C. Beil, 2000.

Bly, Mark. "Bristling with Multiple Possibilities." In *Dramaturgy in American Theater: A Sourcebook*, edited by Susan Jonas, Geoffrey S. Proehl, and Michael Lupu, 48–56. New York: Harcourt, Brace, 1997.

Bogart, Thomas A. *Backstage at the Lincoln Assassination.* Washington, DC: Regnery History, 2013.

Booth, Alison. "From Miranda to Prospero: The Works of Fanny Kemble." *Victorian Studies* 38, no. 2 (Winter 1995): 227–54.

Booth, Edwin. "Edwin Booth to Augustin Daly," December 16, 1886. Folger Shakespeare Library.

———. "Edwin Booth to Augustin Daly," January 27, 1887. Folger Shakespeare Library.

"Booth Family Scrapbook," n.d. Folger Shakespeare Library.

Booth Medal, 1894. Folger Shakespeare Library.

Bordman, Gerald, and Thomas S. Hischak. *The Oxford Companion to American Theatre*. Cary: Oxford University Press, 2004.

Bourdieu, Pierre. *Distinction: A Social Critique of the Judgement of Taste*. Translated by Richard Nice. Cambridge: Harvard University Press, 1984.

———. *The Field of Cultural Production*. Edited by Randal Johnson. New York: Columbia University Press, 1993.

———. *Outline of a Theory of Practice*. Translated by Richard Nice. Cambridge: Cambridge University Press, 1977.

———. *Pascalian Meditations*. Translated by Richard Nice. Stanford: Stanford University Press, 2000.

Bourdillon, F. W. "A Spring Evening." *The Galaxy*, April 1876, vol. 21, issue 4 ed.

Bowdler, Henrietta Maria. *The Family Shakespeare in Four Volumes*. Bath: R. Cruttwell, 1807.

Boyer, Paul. *Urban Masses and Moral Order in America, 1820–1920*. Cambridge: Harvard University Press, 1978.

Bratton, Jacky. "Frances Anne Kemble." In *Great Shakespeareans: Jameson, Cowden Clarke, Kemble, Cushman*, edited by Gail Marshall, vol. 7. London: Continuum, 2011.

Bristol, Michael D. *Big-Time Shakespeare*. London: Routledge, 1996.

"Broadside: Barnum's American Museum," August 19, 1853. New-York Historical Society.

Brown, T. Allston. *A History of the New York Stage*. Vol. 1, 3 vols. New York: Benjamin Blom, 1903.

———. *A History of the New York Stage*. Vol. 3. New York: Dodd, Mead, 1903.

Burrows, Edwin G., and Mike Wallace. *Gotham: A History of New York City to 1898*. Oxford: Oxford University Press, 1999.

Bunting, J. "Biographical Sketch of the Author." In *The Stage*, by James Murdoch, 13–24. Reissued ed. Bronx: Benjamin Blom, 1969.

Butler, Pierce. *Mr. Butler's Statement: Originally Prepared in Aid of His Professional Council*. Philadelphia: J. C. Clark, 1850.

Butler, Pierce, and Fanny Kemble. "Pierce Butler vs. Frances Anne Butler: Libel for Divorce with Answer and Exhibits." Court of Common Pleas of Philadelphia County, 1848.

Carlson, Marvin. *The Haunted Stage*. 2011 paperback reprint. Ann Arbor: University of Michigan Press, 2001.

Carson, William G. B. *Letters of Mr. and Mrs. Charles Kean Relating to Their American Tours*. St. Louis: Washington University Press, 1945.

Cartelli, Thomas. *Repositioning Shakespeare: National Formation, Postcolonial Appropriations*. New York: Routledge, 1999.

Cartwright, William. *Biography of Lawrence Barrett (1838–1891)*. Paterson: Manuscript Club, 1847.

240 | BIBLIOGRAPHY

Catalogue or Guide Book of Barnum's American Museum New York: Containing Descriptions and Illustrations of the Various Wonders and Curiosities of This Immense Establishment. New York: Wynkoop, Hellenbeck and Thomas, Steam Book and Job Printers, 1863. New-York Historical Society.

Catlin, George. *Five Points*, 1827. Oil. WikiCommons, http://en.wikipedia.org/wiki/File:Five_Points_-_George_Catlin_-_1827.jpg.

Cattaneo, Anne. "Dramaturgy: An Overview." In *Dramaturgy in American Theater: A Sourcebook*, edited by Susan Jonas, Geoffrey S. Proehl, and Michael Lupu, 3–15. New York: Harcourt, Brace, 1997.

Chappell, Maria. "Taking Note, Fanny Kemble's Shakespeare." PhD dissertation, University of Georgia, 2018.

Chemers, Michael Mark. *Ghost Light: An Introductory Handbook for Dramaturgy.* Carbondale: Southern Illinois University Press, 2010.

Christian Union. "Ward's Statue of Shakespeare," May 29, 1872, sec. Literature and Arts.

Clarke, Asia Booth. *The Elder and the Younger Booth.* Boston: James R. Osgood, 1882.

———. *John Wilkes Booth: A Sister's Memoir.* Edited by Terry Alford. Jackson: University Press of Mississippi, 1996.

———. *The Unlocked Book: A Memoir of John Wilkes Booth.* Edited by Eleanor Farjeon. New York: G. P. Putnam's Sons, 1938.

Clarke, Charles. "On Booth's Hamlet," n.d. Folger Shakespeare Library.

Cliff, Nigel. *The Shakespeare Riots: Revenge, Drama, and Death in Nineteenth-Century America.* New York: Random House, 2007.

Clinton, Catherine. *Fanny Kemble's Civil War.* Oxford: Oxford University Press, 2000.

"Clippings: The Booth Family," August 2, 1934. New York Public Library Billy Rose Theatre Collection.

"Clippings Related to Lester Wallack," n.d. Harvard Theater Collection, Houghton Library, Harvard University.

Cmiel, Kenneth. *Democratic Eloquence: The Fight over Popular Speech in Nineteenth-Century America.* New York: William Morrow, 1990.

Coffee, Kevin. "The Material Significance of Carriage Drives to the Design of Central Park." *Journal of the Society for Industrial Archeology* 38, no. 1 (2012): 75–92.

Coleman, Marion Moore. *Fair Rosalind: The American Career of Helena Modjeska.* Cheshire: Cherry Hill Books, 1969.

Collins, Mabel. *The Story of Helena Modjeska.* London: W. H. Allen, 1883.

Columbia Democrat. May 12, 1849.

Commercial Advertiser. July 31, 1820.

Commercial Gazette. "Excellent Theatrical," July 19, 1821.

BIBLIOGRAPHY | 241

Conti, Meredith. *Playing Sick: Performances of Illness in the Age of Victorian Medicine.* London: Routledge, 2018.

Cook, James W., ed. *The Colossal P. T. Barnum Reader: Nothing Else Like It in the World.* Urbana: University of Illinois Press, 2005.

Cowper, William. *The Task: A Poem, in Six Books. By William Cowper, . . . To Which Are Added, by the Same Author, An Epistle to Joseph Hill, Esq. . . . To Which Are Added, . . . an Epistle . . . and the History of John Gilpin.* London: J. Johnson, 1785.

Crane, Jacob. " 'One Day Our Warmest Friend; the Next Our Bitterest Enemy': Mordecai Manuel Noah and the Black-Jewish Imaginary." *Studies in American Jewish Literature* 39, no. 2 (September 2020): 182–95.

Curry, Jane Kathleen. "Women in Nineteenth Century American Theatre Management." PhD dissertation, City University of New York, New York, 1991.

Daily Crescent. February 7, 1850.

Daily Intelligencer. " 'Murder Most Foul!': Remembering Lincoln," April 17, 1865.

Daily Picayune. "Wallack's Wish," February 19, 1887.

Daily Richmond Times. January 30, 1850.

Daily Union. November 6, 1849.

David, Deirdre. *Fanny Kemble: A Performed Life.* Philadelphia: University of Pennsylvania Press, 2007.

Davis, Merrell R., and William H. Gilman, eds. *The Letters of Herman Melville.* New Haven: Yale University Press, 1960.

Davis, Tracy. "Acting Black, 1824: Charles Mathews's Trip to America." *Theatre Journal* 63 (2011): 163–89.

———. *The Economics of the British Stage 1800–1914.* Cambridge: Cambridge University Press, 2000.

Deetz, James. "Material Culture and Worldview in Colonial Anglo-America." In *The Recovery of Meaning: Historical Archaeology in the Eastern United States,* edited by Mark P. Leone and Parker B. Potter Jr., 219–34. Washington, DC: Smithsonian Institution, 1988.

Dennett, Andrea Stulman. *Weird and Wonderful: The Dime Museum in America.* New York: New York University Press, 1997.

"Diary of Junius Brutus Booth," n.d. Folger Shakespeare Library.

diZerega, Diana, Nan A. Rothschild, and Meredith B. Linn. "Constructing Identity in Seneca Village." In *Archaeology of Identity and Dissonance,* edited by Diane F. George and Bernice Kurchin, 157–80. Gainesville: University Press of Florida, 2019.

Doctor Who. 2007. Season 3, episode 2, "The Shakespeare Code," directed by Charles Palmer, aired April 7, 2007, on BBC.

Du Bois, W. E. B. *Black Reconstruction in America.* Oxford: Oxford University Press, 2007.

Dudden, Faye E. *Women in the American Theatre: Actresses and Audiences, 1790–1870*. New Haven: Yale University Press, 1994.

Durante, Dianne L. *Outdoor Monuments of Manhattan: A Historical Guide*. New York: New York University Press, 2007.

Dyer, Brainerd. "One Hundred Years of Negro Suffrage." *Pacific Historical Review* 37, no. 1 (February 1968): 1–20.

"Edwin Booth Letters," n.d. Folger Shakespeare Library.

"Edwin Booth Scrapbook," n.d. Folger Shakespeare Library.

"Edwin Booth to JQA Ward," n.d. Typescript copy in research files, the American Wing, Metropolitan Museum of Art.

Elias, Stephen N. *Alexander T. Stewart: The Forgotten Merchant Prince*. Westport: Praeger, 1992.

Engler, Balz. "Shakespeare, Sculpture, and the Material Arts." In *The Edinburgh Companion to Shakespeare and the Arts*, edited by Mark Thornton Burnett, Adrian Streete, and Ramona Wray, 435–44. Edinburgh: Edinburgh University Press, 2011.

Evans, Sara M. *Born for Liberty: A History of Women in America*. New York: Free Press, 1989.

Evening Post. "Communication," October 8, 1821.

———. "From the Richmond Daily Advertiser," July 10, 1821.

"The Evening Telegram," May 21, 1888. Kellogg Family Papers, Box 11, Folder: Notices and Reviews. New-York Historical Society.

Evening World. "5 O'clock Extra," April 19, 1888.

Eytinge, Rose. *The Memories of Rose Eytinge*. New York: Frederick A. Stokes, 1905.

———. "Rose Eytinge to A. M. Palmer," May 18, 1888. Harvard Theater Collection, Houghton Library, Harvard University.

Fanon, Frantz. *Black Skin, White Masks*. Translated by Richard Philcox. New York: Grove Press, 2008.

Fardon, G. R. "San Francisco Album: Photographs of the Most Beautiful Views and Public Buildings of San Francisco," 1856. New-York Historical Society. https://digitalcollections.nyhistory.org/islandora/object/nyhs%3A23971#page/2/mode/1up. Accessed December 14, 2022.

Fazel, Valerie M., and Louise Geddes. *The Shakespeare Multiverse Fandom as Literary Praxis*. New York: Routledge, 2021.

———, eds. *The Shakespeare User*. New York: Palgrave Macmillan, 2017.

Felheim, Marvin. *The Theater of Augustin Daly: An Account of the Late Nineteenth Century American Stage*. Cambridge: Harvard University Press, 1956.

Finn, Robin. "That's Some Key." *New York Times*, September 30, 2012.

Fisherman and Farmer. "Newsy Gleanings," February 3, 1888.

———. January 20, 1888.

Florence, W. J. "Lester Wallack." *North American Review* 147, no. 383 (October 1888): 453–59.

Fort Worth Daily Gazette. May 28, 1888.

Foulkes, Richard. "A Babel of Bardolaters: The 1864 Tercentenary." In *Performing Shakespeare in the Age of Empire*, 58–81. Cambridge: Cambridge University Press, 2002.

Franks, Matthew. *Subscription Theater: Democracy and Drama in Britain and Ireland, 1880–1939*. Philadelphia: University of Pennsylvania Press, 2020.

Fraser, L. M. *Economic Thought and Language*. London: Adam and Charles Black, 1947.

Fredrickson, George M. *The Inner Civil War: Northern Intellectuals and the Crisis of the Union*. New York: Harper and Row, 1965.

Frick, John W. *Theatre, Culture and Temperance Reform in Nineteenth-Century America*. Cambridge: Cambridge University Press, 2003.

Frost, Linda. *Never One Nation: Freaks, Savages, and Whiteness in U.S. Popular Culture 1850–1877*. Minneapolis: University of Minnesota Press, 2005.

Frow, John. *Cultural Studies and Cultural Value*. Oxford: Clarendon, 1995.

Furnas, J. C. *Fanny Kemble: Leading Lady of the Nineteenth-Century Stage*. New York: Dial, 1982.

Furtwangler, Albert. *Assassin on Stage: Brutus, Hamlet, and the Death of Lincoln*. Urbana: University of Illinois Press, 1991.

Gainor, J. Ellen. Introduction to *Performing America: Cultural Nationalism in American Theater*, by Jeffrey D. Mason and J. Ellen Gainor, 7–15. Ann Arbor: University of Michigan Press, 1999.

Garland-Thomson, Rosemarie. *Freakery: Cultural Spectacles of the Extraordinary Body*. New York: New York University Press, 1996.

Gazette. November 29, 1821.

Goffman, Erving. *The Presentation of Self in Everyday Life*. New York: Doubleday, 1959.

Goodrich, S. G., and Thomas G. Bradford. *New York (City). Engraved by G. W. Boynton*. 1841. 36 cm. x 29 cm. David Rumsey Map Collection.

Goodrich, Thomas. *The Darkest Dawn: Lincoln, Booth, and the Great American Tragedy*. Bloomington: Indiana University Press, 2005.

Gronowicz, Antoni. *Modjeska: Her Life and Loves*. New York: Thomas Yoseloff, 1956.

Grossman, Edwina Booth. *Edwin Booth: Recollections by His Daughter Edwina Booth Grossman and Letters to Her and His Friends*. New York: Century, 1894.

"Guide Book to Barnum's American Museum," n.d. Harvard Theater Collection, Houghton Library, Harvard University.

"A Guide to Rapid and Accurate Computation by Professor Hutchings," n.d. Bridgeport Public Library.

Halttunen, Karen. *Confidence Men and Painted Women*. New Haven: Yale University Press, 1982.

"Hamlet Playbill," n.d. Folger Shakespeare Library.

BIBLIOGRAPHY

Harris, Cheryl I. "Whiteness as Property." *Harvard Law Review* 106, no. 8 (1993): 1707–91.

Harris, Wendy Elizabeth, and Arnold Pickman. "Towards an Archaeology of the Hudson River Ice Harvesting Industry." *Northeast Historical Archaeology* 29 (2000): 49–80.

Hartman, Sadakichi. *Shakespeare in Art.* Boston: L. C. Page, 1901.

Hawthorne, Nathaniel. "Recollections of a Gifted Woman." *Atlantic Monthly,* January 1863.

Hay, Samuel A. *African American Theatre in Historical and Critical Analysis.* Cambridge: University of Cambridge Press, 1994.

Hecksecher, Morrison H. "Creating Central Park." *Metropolitan Museum of Art Bulletin,* New Series 65, no. 3 (Winter 2008): 1–3, 5–74.

Heneghan, Bridget T. *Whitewashing America: Material Culture and Race in the Antebellum Imagination.* Jackson: University Press of Mississippi, 2003.

Herald of the Times. June 21, 1849.

———. October 11, 1849.

Hill, Errol. *Shakespeare in Sable: A History of Black Shakespearean Actors.* Amherst: University of Massachusetts Press, 1984.

Hirsch, Leo H., Jr. "The Free Negro in New York." *Journal of Negro History* 16, no. 4 (1931): 415–53.

Hodges, Graham Russell. *Root and Branch: African Americans in New York and East Jersey 1613–1863.* Chapel Hill: University of North Carolina Press, 1999.

Hodin, Mark. "The Disavowal of Ethnicity: Legitimate Theatre and the Social Construction of Literary Value in Turn-of-the-Century America." *Theatre Journal* 52, no. 2 (2000): 211–26.

Holmgren, Beth. *Starring Madame Modjeska.* Bloomington: Indiana University Press, 2012.

Holt, Douglas B. *How Brands Become Icons: The Principles of Cultural Branding.* Boston: Harvard School of Business, 2004.

Hone, Philip. *The Diary of Philip Hone.* Vol. 1, 2 vols. New York: Dodd, Mead, 1889.

Hutter, Michael, and David Throsby, eds. *Beyond Price: Value in Culture, Economics, and the Arts.* Cambridge: Cambridge University Press, 2008.

"Impression from Edwin Booth's Fob Seal," 1893. Folger Shakespeare Library.

Irelan, Scott R., Anne Fletcher, and Julie Felise Dubiner. *The Process of Dramaturgy: A Handbook.* Indianapolis: Hackett, 2010.

Isenberg, Nancy. *Sex and Citizenship in Antebellum America.* Chapel Hill: University of North Carolina Press, 1998.

Jefferson, Thomas. *Notes on the State of Virginia.* Chicago: University of Chicago Press, 1784.

Johnson, Claudia D. *American Actress: Perspective on the Nineteenth Century.* Chicago: Nelson-Hall, 1984.

Kahan, Gerald. "Fanny Kemble Reads Shakespeare: Her First American Tour, 1849–50." *Theatre Survey* 24, no. 1–2 (1983): 77–98.

BIBLIOGRAPHY | 245

Kanellos, Nicolás. *A History of Hispanic Theatre in the United States: Origins to 1940*. Austin: University of Texas Press, 1990.

Kauffman, Michael W. *American Brutus*. New York: Random House, 2004.

Keegan, John. *The American Civil War: A Military History*. New York: Alfred A. Knopf, 2009.

Kellogg, Gertrude. "Diary of Gertrude Kellogg," 1888. New-York Historical Society.

Kemble, Fanny. *The Journal of Frances Anne Butler*. 1970 reprint. New York: Benjamin Blom, 1970.

Kemble, Frances Anne. *Far Away and Long Ago*. New York: H. Holt, 1889.

———. *Further Records*. New York: Henry Holt, 1891.

———. *Journal of a Residence on a Georgia Plantation*. New York: Harper, 1863.

———. *Records of a Girlhood*. Vol. 1, 3 vols. London: H. Holt, 1879.

———. *Records of Later Life*. 2nd ed., vol. 2, 3 vols. London: R. Bentley, 1882.

———. *Records of Later Life*. 2nd ed., vol. 3, 3 vols. London: R. Bentley, 1882.

———. *A Year of Consolation*. London: Moxon, 1847.

Kilman, Bernice W., and Rick Santos, eds. *Latin American Shakespeares*. Madison: Farleigh Dickinson University Press, 2005.

Kimmel, Stanley. *The Mad Booths of Maryland*. 2nd revised and enlarged ed. New York: Dover, 1969.

Kinsley, Elisabeth H. *Here in This Island We Arrived: Shakespeare and Belonging in Immigrant New York*. University Park: Pennsylvania State University Press, 2019.

Knapp, Raymond. *The American Musical and the Formation of National Identity*. Princeton: Princeton University Press, 2005.

Kokai, Jennifer A. *Swim Pretty: Aquatic Spectacles and the Performance of Race, Gender, and Nature*. Carbondale: Southern Illinois University Press, 2017.

Kritzer, Amelia Howe. "Antebellum Plays by Women." In *The Oxford Handbook of American Drama*, edited by Jeffrey H. Richards and Heather S. Nathans, 114–29. Oxford: Oxford University Press, 2014.

Kunhardt, Philip B., Jr., Philip B. Kunhardt III, and Peter W. Kunhardt. *P. T. Barnum: America's Greatest Showman*. New York: Alfred A. Knopf, 1995.

Laird, John. *The Idea of Value*. Cambridge: Cambridge University Press, 1929.

Lamb, Charles, and Mary Lamb. *Tales from Shakespeare*. Illustrated version with Walter Paget. New York: Nister Dutton, 1910.

Langtry, Lillie. *The Days I Knew*. New York: George H. Doran, 1925.

Lanier, Douglas. "Commemorating Shakespeare in America, 1864." In *Celebrating Shakespeare: Commemoration and Cultural Memory*, edited by Clara Calvo and Coppélia Kahn, 140–60. Cambridge: Cambridge University Press, 2015.

———. "Recent Shakespeare Adaptation and the Mutations of Cultural Capital." *Shakespeare Studies (0582-9399)* 38 (January 2010): 104–13.

———. "Shakespeare: Myth and Biographical Fiction." In *The Cambridge Companion to Shakespeare and Popular Culture*, edited by Robert Shaughnessy, 93–113. Cambridge: Cambridge University Press, 2007.

246 | BIBLIOGRAPHY

Lawrence, Philip. "Edwin Booth as Hamlet," November 20, 1876. Folger Shakespeare Library.

Lears, Jackson. *Fables of Abundance: A Cultural History of Advertising in America.* New York: Basic Books, 1994.

Leavitt, Michael Bennett. *Fifty Years in Theatrical Management.* New York: Broadway, 1912.

Lemire, Elise. *"Miscegenation": Making Race in America.* Philadelphia: University of Pennsylvania Press, 2002.

Lepore, Jill. *The Name of War: King Philip's War and the Origins of American Identity.* New York: Alfred A. Knopf, 1998.

———. *New York Burning: Liberty, Slavery, and Conspiracy in Eighteenth-Century Manhattan.* New York: Alfred A. Knopf, 2005.

Lessing, Gotthold Ephraim. *The Hamburg Dramaturgy: A New and Complete Translation.* Edited by Natalya Baldyga. Translated by Wendy Arone and Sara Figal. New York: Routledge, 2019. https://mcpress.media-commons. org/hamburg.

"Lester Wallack Scrapbook," n.d. New York Public Library Billy Rose Theatre Collection.

"Lester Wallack Scrapbook Volume 2," n.d. Folger Shakespeare Library.

"Lester Wallack Scrapbook Volume 3," n.d. Folger Shakespeare Library.

Levenson, Jill L., and Robert Ormsby, eds. *The Shakespearean World.* London: Routledge, 2017.

Levine, Lawrence W. *Highbrow/Lowbrow: The Emergence of Cultural Hierarchy in America.* Cambridge: Harvard University Press, 1988.

Levison, Wallace Goold, Copyright Claimant. "Brooklyn Institute and Adjoining Houses, 192–204 Washington St., Brooklyn, New York," June 10, 1891. Library of Congress. https://www.loc.gov/item/2010648520/. Accessed December 18, 2022.

Lewis, Philip C. *Trouping: How the Show Came to Town.* New York: Harper and Row, 1973.

Lewis, Robert Michael. "Speaking Black, 1824: Charles Mathews's Trip to America Revisited." *Nineteenth Century Theatre and Film* 43, no. 1 (May 2016): 43–66.

The Lily. "Mrs. Kemble and Her New Costume," December 1, 1849.

Litchfield Enquirer. November 29, 1849.

Literary World. "What Is Talked About," November 17, 1849.

Longworth, David, and Andrew Beers. *Longworth's American Almanac, New York Register, and City Directory.* New York: Published at the old established directory office, Shakespeare-Gallery, by David Longworth, 1819.

———. *Longworth's American Almanac, New York Register, and City Directory.* New York: Published at the old established directory office, Shakespeare-Gallery, by David Longworth, 1823.

Lord, Phil, and Christopher Miller, directors. *The LEGO Movie.* Warner Bros. Pictures, 2014. 1 hr., 40 mins.

"The Lost Museum." https://lostmuseum.cuny.edu/. Accessed April 14, 2021.

Lott, Eric. *Love and Theft: Blackface Minstrelsy and the American Working Class.* 20th anniversary ed. Oxford: Oxford University Press, 2013.

Lynchburg Virginian. "Mrs. Kemble's Macbeth," April 4, 1850.

MacDonald, Joyce Green. "Acting Black: 'Othello,' 'Othello' Burlesques, and the Performance of Blackness." *Theatre Journal* 46, no. 2 (May 1994): 231–49.

MacKaye, Percy. *Epoch: The Life of Steele MacKaye.* Reprinted, vol. 1. Grosse Pointe, MI: Scholarly Press, 1968.

Marra, Kim. *Strange Duets: Impresarios and Actresses in the American Theatre, 1865–1914.* Iowa City: University of Iowa Press, 2006.

———. "Taming America as Actress: Augustin Daly, Ada Rehan, and the Discourse of Imperial Frontier Conquest." In *Performing America: Cultural Nationalism in American Theater*, edited by Jeffrey D. Mason and J. Ellen Gainor, 52–72. Ann Arbor: University of Michigan Press, 1999.

Marshall, Gail. *Shakespeare and the Victorian Woman.* Cambridge: Cambridge University Press, 2009.

Marshall, Herbert, and Mildred Stock. *Ira Aldridge: The Negro Tragedian.* Carbondale: Southern Illinois University Press, 1958.

Marx, Karl. *Capital: A Critique of Political Economy.* Edited by Frederick Engels. Translated by Samuel Moore and Edward Aveling. Chicago: Charles H. Kerr, 1912.

———. *The Grundrisse.* Edited by David McLellan. New York: Harper and Row, 1971.

Matthews, Brander, and Laurence Hutton. *The Life and Art of Edwin Booth and His Contemporaries.* Boston: L. C. Page, 1886.

McAllister, Marvin. *White People Do Not Know How to Behave at Entertainments Designed for Ladies and Gentlemen of Color.* Chapel Hill: University of North Carolina Press, 2003.

———. *Whiting Up: Whiteface Minstrels and Stage Europeans in African American Performance.* Chapel Hill: University of North Carolina Press, 2011.

McArthur, Benjamin. *Actors and American Culture, 1880–1920.* Philadelphia: Temple University Press, 1984.

McConachie, Bruce A. *Melodramatic Formations.* Iowa City: University of Iowa Press, 1992.

———. "Museum Theatre and the Problem of Respectability for Mid-Century Urban Americans." In *The American Stage: Social and Economic Issues from the Colonial Period to the Present*, edited by Ron Engle and Tice L. Miller, 65–80. Cambridge: Cambridge University Press, 1993.

Mercantile Advertiser. September 4, 1818.

"Metropolitan Opera House Playbills 1888," n.d. Harvard Theater Collection, Houghton Library, Harvard University.

Middleton, Stephen, David R. Roediger, and Donald M. Shaffer. Introduction to *The Construction of Whiteness: An Interdisciplinary Analysis of Race*

BIBLIOGRAPHY

Formation and the Meaning of a White Identity. Jackson: University Press of Mississippi, 2016.

Miller, Derek. *Copyright and the Value of Performance, 1770–1911*. Cambridge: Cambridge University Press, 2018.

Minnesota Pioneer. "Mrs. Butler—Her Appearance—Dress—Stoutness," March 20, 1850.

Minutes of the Common Council of the City of New York 1675–1776. Vol. 3, 8 vols. New York: Dodd, Mead, 1905.

Minutes of the Common Council of the City of New York 1675–1776. Vol. 4, 8 vols. New York: Dodd, Mead, 1905.

Mirowski, Philip. "Learning the Meaning of a Dollar: Conservation Principles and the Social Theory of Value in Economic Theory." *Social Research* 57, no. 3 (Fall 1990): 689–717.

Modjeska, Helena. *Memories and Impressions of Helena Modjeska: An Autobiography*. New York: Macmillan, 1910.

"Modjeska Scrapbook," n.d. New York Public Library Billy Rose Theatre Collection.

Morris, Clara. *Life on the Stage*. New York: McClure, Phillips, 1902.

Morrison, Toni. *Playing in the Dark: Whiteness and the Literary Imagination*. Cambridge: Harvard University Press, 1992.

Moses, Montrose Jonas. *Famous Actor-Families in America*. New York: T. Y. Crowell, 1906.

Most, Andrea. *Making Americans: Jews and the Broadway Musical*. Cambridge: Harvard University Press, 2004.

"Mr. Booth's Appearance: A Magnificent Return to the Winter Garden," January 3, 1866. Harvard Theater Collection, Houghton Library, Harvard University.

Mullenix, Elizabeth Reitz. "So Unfemininely Masculine: Discourse, True/False, Womanhood, and the American Career of Fanny Kemble." *Theatre Survey* 40, no. 2 (November 1999): 27–42.

Mullenneaux, Nan. *Staging Family: Domestic Deceptions of Mid-Nineteenth-Century American Actresses*. Lincoln: University of Nebraska Press, 2018.

Nathans, Heather. *Early American Theatre from the Revolution to Thomas Jefferson: Into the Hands of the People*. Cambridge: Cambridge University Press, 2003.

———. *Hideous Characters and Beautiful Pagans: Performing Jewish Identity on the Antebellum American Stage*. Ann Arbor: University of Michigan Press, 2017.

———. "A Much Maligned People: Jews on and off the Stage in the Early American Republic." *Early American Studies* 2, no. 2 (2004): 310–42.

The Nation. "A Word about Museums," July 27, 1865.

National Advocate. "African Amusements," September 21, 1821.

———. "African Amusements," September 25, 1821.

———. "Mr. Booth; Attend; Theatre; Witness; Present," October 8, 1821.

"NativeLand.Ca." Native-land.ca—Our home on native land. https://native-land.ca/. "NativeLand.Ca." Accessed January 25, 2021.

Nayar, Pramod. "Branding Bill: The Shakespearean Commons." *Economic and Political Weekly* 50, no. 12 (March 21, 2015): 41–47.

Neilson, Peter. *Recollections of a Six Years' Residence in the United States of America.* Glasgow: David Robertson, 1830.

"A Nestor of the Stage." *The Star*, n.d. The Gen Ts 211.5.3 F. Harvard Theater Collection, Houghton Library, Harvard University.

New York Daily Advertiser. January 4, 1821.

———. January 6, 1821.

New-York Daily Tribune. "Edwin-Booth at the Winter Garden," January 4, 1866.

———. "Mrs. Kemble's Reading in Aid of the Hungarian Exiles," January 25, 1850.

———. "The Reappearance of Edwin Booth," January 3, 1866.

New York Herald. "A Herald Cast for 'Hamlet,'" January 9, 1888.

———. "The Celebration of Shakespeare's Birthday," January 31, 1864.

———. "The Ideal Hamlet," May 22, 1888.

———. "Mr. Wallack's Benefit," January 22, 1888.

———. "The Three Hundredth Anniversary of Shakespeare's Birth," April 20, 1864.

"New York Theatre and the Moral Drama." *United States Magazine of Science, Art, Manufactures, Agriculture, Commerce, and Trade* 1 (May 15, 1854): 22–23.

New York Times. "The Changes at Wallack's: Arrangements and Plans of the New Management." May 11, 1887

———. "Changes at Wallack's: Mr. Abbey's Assumption of the Management," August 21, 1887.

———. "Charles Coghlan Is Dead," 1899.

———. "Classified Ads 18," September 5, 1865.

———. "Couldock's Long Career," May 12, 1895.

———. "Death of Henry E. Abbey," October 18, 1896.

———. "Disastrous Fire," July 14, 1865.

———. "Once Well-Known Actress Succumbs to Heart Disease—Was Engaged to Be Married," 1903.

———. "Rebel Plot Attempt to Burn City; All Principal Hotels Simultaneously Set Fire," November 26, 1864.

New-York Tribune. "Barnum's Museum," June 19, 1850.

———. "The Shakespeare Statue Fund," April 23, 1864.

Nora, Pierre. "Between Memory and History: *Les Lieux de Mémoire.*" *Representations* 26 (Spring 1989): 7–24.

Odell, George Clinton. *Annals of the New York Stage.* New York: Columbia University Press, 1927.

———. *Annals of the New York Stage.* Vol. 3. New York: Columbia University Press, 1928.

Oggel, L. Terry. *Edwin Booth: A Bio-bibliography.* New York: Greenwood, 1992.

Oliver, Egbert S. "Melville's Goneril and Fanny Kemble." *New England Quarterly* 18, no. 4 (December 1945): 489–500.

250 | BIBLIOGRAPHY

Olmsted, Frederick Law, Jr. *Frederick Law Olmsted, Landscape Architect, 1822–1903.* New York: B. Blom, 1970.

Olson, Edwin. "The Slave Code in Colonial New York." *Journal of Negro History* 29, no. 2 (April 1944): 147–65.

Over, William. "New York's African Theatre: Shakespeare Reinterpreted." In *Shakespeare without Class: Misappropriations of Cultural Capital*, edited by Donald Hedrick and Bryan Reynolds, 65–84. New York: Palgrave, 2000.

Painter, Nell Irvin. *The History of White People.* New York: W. W. Norton, 2010.

Palmer, A. M. "A. M. Palmer to Augustin Daly," December 31, 1886. Folger Shakespeare Library.

———. "A. M. Palmer to Augustin Daly," January 28, 1887. Folger Shakespeare Library.

———. "A. M. Palmer to Augustin Daly," February 10, 1887. Folger Shakespeare Library.

———. "A. M. Palmer to Augustin Daly," March 1888. Y.C. 4689 47–51. Folger Shakespeare Library.

———. "A. M. Palmer to Augustin Daly," April 6, 1888. Folger Shakespeare Library.

———. "A. M. Palmer to Augustin Daly," April 10, 1888. Y.C. 4689 57–62. Folger Shakespeare Library.

———. "A. M. Palmer to Augustin Daly," May 1888. Y.C. 4689 57–62. Folger Shakespeare Library.

———. "A. M. Palmer to Augustin Daly," May 22, 1888. Folger Shakespeare Library.

———. "Palmer's Account of the Testimonial Benefit Performance to Mr. Lester Wallack." Thoe L. Devinne, May 1893. Folger Shakespeare Library.

"Papers of the Kellogg Family," n.d. New-York Historical Society, New York, New York.

Perry, John. "P. T. Barnum's American Museum." *Early American Life* 7, no. 56 (June 1976): 14–17.

Perry, Ralph Barton. *General Theory of Value.* Cambridge: Harvard University Press, 1967.

Plain Dealer. "Lester Wallack Declines a Testimonial Performance of Brother Professionals," February 19, 1887.

The Post. "The Wallack Testimonial," May 21, 1888.

"Record of Assessed Valuation of Real Estate (Ward 2)," 1821. New York Municipal Archive.

Reiss, Benjamin. *The Showman and the Slave: Race, Death and Memory in Barnum's America.* Cambridge: Harvard University Press, 2001.

The Republic. October 8, 1849.

Rhodehamel, John, and Louise Taper, eds. *"Right or Wrong, God Judge Me": The Writings of John Wilkes Booth.* Urbana: University of Illinois Press, 1997.

Richards, Jeffrey H. *Drama, Theatre, and Identity in the American New Republic.* Cambridge: Cambridge University Press, 2009.

Richardson, Heather Cox. "North and West of Reconstruction: Studies in Political Economy." In *Reconstructions: New Perspectives on Postbellum America*, edited by Thomas J. Brown, 66–90. Oxford: Oxford University Press, 2006.

Richter, Amy G. *At Home in Nineteenth-Century America: A Documentary History*. New York: New York University Press, 2015.

Rinear, David L. *Stage, Page, Scandals, and Vandals: William E. Burton and Nineteenth-Century American Theatre*. Carbondale: Southern Illinois University Press, 2004.

Ripley, John. *Julius Caesar on Stage in England and America 1599–1973*. Cambridge: Cambridge University Press, 1980.

Roach, Joseph. *Cities of the Dead*. New York: Columbia University Press, 1996.

Robins, Edward. *Twelve Great Actors 1862–1943*. New York: Knickerbocker Press, 1900.

"Robinson Locke Collection of Theatrical Scrapbooks," n.d. New York Public Library Billy Rose Theatre Collection.

Roediger, David R. *The Wages of Whiteness: Race and the Making of the American Working Class*. London: Verso, 1991.

Root, Harvey W. *The Unknown Barnum*. New York: Harper and Brothers, 1927.

Rosen, Zvi S. "The Twilight of the Opera Pirates: A Prehistory of the Exclusive Right of Public Performance for Musical Compositions." *Cardozo Arts and Entertainment Law Journal* 24 (2007): 1157–1218.

Rosenfield, Lawrence W. "Central Park and the Celebration of Civic Virtue." In *American Rhetoric: Context and Criticism*, 222–66. Carbondale: Southern Illinois University Press, 1989.

Rosenzweig, Roy, and Elizabeth Blackmar. *The Park and the People: A History of Central Park*. Ithaca: Cornell University Press, 1992.

———. "Pig Keepers, the Story of Bone Boilers, and Central Park." *Humanities* (November 2003): 22–25.

Ross, Thomas. "The Rhetorical Tapestry of Race." In *Critical White Studies: Looking Behind the Mirror*, edited by Richard Delgado and Jean Stefancic, 89–97. Philadelphia: Temple University Press, 1997.

Rosvally, Danielle. "Off with His Head! . . . So Much for Hewlett/Brown': The African Grove Theatre Presents Richard III." In *Shaping Shakespeare for Performance: The Bear Stage*, by Catherine Loomis and Sid Ray, 127–40. Madison: Farleigh Dickinson University Press, 2015.

Round Table: A Saturday Review of Politics, Finance, Literature, Society, and Art. "Personal," May 7, 1864.

Rowe, Nicholas. *Some Account of the Life of Mr. William Shakespear*. Samuel H. Monk, 1709.

Rumbold, Kate. "Brand Shakespeare?" *Shakespeare Survey* 64, no. 1 (2011): 25–37.

Russell, Anne. " 'Playing the Men': Ellen Tree, Fanny Kemble, and Theatrical Constructions of Gender." *Borrowers and Lenders* 7, no. 1 (April 2013): 6.

Samples, Gordon. *Lust for Fame: The Stage Career of John Wilkes Booth*. Jefferson: McFarland, 1982.

Saturday Evening Gazette. "Letters from New York," May 7, 1864.

Saxon, A. H. *P. T. Barnum: The Legend and the Man*. New York: Columbia University Press, 1989.

———, ed. *Selected Letters of P. T. Barnum*. New York: Columbia University Press, 1983.

Schneider, Bethany. "Thus, Always: Julius Caesar and Abraham Lincoln." In *Shakesqueer: A Queer Companion to the Complete Works of William Shakespeare*, edited by Madhavi Menon, 152–62. Durham: Duke University Press, 2011.

Schneider, Rebecca. *Performing Remains: Art and War in Times of Theatrical Reenactment*. Florence: Taylor and Francis, 2011.

Scott, William Wallace. *Edwin Booth as Hamlet*, 1870. National Portrait Gallery, 83.2 cm. x 58.2 cm. https://npg.si.edu/object/npg_MA250730.

"Scrapbook: Lester Wallack," n.d. Folger Shakespeare Library.

Seitz, Don C. *The James Gordon Bennetts, Father and Son, Proprietors of the New York Herald*. Indianapolis: Bobbs-Merrill, 1928.

Seltzer, Thomas. *The Central Park*. New York: Central Park Association, 1926.

Seymour, Charles Bailey (Figaro). "Dramatic Feuilleton." *New York Saturday Press*, December 30, 1865.

———. "Dramatic Feuilleton." *New York Saturday Press*, January 6, 1866.

Shafer, Yvonne. "Black Actors in the Nineteenth-Century American Theatre." *CLA Journal* 20, no. 3 (1977): 387–499.

"Shakespeare at the Winter Garden," November 28, 1864. Folger Shakespeare Library.

Shakespeare, William. *As You Like It*. Edited by Juliet Dusinberre. Arden third series. London: Thomson Learning, 2006.

———. *Julius Caesar*. Edited by David Daniell. Arden Shakespeare. London: Thomson Learning, 2005.

Shakespeare in Love. Directed by John Madden, Miramax, 1998, 2 hr., 3 min.

Shaler, Nathaniel Southgate. *The Negro Problem*. Boston: Atlantic Monthly, 1884.

———. *The Neighbor; the Natural History of Human Contacts*. Boston: Houghton Mifflin, 1904.

Shapiro, James. *Shakespeare in a Divided America: What His Plays Tell Us about Our Past and Future*. Digital ed. New York: Penguin, 2020.

Sharp, Lewis I. *John Quincy Adams Ward: Dean of American Sculpture*. Newark: University of Delaware Press, 1985.

Shattuck, Charles H. *The Hamlet of Edwin Booth*. Urbana: University of Illinois Press, 1969.

Silber, Nina. "Emancipation without Slavery: Remembering the Union Victory." In *In the Cause of Liberty: How the Civil War Redefined American Ideals*, by William J. Cooper Jr. and John M. McCardell Jr., 105–25. Baton Rouge: Louisiana State University Press, 2009.

Smith, Adam I. P. *The American Civil War*. New York: Palgrave Macmillan, 2007.

Smith, Andrew F. *Eating History: Arts and Traditions of the Table*. New York: Columbia University Press, 2009.

Smith, Anthony D. *National Identity*. Reno: University of Nevada Press, 1991.

Smith, Barbara Herrnstein. *Contingencies of Value*. Cambridge: Harvard University Press, 1988.

Smith, Gene. *American Gothic: The Story of America's Legendary Theatrical Family Junius, Edwin, and John Wilkes Booth*. New York: Simon and Schuster, 1992.

Soltow, Lee, and Edward Stevens. *The Rise of Literacy and the Common School in the United States: A Socioeconomic Analysis to 1870*. Chicago: University of Chicago Press, 1981.

Sondheim, Stephen, and John Weidman. *Assassins*. New York: Theatre Communications Group, 1991.

Southern, Eileen. "The Origin and Development of the Black Musical Theater: A Preliminary Report." *Black Music Research Journal* 2 (1982–1981): 1–14.

Staunton Spectator and General Advertiser. "Mrs. Butler," October 17, 1849.

Stone, Mary Isabella. "Mary Isabella Stone Notes on Edwin Booth, 1879–1884," n.d. Harvard Theater Collection, Houghton Library, Harvard University.

Stubbs, Naomi J. *Cultivating National Identity through Performance: American Pleasure Gardens and Entertainment*. New York: Palgrave Macmillan, 2013.

Sturgess, Kim. *Shakespeare and the American Nation*. Paperback reissue. Cambridge: Cambridge University Press, 2004.

The Sun. May 19, 1888.

———, n.d. The Gen Ts 211.5.3 F. Harvard Theater Collection, Houghton Library, Harvard University.

Takaki, Ronald T. *Iron Cages: Race and Culture in Nineteenth-Century America*. New York: Alfred A. Knopf, 1979.

Taylor, Diana. *The Archive and the Repertoire: Performing Cultural Memory in the Americas*. Durham: Duke University Press, 2003.

Taylor, Gary. *Reinventing Shakespeare: A Cultural History from the Restoration to the Present*. New York: Weidenfeld and Nicolson, 1989.

Taylor, Yuval, and Jake Austen. *Darkest America: Black Minstrelsy from Slavery to Hip-Hop*. New York: W. W. Norton, 2012.

Teacup and Saucer Set, circa 1895. Folger Shakespeare Library.

Theis, Jeffrey. "The 'Ill Kill'd' Deer: Poaching and Social Order in *The Merry Wives of Windsor*." *Texas Studies in Literature and Language* 43, no. 1 (2001 Spring 2001): 46–73.

"Third Annual Message: The American Presidency Project." https://www.presidency.ucsb.edu/documents/third-annual-message-10. Accessed March 29, 2921.

254 | Bibliography

Thomas, Julia. "Bidding for the Bard: Shakespeare, the Victorians, and the Auction of the Birthplace." *Nineteenth-Century Contexts* 30, no. 2 (2008): 215–28.

Thompson, Ayanna. *Blackface*. London: Bloomsbury, 2021.

Thompson, George A., Jr. *A Documentary History of the African Theatre*. Evanston: Northwestern University Press, 1998.

Throsby, David. *Economics and Culture*. Cambridge: Cambridge University Press, 2004.

The Times. February 25, 1887.

Titone, Ora. *My Thoughts Be Bloody: The Bitter Rivalry between Edwin and John Wilkes Booth That Led to an American Tragedy*. New York: Free Press, 2010.

Toll, Robert C. *Blacking Up: The Minstrel Show in Nineteenth-Century America*. Oxford: Oxford University Press, 1977.

Townsend, Horace. "Lester Wallack's Successor." *North American Review* 147, no. 385 (1888): 703–04.

Townsend, Mrs. John D. "Mrs. John D. Townsend to A. M. Palmer and Augustin Daly," December 7, 1887. Folger Shakespeare Library.

Toynbee, William. *The Diaries of William Charles Macready 1833–1851*. New York: G. P. Putnam's Sons, 1912.

Trace, Ciaran B. "What Is Recorded Is Never Simply 'What Happened': Record Keeping in Modern Organizational Culture." *Archival Science* 2, no. 1–2 (March 2002): 137–59.

Umland, Rebecca A. "Lillie Langtry: From 'Professional Beauty' to International Icon." In *Women in the Arts in the Belle Epoque*, edited by Paul Fryer, 48–60. Jefferson: McFarland, 2021.

Union Vedette. "A Deed without a Name," April 17, 1865.

United States Magazine of Science, Art, Manufactures, Agriculture, Commerce, and Trade. "New York Theatre and the Moral Drama," May 15, 1854.

Vaughan, Virginia Mason, and Alden T. Vaughan. *Shakespeare in America*. Oxford: Oxford University Press, 2012.

Veblen, Thorstein. *The Theory of the Leisure Class*. Edited by Martha Banta. Oxford: Oxford University Press, 2007.

Vogel, Todd. *Rewriting White: Race, Class, and Cultural Capital in Nineteenth-Century America*. New Brunswick: Rutgers University Press, 2004.

Wainwright, Nicholas B., ed. *A Philadelphia Perspective: The Diary of Sidney George Fisher Covering the Years 1834–1871*. Philadelphia: Historical Society of Pennsylvania, 1967.

Waldstreicher, David. *In the Midst of Perpetual Fetes: The Making of American Nationalism, 1776–1820*. Chapel Hill: University of North Carolina Press, 1997.

Wall, Diana diZerega, Nan A. Rothschild, and Cynthia Copeland. "Seneca Village and Little Africa: Two African American Communities in Antebellum New York City." *Historical Archaeology* 42, no. 1 (2008): 97–107.

BIBLIOGRAPHY | 255

Wallace, Irving. *The Fabulous Showman: The Life and Times of P. T. Barnum*. New York: Alfred A. Knopf, 1959.

"The Wallack Testimonial." *Tribune*, n.d. The Gen Ts 211.5.3 F. Harvard Theater Collection, Houghton Library, Harvard University.

Ward, JQA, March 1910. Box 4, Folder 7. JQA Ward Papers, Albany Institute of History.

Warner, Michael, Natasha Hurley, Luis Iglesias, Sonia Di Loreto, Jeffrey Scraba, and Sandra Young. "A Soliloquy 'Lately Spoken at the African Theatre': Race and the Public Sphere in New York City, 1821." *American Literature* 73, no. 1 (2001): 1–46.

Washington Critic. "Testimonial to Wallack," March 21, 1888.

Washington Gazette. "Mr. Booth," November 9, 1821.

———. "New York October 7," October 9, 1821.

Watermeier, Daniel J., ed. *Between Actor and Critic: Selected Letters of Edwin Booth and William Winter*. Princeton: Princeton University Press, 1971.

———, ed. *Edwin Booth's Performances: The Mary Isabella Stone Commentaries*. Ann Arbor: University of Michigan Press, 1990.

Welch, Deshler. "Necroloy of 1888." *The Theatre*. January 18, 1889, vol. 5, no. 3. ed.

Werner, M. R. *Barnum*. New York: Harcourt, Brace, 1923.

West, Robert Craig. *Banking Reform and the Federal Reserve, 1863–1923*. Ithaca: Cornell University Press, 1977.

"What the Theatres Are Doing." *Watson's Art Journal* 8, no. 15 (1868): 209.

White, Shane. *Somewhat More Independent: The End of Slavery in New York City, 1770–1810*. Athens: University of Georgia Press, 1991.

———. *Stories of Freedom in Black New York*. Cambridge: Harvard University Press, 2002.

White, Shane, and Graham White. *Stylin': African-American Expressive Culture, from Its Beginnings to the Zoot Suit*. Ithaca: Cornell University Press, 1999.

Williams, Gary Jay. "Edwin Booth: What They Also Saw When They Saw Booth's Hamlet." In *Macready, Booth, Terry, Irving: Great Shakespeareans*, vol. 6, edited by Richard Schoch, 57–89. London: Bloomsbury, 2011.

Wilmeth, Don, and Rosemary Cullen. *Plays by Augustin Daly*. Cambridge: Cambridge University Press, 1984.

Wilmington Journal. "From the Editor," October 12, 1849.

Winter Garden (Theater New York, N.Y. 1859–1867). "Broadside: Winter Garden, Farewell Benefit of Mrs. Barney Williams." Herald Print, 1862. American Antiquarian Society.

Winter, William. "Drama." *Albion, a Journal of News, Politics, and Literature* 42, no. 8 (February 20, 1864): 91.

———. *The Life and Art of Edwin Booth*. New York: Macmillan, 1894.

———. *Shakespeare on the Stage*. New York: Moffat Yard, 1911.

———. *A Sketch of the Life of John Gilbert: Together with Extracts from His Letters and Souvenirs of His Career*. New York: Dunlap Society, 1890.

Wister, Fanny Kemble. *Fanny: The American Kemble*. Tallahassee: South Pass Press, 1972.

Yim, Laura Lehua. "Reading Hawaiian Shakespeare: Indigenous Residue Haunting Settler Colonial Racism." *Journal of American Studies* 54, no. 1 (2019): 36–43.

Index

Note: page references in *italics* indicate illustrations; 'n' indicates chapter notes; all places are in New York City unless otherwise stated.

Abbey, Henry E., 170
access, 66–67, 108
African Theatre, 31–32, 35, 36, 37, *46*, 46–47; advertising, 41, 46, 57; arrests, 56–57; at Hampton's Hotel/ Park Theatre Hotel, 40–48, *41*, *46*, 56–57, 205n45; legitimacy of, 30, 31, 32–35, 41, 42, 43, 46, 47, 48, 57; locations, *x*, 31, 45–47, *46*, 55; playbills, 37, 43–44, 207n63; *Richard III* at, 30, 31, 37, *46*, 49–53, 54, 56, 207n63; as "The African Grove," 55–56; ticket pricing, 37–38; white audiences, 30, 31, 36, 38, 40, 47, 53; and whiteness, 53–55
agency, 31, 52, 91, 108, 111
Agnew, Jean-Christophe, 17–18
Albion, The, 142–43, 145, 152
Aldine, The, 158–59
Alexandria Gazette, 113
American Museum and Lecture Room, *x*, 59–64; advertising, 67, 75, 83; "Barnum's American Museum Illustrated" pamphlet, 62; class performance at, 63–67; domestic setting, 73–75; entry pricing, 63–64, 210n25; plays performed at, 71,

76–83, *78*, *79*, *80*; print of, 191; segregation at, 67; Shakespearean ephemera at, 83–86
American Museum of Natural History, 66
American theatre, 32–34, 142, 201n64
Anbinder, Tyler, 70
Anderson, Benedict, 21, 143, 146, 150
Astor Place Riots, *x*, 1–2, 10
Atlantic, The, 85

Bache, Meade, 130
Barker, Jebediah, 97
Barnum, Phineas Taylor, 59, 69; autobiographies, 63, 65–66, 208n1. *See also* American Museum and Lecture Room
Barrett, Lawrence, 161, 165–66, 172, 175–76, 179, 186
Beekman, James, 146
Bennett, James Gordon Jr., 183
Bernstein, Robin, 8, 151
Black New Yorkers: emancipation, 31–32, 38–40, 125–26, 204n27–28; free households, *46*, 46–47, 57, 205n47; laborers, 123; museum patrons, 67; pleasure garden, 35–36,

258 | INDEX

Black New Yorkers (continued)
207n68; Seneca Village, x, 146–47,
226n31; voting rights, 29–30, 147,
202n2. See also African Theatre
Black theatre, 30–31
Blackmar, Elizabeth, 141, 146
Blackness, 126, 129–30
Blackwood, Sarah, 124
Bly, Mark, 3
Bobalition broadsides, 50
body/mind divide, 119, 123–25, 132
Booth, Edwin, 4, 26, 51, 123–24,
132–35, 139, 145, 152–58, 155,
175–77; as Hamlet, 116–18, 119,
120–21, 121, 122, 124–25, 128–31,
135–38, 161, 165, 171, 174–75, 186,
192, 193, 194–95, 235n4
Booth, John Wilkes, 115–16, 117,
118, 119–20, 123, 129, 131–33, 137,
152–55, 155, 219n6
Booth, Junius Brutus Sr., 116–17, 118,
134, 137, 220n20
Booth, Junius Jr., 152–55, 155
Booth brothers' brand, 115–38,
152–56, 194–95, 219n4; production
of Julius Caesar, 152, 154–55, 155,
195
Boston Daily Mail, 110
Boston Theatre, 133–34
Bourdieu, Pierre, 13–14, 15, 19, 20,
24, 25
Bowers, Elizabeth (née Crocker), 178
brand, 16–17, 23–24, 26, 27, 61,
68–69, 75, 103, 114, 164–65, 194,
201n73. See also Booth brothers'
brand
Bristol, Michael, 16
Brooklyn Lyceum, 87, 101, 214n2
Brown, T. Allston, 76
Brown, William, 30–32; tea/pleasure
garden, 35–37, 40–41, 46, 54. See
also African Theatre

Butler, Pierce, 87, 88, 89–90, 93, 96,
100, 104–5, 109, 113–14

Capen, Nahum, 132
capital, 19–20, 21, 27, 30, 123;
economic, 15, 33–34, 92, 99;
linguistic, 50; social, 4, 33, 99,
111, 185; symbolic, 19–20. See also
cultural capital
Cartelli, Thomas, 23, 24, 48–49
Catlin, George, Five Points, 70, 70
Central Park statue of Shakespeare,
x, 139–60, 193, 194–95, 224n2,
225n21; benefit performance, 152,
154–55, 155, 195; production of,
139, 156–59, 228n66
Chappell, Maria, 102
charity, 70–71
Charles Street Theatre, Baltimore, 118
Chipman, George R., 184
Choate, Rufus, 117
Christian Union, 160
Civil Rights Cases (1883), 126
Civil War, 4, 21, 22, 31, 38–39, 90–91,
124, 132–33, 137, 140, 143, 156
Clarke, Asia Booth, 117, 118, 131–33,
152–53
Clarke, Charles, 129
class, social, 1–2, 10, 14–15; and
Barnum's American Museum, 60,
61, 62, 63–67, 69, 70, 71, 73, 85–86;
and the Booth brothers, 123, 125,
126, 128, 130, 131, 132, 136–38;
and Brown's African Theatre, 35,
36, 50, 53–54; and the Central
Park statue of Shakespeare, 140,
141, 147, 148, 149, 150, 151; and
Wallack's benefit performance,
183–85
Cleveland Democrat, 109
Coffee, Kevin, 150
Columbia Democrat, 112

INDEX | 259

Commercial Advertiser, 43
commodity, 11, 15–18, 19, 195,
    203n11; and the Booth brothers,
    121–23, 127, 128; and Brown's
    African Theatre, 30, 34, 35, 38, 44;
    and Kemble's reading career, 90,
    92–93, 96–99, 102, 106, 109, 114
consumption, 10–12, 61; conspicuous,
    66, 71, 131, 198n11
Cook, James, 67
Couldock, Charles Walter, 174–75
cultural capital, 4, 8, 14–15, 19–20,
    22, 23, 27, 35, 60, 76, 83–84, 88,
    92, 103, 116, 141–42, 193–94, 195

Daily Intelligencer, 115
Daily Union, 104
Daly, Augustin, 161–62, 165–90
Daly, Charles P., 139
Davis, Tracy, 11
Deetz, James, 127
Delmonico's restaurant, 164–65
Dennett, Andrea Stulman, 74
Dittenhoefer, Abram Jesse, 166
Doctor Who, "The Shakespeare Code,"
    193, 235n3
domesticity, 73–75, 99–106
dramaturgy, defining, 3
dramaturgy of value: concept of, 1–4;
    at large, 191–96
Dred Scott case (1856–1857), 126
Drunkard, The, 71, 83
Du Bois, W. E. B., 126
Dudden, Faye, 95

Emerson, Ralph Waldo, "American
    Scholar" address, 123–24
England/Englishness, 23–24, 49, 87,
    88, 102, 140, 144
English theatre, 32, 54, 116–17, 142;
    London patent theatres, 34–35
esteem-value, 9, 10, 127, 128

ethics. *See* moral and ethical health
Evans, Sara M., 101
Evening News, 189
Evening World, 178
exchange-value, 9–10, 15
Eytinge, Rose, 123–24, 178–79

Fanon, Frantz, 49–50
Fisher, Sidney George, 112–13
Fisherman and Farmer, 172, 173
Five Points district, x, 69–71, *70*
Forrest, Edwin, 1
Frank Leslie's Illustrated Newspaper,
    191
Fraser, L. M., 9, 11, 15–16, 19
Fredrickson, George M., 123
Frost, Linda, 67, 130–31
Frow, John, 15
Furnas, J. C., 94, 104, 106

gender, 87–88, 91, 94, 95, 107–11
Gramercy Park, x, 120, *121*, 192–93
Greeley, Horace, 66
Grossman, Edwina Booth, 117

habitus, 14, 19
Hackett, James Henry, 139, 145, 152
Hamburg Dramaturgy, The, 3, 198n8
Hamlet, 4, 56, 76, 77, 101, 161,
    171–72, 177–80, 186, 193–94,
    222n55; Edwin Booth as Hamlet,
    116–18, 119, 120–21, *121*, *122*,
    124–25, 128–31, 135–38, 161, 165,
    171, 174–75, 186, 192, 193, 194–95,
    235n4
Hampton, Ephraim, *41*, 41–42. *See
    also* Park Theatre
Harris, Cheryl, 126–27
Hartman, Sadakichi, 224n2
Hawthorne, Nathaniel, 85
Hay, Samuel, 44, 45, 56
Heneghan, Bridget, 127–28

260 | INDEX

Herald of the Times, 104
Hewlett, Mr., 37, 50, 51–52, 56, 208n77
Hodin, Mark, 33, 34
Hoey, Mrs. John (née Josephine Shaw), 183
Holt, Douglas B., 17
Hone, Philip, 95, 114

intellectualism, 123–25, 129, 137
Isenberg, Nancy, 108

Jackson, Andrew, 123
Jarrett, Henry C., 133
Jefferson, Joseph, 161, 166, 187
Jefferson, Thomas, *Notes on the State of Virginia*, 129–30
Jerrold, Douglas, 32–33
Johnson, Andrew, 130

Kahan, Gerald, 102
Kean, Edmund, 116
Keen, Ellen (née Tree), 107–8
Keene, Laura, 183
Kellogg, Gertrude, 179, 185, 233n72
Kemble, Charles, 102–3, 215n10
Kemble, Mrs. Fanny, 87–114, 214n4; appellations, 104–5, *105*; and commodity, 92–93, 96–99, 102, 106, 109, 114; divorce narrative, 93–95; earnings, 111–14; equestrian talent, 91, 109; gendered performance, 107–11; Hanmer reading edition, 102–3; journals, 88–92, 96–97, 103
Knapp, Raymond, 201n64

labor/laborers, 123–25, 132
Lady of Lyons, The, 77
LaFarge House fire, 155–56
Laird, John, 12
Langtry, Lillie, 166, 173, 177
language, 49–52, 126

Lanier, Douglas, 62, 74
Lawrence, Philip, 129
legitimacy, 24, 74, 82; and Brown's African Theatre, 30, 31, 32–35, 41, 42, 43, 46, 47, 48, 57
LEGO Movie, 193
Levine, Lawrence, 10, 14, 32, 34
Lily, The, 110–11
Lincoln, Abraham, assassination, 115–16, 118, 120, 132, 133–34, 195
Litchfield Enquirer, 110
literacy, 51, 206n58
literary blackface, 50, 206n53
literary value, 33–34
Lott, Eric, 130
Lynchburg Virginian, 111

McAllister, Marvin, 34, 44
McConachie, Bruce, 61, 63
MacKaye, Percy, 158
MacKaye, Steele, 158–59
Macready, William Charles, 1, 33
market, 17–18, 20, 25, 60–61, 106, 140, 195–96
Marshall, Gail, 94–95
Marx, Karl, 10–11, 15–16, 17–18, 19, 33, 66, 200n56, 203n11
material culture, 127–28
Mathews, Charles, 56
Melville, Herman, 107, 109, 111
memorialization, 159–60
memory, sites of (*lieux de mémoire*), 144–45
Metropolitan Museum of Art, 66
Metropolitan Opera House, 161, 166, 170, 184
Miller, Derek, 17, 19
mind/body divide, 119, 123–25, 132
Minnesota Pioneer, 105, 110
minstrelsy, 56, 130
Mirowski, Philip, social theory of value, 11–12, 185

Mitchell, John, 97–98
Modjeska, Helena, 161, 177, 185, 186–87
Molière, 33
moral and ethical health, 68, 71, 72, 73, 74, 82–83, 99, 102, 106, 112, 148–49
Morris, Clara, 117
Moss, Theodore, 168
Most, Andrea, 201n64
Mullenix, Elizabeth, 109
Mullenneaux, Nan, 100, 102, 104
myth, 22, 144–45, 159, 160

Nation, The, 59–60, 68, 74
National Advocate, 29–30, 37, 38, 42, 51–52, 56–57, 208n77. See also Noah, Mordecai
national identity, 20–24, 26, 32, 34–35, 67, 131, 139–60, 194
Nayar, Pramod, 16–17, 62
Neilson, Peter, 51–52
New York City, 4, 9, 72–73; carriage use, 150–51; churches, 57. See also Black New Yorkers; white New Yorkers; specific places in
New York Daily Advertiser, 43
New York Herald, 22–24, 134–35, 145, 171–73, 183, 231n38
New York Post, 184–85
New York Saturday Press, 135
New York State Constitutional Convention (1821), 29
New York Times, 69
New York Tribune, 68, 186
Noah, Mordecai, 31, 32, 34, 36–37, 38, 40, 42, 43, 47, 48, 49–51, 53, 54, 55–57, 206n53
Nora, Pierre, 144

Odell, George C., 76; Annals of the New York Stage, 37, 76

Olmsted, Frederick Law, 148
Our American Cousin, 175
Our Irish Cousin, 77

Painter, Nell Irvin, 127
Palmer, Albert Marshman, 162–63, 165–90
Park Theatre, x, 31, 41, 42, 43–44, 46, 47–48, 76–77, 81, 82, 117, 205n44
Perry, Ralph Barton, theory of value, 11, 34, 185
Players, The, x, 119, 120, 192
pleasure gardens, 35–37, 40–41, 46, 53–54, 207n68
Plessy v. Ferguson (1896), 126
Plympton, Eben, 186
postcoloniality, 48–49
power, 14–15, 19, 20, 50, 52, 91, 92, 123
Price, Stephen, 43, 44–45, 46, 47, 49, 57
privacy, 123–24
property, 127, 130, 198n16
public parks, 145–46, 148, 149–51

race, 67, 126, 128, 130
racism, 32, 46, 56, 123, 147–48. See also minstrelsy; segregation
rebellion, 15, 35
Rehan, Ada, 178
Republic, The, 105
Rhodehamel, John, 119
Richards, Jeffrey, 201n64
Richelieu, 174–75
Richter, Amy, 73, 102
Ripley, John, 154
Roach, Joseph, 159–60
Roediger, David, 126
Rosenzweig, Roy, 141, 146
Rumbold, Kate, 17, 61

St. Leger, Harriet, 114

262 | INDEX

Saxon, A. H., 63
Schneider, Rebecca, 90
Scudder, George, 63
segregation, 67, 126
self, performance of, 72, 73, 88, 89, 90
Seneca Village, *x*, 146–47, 226n31
Seymour, Charles Bailey, 135
Shakespeare, William, 2, 4; and value,
   9–11; defining "Shakespeare," 8–9,
   26–27; cutting/editing of plays,
   51, 148–49; *Comedy of Errors*, 76;
   Henry IV, 152; *Julius Caesar*, 77,
   115, 119–20, 131–32, 152, 154–55,
   155, 195; *King John*, 77; *King Lear*,
   77, 133; *Macbeth*, 1, 54, 69, 76,
   77; *The Merchant of Venice*, 76, 77,
   213n75; *Much Ado about Nothing*,
   76, 77; *Othello*, 51, 76, 77; *Richard
   III*, 30, 31, 37, 46, 49–53, 54, 56,
   76–77, 116, 117, 118, 119, 207n63;
   Romeo and Juliet, 76, 77, 101, 107,
   108, 152; *Two Gentlemen of Verona*,
   77; *As You Like It*, 65, 76, 77, 113.
   See also Central Park statue; *Hamlet*
Shakespeare in Love (film), 193, 235n3
Shakespeare realia, 83–86, 120–23,
   122, 191–92
She Stoops to Conquer, 77
Sheridan, Richard Brinsley, 33
slavery, 126, 129, 131–38, 204n28.
   See also Black New Yorkers:
   emancipation
Smith, Anthony D., 21–22, 23, 143
Smith, Barbara Herrnstein, 12–13,
   139
Smith, Dr., 36
*Staunton Spectator and General
   Advisor*, 109, 112
Stewart's dry goods store, 164–65
Stone, Mary Isabella, 117
Stratford-upon-Avon, UK, 61–62

Stubbs, Naomi, 53–54, 64
Stuyvesant Institute, *x*, 87, 95, 99, 101
subscriptions, 182–83
subversion, 30, 40
Sun, The, 179, 189
Supreme Court, 126

Takaki, Ronald, 18
Taper, Louise, 119
Taylor, Diana, 21
temperance, 69–72
territory, cultural, 53, 55
Theatre Alley, 41, 46–47
theatre of value, concept of, 25
Thompson, George A., 45, 55, 57
Times, The (Owosso, Michigan), 169,
   181
Townsend, Mrs. John D. (Margaret
   Townsend Tagliapietra), 169–70,
   230n32
Trace, Ciaran, 91
Tracy, Agnes Ethel, 183

Uncle Tom's Cabin, 77
Unemployed Philosophers Guild,
   191–92
Union Square Holiday Market, 191
Union Vedette, 115
*United States Magazine of Science,
   Art, Manufactures, Agriculture,
   Commerce, and Trade*, 68
urban environments, 72–75
utility/use-value, 9, 10, 31, 62, 127

value, concept of, 2, 9–15
Veblen, Thorstein, 66
Vogel, Todd, 50

Waldstreicher, David, 206n53
Wallack, Lester, 161, 164, 167–68,
   181, 182

Wallack, Mrs., 170–71

Wallack benefit, 161–90, 195; advertisements, 168–69, 178; reporting on, 181–85; souvenir program, 162–63, 173–74, 176, 178, 180, 189–90; witness marks, 162, 175, 182, 190

Wallack's Lyceum Theatre, 76–77, *80, 81,* 112, 164–65

Ward, John Quincy Adams, statue of Shakespeare, 139, 156–59, 228n66

Warner, Michael, 47, 57

Welsh, S., 50–51, 206n58

Wheatley, William, 139, 145

White, Shane, *46,* 46–47, 53, 55, 57

white New Yorkers, 29, 40–41, 47–48, 67, 137; at the African Theatre, 30, 31, 36, 38, 40, 47, 53; labor/laborers, 123–25, 126

whiteness, 53, 116, 125–31, 138

Wife's Secret, The, 77

Williams, Gary Jay, 118

Wilmington Journal, 104

Winter, William, 125, 134, 136–37, 142–43, 144, 145, 152

Winter Garden Theatre, 118, 135, 152–56

witness marks, 162, 175, 182, 190

women patrons, 74. *See also* gender

worth, 9–15, 27, 34, 62, 63, 140, 160

www.ingramcontent.com/pod-product-compliance
Lightning Source LLC
Chambersburg PA
CBHW022038020325

22763CB00020B/498